A NOVEL BY AYI KWEI ARMAH

# two thousand seasons

Third World Press    Chicago

Cover design by L.F. Crowe

AYI KWEI ARMAH

# two thousand seasons

**By the same author**

*The Beautyful Ones Are Not Yet Born* (H.E.B.)

*Fragments* (E.A.P.H.)

*Why Are We So Blest?* (E.A.P.H.)

*The Healers* (E.A.P.H.

*for Ekua Korkoi Armah and Li Chun Hi*

# Contents

*Springwater flowing to the desert, where you flow there is no regeneration. The desert takes. The desert knows no giving. To the giving water of your flowing it is not in the nature of the desert to return anything but destruction. Springwater flowing to the desert, your future is extinction.*

*Hau, people headed after the setting sun, in that direction even the possibility of regeneration is dead. There the devotees of death take life, consume it, exhaust every living thing. Then they move on, forever seeking newer boundaries. Wherever there are living remnants undestroyed, there lies more work for them. Whatever would direct itself after the setting sun, an ashen death lies in wait for it. Whichever people make the falling fire their aim, a pale extinction awaits them among the destroyers.*

*Woe the headwater needing to give, giving only to floodwater flowing desertward. Woe the link from spring to stream. Woe the link receiving springwater only to pass it on in a stream flowing to waste, seeking extinction.*

*You hearers, seers, imaginers, thinkers, rememberers, you prophets called to communicate truths of the living way to a people fascinated unto death, you called to link memory with forelistening, to join the uncountable seasons of our flowing to unknown tomorrows even more numerous, communicators doomed to pass on truths of our origins to a people rushing deathward, grown contemptuous in our ignorance of our source, prejudiced against our own survival, how shall your vocation's utterance be heard?*

This is life's race, but how shall we remind a people hypnotized by death? We have been so long following the falling sun, flowing to the desert, moving to our burial.

In the living night come voices from the source. We go to find our audience, open our mouths to pass on what we have heard. But we are fallen among a fantastic tumult. The noise the hypnotized make, multiplied by every echoing cave of our labyrinthine trap, is heavier, a million times louder than the sounds we carry.

Hoarsened, we whisper our news of the way. In derisive answer the hurtling crowds shriek their praise songs to death. All around us the world is drugged white in a deathly happiness while from under the falling sun powerful engines of noise and havoc emerge to swell the cacophony. Against their crashing riot nothing whispered can be heard, nothing said. Indeed the tumult welcomes who would shout and burst the veins on his own neck. His message murdered before birth, the shouter only helps confusion.

Giver of life, spring whose water now pours down destruction's road a rushing cataract, your future is destruction, your present a giving, giving into a void with no return. Your flow knows no regeneration.

Say it is the nature of the spring to give; it is the nature of the desert's sand to take. Say it is the nature of your given water to flow; it is the nature of the desert to absorb.

It is your nature also, spring, to receive. Giving, receiving, receiving, giving, continuing, living. It is not the nature of the desert to give. Taking, taking, taking, taking, the desert blasts with destruction whatever touches it. Whatever gives of itself to *the desert parts from regeneration.*

*It is for the spring to give. It is for springwater to flow. But if the spring would continue to give and the springwater continue flowing, the desert is no direction. Along the desert road spring-water is the sap of young wood prematurely blazing, meant to carry life quietly, darkly from roots to farthest veins but abruptly betrayed into devouring light, converted to scalding pus hissing its own vessel's destruction. Along the desert road springwater is blood of a murdered woman when the sun leaves no shadow.*

*No spring changes the desert. The desert remains; the spring runs dry. Not one spring, not thirty, not a thousand springs will change the desert. For that change floods, the waters of the universe in unison, flowing not to coax the desert but to overwhelm it, ending its regime of death, that, not a single perishable spring, is the necessity.*

*Receiving, giving, giving, receiving, all that lives is twin. Who would cast the spell of death, let him separate the two. Whatever cannot give, whatever is ignorant even of receiving, knowing only taking, that thing is past its own mere death. It is a carrier of death. Woe the giver on the road to such a taker, for then the victim has found victorious death.*

*Woe the race, too generous in the giving of itself, that finds a road not of regeneration but a highway to its own extinction. Woe the race, woe the spring. Woe the headwaters, woe the seers, the hearers, woe the utterers. Woe the flowing water, people hustling to our death.*

*What remains? To sing regret, curse ancestors and throughout stagnant lives pass down the malediction on those yet to come? Easy that lazy existence, sweetly drugged the life spent waiting* upon death. Easy the falling slide, even for rememberers.

We who hear the call not to forget what is in our nature, have we not betrayed it in this blazing noonday of the killers? Around us they have placed a plethora of things screaming denial of our nature, things welcoming us against ourselves, things luring us into the whiteness of destruction. We too have drunk oblivion, and overflowing with it, have joined the exhilarated chase after death.

We cannot continue so. For a refusal to change direction, for the abandonment of the way, for such perverse persistence there are no reasons, only hollow, unconvincing lies.

And the seers, the hearers, the utterers? What sufficiency is there in our hearing only this season's noise, seeing only the confusion around us here, uttering, like cavernous mirrors, a wild echo only of the howling cacophony engulfing us? That is not the nature of our seeing, that is not our hearing, not our uttering. Only our drugged weariness, unjustified, unjustifiable, keeps us bound to the present.

How have we come to be mere mirrors to annihilation? For whom do we aspire to reflect our people's death? For whose entertainment shall we sing our agony? In what hopes? That the destroyers, aspiring to extinguish us, will suffer conciliatory remorse at the sight of their own fantastic success? The last imbecile to dream such dreams is dead, killed by the saviours of his dreams. Such idiot hopes come from a territory far beyond rebirth. Those utterly dead, never again to wake, such is their muttering. Leave them in their graves. Whatever waking form they wear, the stench of death pours ceaseless from their mouths. From every opening of their possessed carcases comes death's excremental pus. Their soul itself is dead and long since putrified.

xii

*Would you then have your intercourse with these creatures from the graveyard? Go to them, and speak your message to long rotted ash.*

*This sight, this hearing, this our uttering: these are not for dumb recording of the senseless present, unless the vocation we too have fallen into wanting is merely to be part of the cadaverous stampede, hurrying on the rush to destruction.*

*The linking of those gone, ourselves here, those coming; our continuation, our flowing not along any meretricious channel but along our living way, the way: it is that remembrance that calls us. The eyes of seers should range far into purposes. The ears of hearers should listen far toward origins. The utterers' voice should make knowledge of the way, of heard sounds and visions seen, the voice of the utterers should make this knowledge inevitable, impossible to lose.*

*A people losing sight of origins are dead. A people deaf to purposes are lost. Under fertile rain, in scorching sunshine there is no difference: their bodies are mere corpses, awaiting final burial.*

*What when the tumult and the rush are yet too strong for the voice to prevail uttering heard sounds of origins, transmitting seen visions of purposes? What when all our eyes are raped by destruction's furious whiteness?*

*Easy then the falling slide, soft the temptation to let despair absorb even the remnant voice. Easy for unheeded seers, unheard listeners, easy for interrupted utterers to clasp the immediate destiny, yield and be pressed to serve victorious barrenness. Easy the call to whiteness, easy the welcome unto death.*

*Have we not seen the devotees of death? They are beyond the* source's beckoning. Purpose has no power to draw them forward from dead todays. Make way for them along the easy road. Those with their guts cracked out of them, those with minds so minced all their remembrance would turn to pain, leave them along the easy road. Do not condemn, do not pity them. Let them go. Or would you try reminding them of their murdered selves? As well graft back blighted leaves. Some restful night after the first thousand and the second thousand seasons the loss of such, devoted to whiteness in their souls, will appear justly: a gain.

But among the rushing multitude remember well the many rushing just because that is the present road—rushing not out of devotion but because they are of a nature to take their internal order from the present season's surroundings. It is a waste of the seer's thought, the hearer's breath, a waste of the utterer's spirit to pour blame on such natures. Were the surrounding order the order of the way, these also would again be people of the way. It is their nature to flow along channels already deepened by recent flow. It is not in their nature to wonder, threatening their easy peace with thinking if channels already found run true. Finders they are, not makers. Would you too, in pride miming the white, deathly people, would you also heap contempt on them? Do it directly then, and for your own satisfaction undisguised. Only plead no disappointment that the ones you so contemn, they too have not turned out to be makers. Finders they are—never did they deceive you with any promise to be creators.

And if the mind-channels of the way are all destroyed, and the only channels left lie along the white road? Drawing from remembrance, from knowledge of future purpose, it is for the hearers to listen, for the hearers to glean what through accident

xiv

death's messengers have not found to silence.

And if all around has indeed been touched by them? The destroyed who retain the desire to remake themselves and act upon that desire remake themselves. The remade are pointers to the way, the way of remembrance, the way knowing purpose.

In this present season the flow is so powerful in the direction of death. It has been so long, even since before Anoa spoke her prophecy of a thousand seasons and another thousand seasons: a thousand seasons wasted wandering amazed along alien roads, another thousand spent finding paths to the living way.

The reign of the destroyers has been long. It will be longer. But what is our present despair against the sharp abandonment of those first snatched away to waste? What puniness is this our anxiety against the howling agony of their murdered soul?

Remember this: against all that destruction some yet remained among us unforgetful of origins, dreaming secret dreams, seeing secret visions, hearing secret voices of our purpose. Further: those yet to appear, to see, hear, to utter and to make—little do we know what changes they will come among. Idle then for us to presume despair on their behalf; foolish when we have no knowledge how much closer to the way their birth will come, how much closer than our closest hopes.

Not all our souls are of a nature to answer the call of death, however sweetened. Easy these seasons to forget this too. Seasons, seasons and seasons ago the first thousand seasons passed. Before the passing of the second thousand, even before then, the time will come when those multitudes starting out on the road of death must meet predecessors returning scalded from the white taste of death.

These first returners, their wounds are so raw, their minds so *butchered with the enormity of a fate so recently, so closely grazed, that the very sound of their voices, the very sight they present is unacceptable, unreal, impossible to the hastening, careless, prancing, advancing multitudes. These first returners, amid the general oblivious happiness they appear mere capricious night-mares, specific, unfortunate accidents, particular mishaps to be sidestepped on the jubilant white road, single apparitions easy to ignore, most pleasantly easy to forget.*

*But farther along the road more returning apparitions arise. They are intermittent still, but frequenter. Minds still unwounded in the dizzy, happy deathward rush, chancing upon this frequency of warning casualties, begin to wonder if the advancing dance will really be the promised revelry.*

*More apparitions. The thoughtful are given greater pause. There are many now, some half concealed in the other wreckage along the happy highway. Completely ruined, bled of life's juices, they have staggered groping for the source, their purpose now the contemned past. Unable to stagger farther, they lie unburied by the common road, their corpses multiplying, their feet pointing to their destruction.*

*Returning casualties, many now and desperate, challenge the progressing revellers for right of way. When the numbers of the hopeful going and the desperate fleeing back are almost even, then the interrupted revelry becomes pure carnage. For those with no understanding of the source, those blest in their ignorance of doom's whiteness, the blind revellers, are anxious to cascade away, to obey the highway's call. Those who have seen the white destination and yet escaped death, stampeding back, crash in unbuffered collision against the revellers. In their spirits contempt from those escaping* death—contempt against the others for seeking what so recently they themselves sought—clashes with pure incomprehension from the hopeful revellers.

How indeed would a living understanding come to those who have fled knowledge of the source? And those running back to the source in their new desperation, have they not more fear of death's horror than love of life? Whiteness indeed they have known; of our own blackness they have yet to learn.

You who yearn to be hearers, you who would see, you the utterers of the future, this is not the season for contempt. Look upon those in whose nature it is to wait upon death to create in them a need to know life. Look upon them, but in this season do not look too steeply.

Say then the multitude is noisier after the shaking, shattering knowledge of the pale road of death. Are your ears also dead? This noise is not the recent uniform cacophony of death victorious, death alone ruling. Now the customary noises of triumphant death have the tone of lies to some of our ears. In such a season the voice informed with knowledge of the way, that voice whose utterance is inseparable from life, that voice will be heard. For there are ears straining against the loud nonsense of the destroyers, ears that have heard all the sweet and easy sounds of death and found them false.

Would you lock your gift away in pallid silence? Know then that in the absence of the utterers' work the carnage will be long and pure, and not the wisest mind can in the absence of the utterers' work trace in all our flowing blood even one broken ring of meaning. For those returning, salvaging blistered selves from death, and those advancing still hypnotized by death, in the *absence of the utterers' work what will they be but beasts devouring beasts, zombis fighting zombis, a continuation along the road of death in place of regeneration, the rediscovery of our way, the way?*

*Leave the killers' spokesmen; the predators' spokesmen, leave the destroyers' spokesmen to cast contemptuous despair abroad. That is not our vocation. That will not be our utterance.*

# 1

# the way

We are not a people of yesterday. Do they ask how many single seasons we have flowed from our beginnings till now? We shall point them to the proper beginning of their counting. On a clear night when the light of the moon has blighted the ancient woman and her seven children, on such a night tell them to go alone into the world. There, have them count first the one, then the seven, and after the seven all the other stars visible to their eyes alone.

After that beginning they will be ready for the sand. Let them seek the sealine. They will not have to ponder where to start. Have them count the sand. Let them count it grain from single grain.

And after they have reached the end of that counting we shall not ask them to number the raindrops in the ocean. But with the wisdom of the aftermath have them ask us again how many seasons have flowed by since our people were unborn.

The air everywhere around is poisoned with truncated

tales of our origins. That is also part of the wreckage of our people. What has been cast abroad is not a thousandth of our history, even if its quality were truth. The people called our people are not the hundredth of our people. But the haze of this fouled world exists to wipe out knowledge of our way, the way. These mists are here to keep us lost, the destroyers' easy prey.

Pieces cut off from their whole are nothing but dead fragments. From the unending stream of our remembrance the harbingers of death break off meaningless fractions. Their carriers bring us this news of shards. Their message: behold this paltriness; this is all your history.

Beware the destroyers. It is their habit to cut off fingers from the hand itself uprooted from its parent body, calling each fallen piece a creature in itself, different from ears, eyes, noses, feet and entrails, other individual creatures of their making. Is it a wonder we have been flung so far from the way? That our people are scattered even into the desert, across the sea, over and away from this land, and we have forgotten how to recognise ourselves?

We are not a people of yesterday. Until the utterance of Anoa the reason itself for counting seasons had been forgotten. It had been swallowed up among a people sure of our past, unharried in our present, assured of a thousand thousand tomorrows easily flowing. Ours then was the way of creation. From the cycle of regeneration we had not yet strayed on this exile road, though even then the hearers and the seers, listening to sounds not yet arrived in the present, their eyes peering at entrails yet embowelled,

2

these silent utterers had begun thinking uncertainly about disasters growing out of too secure, too sure a harmony.

We wander now along steep roads declining into the whitest deaths. Along these highways whatever we may do will fight against our self—how could there be other possibilities? For seasons and seasons and seasons all our movement has been a going against our self, a journey into our killers' desire. Killers who from the desert brought us in the aftermath of Anoa's prophecy a choice of deaths: death of our spirit, the clogging destruction of our mind with their senseless religion of slavery. In answer to our refusal of this proffered death of our soul they brought our bodies slaughter. Killers who from the sea came holding death of the body in their right, the mind's annihilation in their left, shrieking fables of a white god and a son unconceived, exemplar of their proffered, senseless suffering.

We were not always outcasts from ourselves. In that fertile time before far-listening Anoa made her vatic utterance we were a refuge on this earth for those—hau, too many—bitten hard among their own. In our generosity they found their denied sustenance.

A ruinous openness we had, for those who came as beggars turned snakes after feeding. The suspicious among us had pronounced fears incomprehensible to our spirit then, words generosity failed to understand.

"These are makers of carrion," the wary ones said, "do not shelter them. See their eyes, their noses. Such are the beaks of all the desert's predatory birds."

We laughed at the fearful ones, gave the askers shelter

and watched them unsuspicious, watched them turn in the fecundity of our way, turn into the force that pushed us till the proper flowing of all our people, the way itself, became a lonely memory for abandoned minds.

It is not that we had not travelled before. We are not a stagnant people, hating motion. But in that fertile time before Anoa's utterance even our longer journeys were absorbed in a lasting evenness. From that long, forgetful peace our exile has been harsh and steep has been our descent.

That we the black people are one people we know. Destroyers will travel long distances in their minds and out to deny you this truth. We do not argue with them, the fools. Let them presume to instruct us about ourselves. That too is in their nature. That too is in the flow of their two thousand seasons against us.

How the very first of us lived, of that ultimate origin we have had unnumbered thoughts and more mere fables passed down to us from those gone before, but of none of this has any of us been told it was sure knowledge. We have not found that lying trick to our taste, the trick of making up sure knowledge of things possible to think of, things possible to wonder about but impossible to know in any such ultimate way. We are not stunted in spirit, we are not Europeans, we are not Christians that we should invent fables a child would laugh at and harden our eyes to preach them daylight and deep night as truth. We are not so warped in soul, we are not Arabs, we are not Muslims to fabricate a desert god chanting madness in the wilderness, and call

4

our creature creator. That is not our way.

What we do not know we do not claim to know. Who made the earth and when? We have no need to claim to know. Many thoughts, growing with every generation, have come down to us, many wonderings. The best have left us thinking it is not necessary for the earth to have been created by any imagined being. We have thought it better to start from sure knowledge, call fables fables, and wait till clarity. But from the desert first, then from the sea, the white predators, the white destroyers came assailing us with the maddening loudness of their shrieking theologies.

Of our first home we have more certainty. That it was here, on this same land, we know. We have crossed lakes and forded rivers changing resting places, but never have we had to leave our land itself, though we have roamed thousands of days over it, and lit a thousand thousand fires in thirty thousand varying places.

This land is ours, not through murder, not through theft, not by way of violence or any other trickery. This has always been our land. Here we began. Here we will continue even after the thousand seasons' scattering and the thousand seasons' groping, though the white death sometimes openly, often covertly, seductively now, brutally at other times, changes means but always seeks one end: our extermination.

Our clearest remembrances begin with a home before we came near the desert of the falling sun. Thousands upon thousands the seasons that have passed since the heavy time of parting, countless those among us who have

5

rejoined the ancestors since we left, but the knowledge has come surely down of the skirting of great waters, kin to the sea, lacking only salt; of long and tiring seasons spent journeying through high forests; of our settling down at the foot of beautiful mountains joining earth to sky again; of the fearful wailing rush when these same mountains of our admiration, now belching smoke, vomiting hot mud, throwing on our bewildered heads ashes and rocks of fire, like demented demons forced us out of all shelter; of other forests where, astonished, we met predecessors we thought had disappeared along other paths, people who had lost half our language but still had our ways, who gave us the water of welcome and after we had rested long with them guided us the length of all the paths they knew; of a hundred seasons spent journeying till we came to the wide, clear plains before the desert, that place in spirit so like other remembered places our people have called home.

There before the desert the howling regret, the longing for homes left behind, was sweetened by the promise of new homes found. So much of familiarity the place had in it, it called our weary spirits to rest. Tired from long journeys we answered the welcome of the place. We built homes it was not our intention to leave again. We lost count of stable seasons, lost count of droughts, lost count of good rains and in the ease of thirty thousand seasons forgot all anxiety.

Yes, there was motion. The surrounding soil, the air, the rivers called our younger blood. Generation after generation, growing groups journeyed a day, three days from our outer reaches looking not for escape but for greater space in an open land. Disasters there were, but the land was always larger than any calamity. It absorbed them. We continued, mothers, brothers, spreading connected over this land.

There were those who also travelled but not over land and not over water. Movers in the mind, their news was of communities we would have forgotten without them, roots to ours but gone from our waking sight. Their news was of communities too far off for us immediately to remember, places where the sun rising approaches over sea, not land. Their news was also of relationships of a beauty still to be realized, of paths still to be found. Their news was of the way, the forgotten and the future way.

Our fears are not of motion. We are not a people of dead, stagnant waters. Reasons and promptings of our own have urged much movement on us—expected, peaceful, repeated motion.

At times, in the aftermath of good seasons when for too long a time none among us had had to think of such motion, when our people grown in numbers had been surprised by some unexpected change—furious weather, drought longer than usual, spastic rains too staggered to be helpful—the urge to motion swelled.

Then the time and our need for continuation called for motion. The flow of our warmest blood answered the call. We spread connected over an open land.

Of those that journeyed most stopped close by, their new

homes soon mere extensions of our old. A few went farther in the heat of some small anger or some unusual fear. Such, to pause briefly here, was the hunter Brafo.

In the thirty-fourth season of Brafo's life his father—may like disasters strike those among our elders whose greed overwhelms their knowledge of the way—saw the amazing beauty of his own ward Ajoa and grew helpless before his dotard passion. The girl was in the thirtieth of her seasons, a few seasons' woman in body, in her spirit still a child. Brafo's father was close to a hundred seasons.

Growing up together, Ajoa saw in Brafo a hunter greater than his father. Brafo saw in Ajoa a beauty and a skill to match his mother's. The father, surprised by the discovery, was first struck impotent with rage, then maddened with a desire to destroy both his son and the beloved child.

The children were wiser than their elder. Silently— distance is the hatred of those who love—they moved away. With them went Brafo's mother, together with others of the family tired of an old man's greed. Such was the knowledge of the father's vengefulness that the fugitives ran far, so far that even news of them became uncertain, and in only thirty seasons had taken on the sound of legend. Such as Brafo travelled far, but always we knew this land would keep them, would not let them disappear.

To return. But that a new thing would interfere, that an external force would add its overwhelming weight to the puny tearing efforts of the ostentatious cripples, to the attritive attempts of the askaris, those whose fulfilment lay in our abasement, that even the seers and the hearers did not know till Anoa spoke.

Before Anoa's utterance then, our migrations were but an echo to the alternation of drought and rain. Who is it calling for examples? The people of Antobam spared exhausted soil and moved closer to the forests. True it was the drought was fierce that season. Three baobab trees were struck at once by the same instant bolt of lightning, three trees standing far apart. In their places not one faggot of wood was left, only ash.

Another: Tano and his people moved from land turned to soggy dough after ceaseless rains had brought the Kwarra into our homes and turned us into neighbours for crocodiles. They left vowing never again to curse dryness, for the rain had blotted out the sun it seemed a whole season, and it was not even a reasonable season for ordinary rain.

Another: In the slow drought Ambantem, every day for two seasons promised rain, promised and held back. The baobabs themselves drank up all their water. Those who left then we also came to call Ambantem after the cruel rain.

Another time there was no flooding surface rain, but water lying too near the air held soil together so fast it was great labour making the earth ready for seed, greater labour still for inserted seed to sprout. But why should we make an unending remembrance of drought and rain, the mere passage of seasons? The desert was farther then. Close to it, close against it we brought a fecundity unimagined there now in the glare of all the present barrenness, eternal in its aspect.

It was not always so. The desert was made the desert, turned barren by a people whose spirit is itself the seed of death. Each single one of them is a carrier of destruction. The spirit of their coming together, the purpose of their existence, is the spread of death over all the earth. An insatiable urge drives them. Wherever there is life, even if it be only a possibility, the harbingers of death must go— to destroy it. See the footsteps they have left over all the world. Wherever they have been they have destroyed along their road, taking, taking, taking. They have wiped the surface barren with their greed. They have dug deep to take what the earth needed for itself to stay fertile earth. They have taken everything within their reach, things that made the earth good, and they have put nothing back but hard, dead things in place of life destroyed. Even their putting back has nothing of a sense of reciprocity. Their semblance of giving is parcel of their greed. It is their habit to put dead, useless things in the hollowed earth to help them take more coveted things.

You do not understand how the destroyers turned earth to desert? Look around you. You are ignorant of death, but sleep you know. Have you not seen the fat ones, the hollow ones now placed above us? These the destroyers have already voided of their spirits, like the earth of its fertility. Barren, unproductive pillars have been driven into their brains. Then, left to walk the land, they do their zombi work, holding up the edifice of death from falling in vengeance on the killers' heads.

We have been handed down a vision of a slave man

10

roaming the desert sand—a perfect image of our hollowed chiefs today. Language he had not, not ours, and not his own. It had been voided out of him, his tongue cut out from his mouth. He pointed to the gaping cavity. Thinking he still had a soul, even mutilated, we imagined he was after sympathy. We were mistaken—he was pointing to the hole with pride. They who had destroyed his tongue, they had put pieces of brass in there to separate the lower from the upper jaw. The slave thought the brass a gift. Its presence made sweet to him the absence of his tongue. He communicated his haughty pride to us, indicating in the sand with precise remembrance when he had achieved each piece of brass, what amazing things he had been made to do in order to be given them.

Hau! It is not only rife among the fatted chiefs, this idiocy of the destroyed. Among ourselves we have seen beings thus voided of their souls, sent deep into earth on their mission of destruction, injected with the white people's urge to devastation, sending what they take across the sea to the white destroyers' homes.

The destroyers take. That is their way. They know nothing of reciprocity. The road to death—that is their road.

Follow the falling sun, you who still are fascinated by glittering death. When you reach your destination, there too you will find our people scattered, sold to destruction. Most are already pulverized. Those not yet visibly broken into fragments, they are zombis, death's inspired vessels, voided of our soul. There you too will wonder, looking

11

upon them, whether any can still retain the seed of life in them in the center of death's empire. Their destroyers are friends of themselves alone. All else is prey. They themselves, they are not friends even of their isolate selves. Split, each victim fraction warring against every other, they prepare the way for their only possible victor, our enemy. Among them you will find it impossible to remember that the smallest self is the self most destroyed; that our best self is our people; that if we have shrunk from all the black people to the portions that moved on the longest of journeys, from those to the fraction that came to Anoa, and among these have further shrunk till we are dwindled to the friendship of utterers, all that is merely destruction's work.

Creation calls the utterer to reach again the larger circle. That communication must be the beginning of destruction's destruction, the preparation for creation's work. That, not an incestuous, unproductive, parasitic gathering, is our vocation, that our purpose. We will not betray this remembrance: that all unconnected things are victims, tools of death.

The disease of death, the white road, is also unconnected sight, the fractured vision that sees only the immediate present, that follows only present gain and separates the present from the past, the present from the future, shutting each passing day in its own hustling greed.

The disease of death, the white road, is also unconnected hearing, the shattered hearing that listens only to today's brazen cacophony, takes direction from that alone and stays deaf to the whispers of those gone before, deaf to the soft voices of those yet unborn.

The disease of death, the white road, is also unconnected thinking, the broken reason that thinks only of the immediate paths to the moment's release, that takes no care to connect the present with past events, the present with future necessity.

Our vocation goes against all unconnectedness. It is a call to create the way again, and where even the foundations have been assaulted and destroyed, where restoration has been made impossible, simply to create the way.

Remembrance has not escaped us. Trapped now in our smallest self, we, repositories of the remembrance of the way violated, we, portion that sought the meaning of Anoa's utterance in full and found another home on this same land, we, fraction that crossed mountains, journeyed through forests, shook off destruction only to meet worse destruction, we, people of the fertile time before these schisms, we, life's people, people of the way, trapped now in our smallest self, that is our vocation: to find our larger, our healing self, we the black people.

Of the time still known as the time of men our knowledge is fragile. The time is bound in secrets. Of what is revealed, all is in fragments. Much of it was completely lost in that ashen time when loneliness, bringer of madness, nearly snapped the line of rememberers.

That was the long time of single, despairing dwellers in the farthest grove. One rememberer herself lost speech before she could finish telling of that time, and there was

13

none to give even borrowed voice to what her dying body held.

Nothing good has come to us of that first time. The remembrance is of a harsh time, horrid, filled with pains for which no rememberer found a reason, choked with the greed, the laziness, the contempt for justice of men glad to indulge themselves at the expense of their own people. The time's tale is of jealous, cowardly men determined to cling to power, and the result of that determination: the slaughter of honest people, the banishment of honest words, the raising of flattery and lies into the authorized currency of the time, the reduction of public life to an unctuous interaction.

Below the powerful the ordinary multitudes, in their turn seized by the fever of jealous ownership, turned our people into a confused competition of warring gangs, each gang under its red-eyed champion seeking force or ruse to force its will against the others. In the end it was this hot greed itself that destroyed the power of the men. They had smashed up everything, and in their festival of annihilation they had forgotten to spare each other and themselves. It was left to the women to begin the work of healing.

It was not any violence from females that cracked the rule of fathers. It was the fathers themselves who, splitting in their headlong greed for power into seven warring factions, broke each other's strength and left themselves impotent against the coming of more reasonable nights. Always above the horror brought by the memory of such unthinking carnage rides the utterers' shame that murderous

14

gluttony such as this has had power to hurl our clans one against the other.

The remembrance is of the leopard and the dupon together waylaying the lion; of the wild eagle snatching the ram, the duiker lying surprised under the claws of the parrot turned from eloquence to war; of eagle and parrot both self-hurled against the lion and the dupon tree. All the clans clawed each other, so that in the end exhaustion, not reason, not persuasion, not the women's voice speaking of the future now forgotten, exhaustion was the real peacebringer.

So the end of the rule of the fathers was violent. The beginning of the rule of women was not. Here was easy movement, natural, imperceptible to impatient, unconnected eyes.

The masculine carnage had exhausted everyone. As after all destruction, there was much heavy building left to do, and after that there still remained the steady, patient work of maintenance. For this the men—opprobrium fill their new-grown paunches—showed no extraordinary stomach, preferring to sit in the shade of large bodwe trees or beneath the cool grass of huts built by women, drinking ahey, breathing the flattering air of the shade, in their heads congratulating the tribe of men for having found such easy means to spare itself the little inconveniences of work while yet enjoying so much of its fruit—so easy it is for men's feet to dance off the way of reciprocity.

The men, at length announcing a necessity to nurse their strength for the work of elephants, with the magic of words

15

made weightier with furrowed brows successfully pulled themselves out of all ongoing work, leaving only phantom heroic work, work which never found them, while generously they welcomed the women into all real work, proclaiming between calabashes of sweet ahey how obvious it was that all such work was of its nature trivial, easy, light and therefore far from a burden on any woman.

The peace of that fertile time spread itself so long, there was such an abundance of every provision, anxiety flew so far from us, that men were able to withdraw from even those unusual jobs they claimed they were holding themselves ready for, and their absence left no pain. They had elected to go with the women every farming day to sit in shady places guarding against danger. Danger came seldom. Pleading boredom the men replaced the shady places on the farm with shades closer home, next to the fragrant breweries of ahey. After this, even on those rare occasions when such work as the men had named their work happened, there were no men in sight.

The women were maintainers, the women were their own protectresses, finders and growers both. The lost exile seeking an end to his loneliness in rape out on the open farms; the huge python blindly spreading the terror gripping it in sudden discovery; the cat of the fields hunting unusual food; the maddened elephant: every danger the women tamed, bringing tales and skins and meat home to triumphant husbands.

Drought came. The men grew eloquent describing to each other the terrors of a long dryness. That was when

Yaniba, a woman unwilling to tolerate the dryness outside and the indolence of mind among us, went past the farthest tributary here of the dry river, obsessed with our people's need of water.

Those seasons fords were things to laugh at. For six seasons babies did not fear to crawl along the riverbed itself. The water was so far we forgot the blackness of its flowing. The clouds left in the sky were streaky, wispy, barren, white. It has come down that the men—cursed the tyranny of belly and tongue—were most concerned to have water enough to mix their ahey in, and then they sat through moistureless afternoons season after season consuming stored supplies, staring up at the clear white skies, muttering mutual incoherencies about the beauty of such skies—how often the unconnected eye finds beauty in death—while the women looked at the same whiteness, saw famine where the men saw beauty, and grew frightened for our people.

Yaniba went past the farthest tributary to its source. She lifted a rock, one after many, and revealed to thirsty eyes a pool, the feeder of springs then dry. Other women came bringing help to her. It was ordained the scarce water was not to be wasted cooking selfish food. No one was to brew the drink ahey, a thirsty drink, till rain in abundance fell again.

The men succumbed to the reasoned beauty of this ordinance. But already the ahey had brought forth a strange, new kind of man, his belly like a pregnant woman's, of a habit to consume more food and drink than he gives out in work and energy.

It came simply, the rule of women. They razed the men's unearned privileges, refused to work to supply the unnecessary wants of men. All enjoyment, the new order said, was to be the result of work accomplished. The men were resentful, but this was not a venomous resentment. It was an embarrassed kind, impotent to cause any spilling of our blood. Whether from sheer astonishment or from their drunken lethargy, they attempted nothing disastrous.

The time following—it is that we still call the fertile time—was creation's time. In its abundance generosity became our vice. We lost the quick suspiciousness of the deprived, gained unwisely generous reflexes, grew able to give without having to worry about receiving, became accustomed to producing without taking thought of the future depredations of destroyers. As yet this fateful generosity disturbed no one—there was no hardship. A fertile softness enfolded all our life. Ease, the knowledge tomorrow would sing as sweetly as the present day, made all willing to forget the past, to ignore the future. Past and future, neither weighed unpleasantly upon our mind.

The general astonishment was therefore sudden, shattering, when with no warning save five brief, uncomprehended, easily forgotten fragments twin voices rose from one breast prophesying pain. They were not ugly voices. But in the common ease of our surroundings then, with nothing to put danger in the front of our mind, the voices shook us. Their message, like shouts in the middle of long, restful sleep, angered us, like screams interrupting slow, restful dreams.

Who was it prophesying? And what was it she said to pierce our comfort, the ease of ages?

Concerning the two thousand seasons thrown away to destruction—we speak of the central prophecy that heard the curse of our present coming before its violence burst upon our heads, we speak of the vision that saw our scattering before the first shattering stroke exploded from the desert's white light—of destruction's two thousand seasons against us Anoa was not the first to speak. Three we remember who spoke before her birth; and after, in her childhood, two.

The three spoke of a time impending, a time heavy with carnage. Fire, and in the fire blood hissing out its life: that was the definite burden of their brief utterance.

Concerning reasons why this fearful holocaust was to come upon us, whether truly it was a vision directed unto us and not something that merely chanced unluckily to glance across the mind of one, two, three among us; concerning all this the first three were mute as the mighty odum tree.

The two who spoke after were no more definite. They spoke of a different portion of our destruction. Their hearing was of fantastic journeys over land, one long, incredible traversing of a place neither land nor water, and after, worse: the forced crossing of oceans with no life at the other end, only lifelong slavery. They heard also how our people would come to know the howling agony of humans craving death itself not from impatience for reunion with ancestors, not for any reason of peace but to escape a life turned into an endless cycle of ever sharper cruelties.

Concerning causes why this fantastic destruction was to visit us, whether we were fated completely to disappear or to emerge from the whiteness of this fire living still, concerning all this the two spoke too briefly, stopped too abruptly to utter any indication.

The three and then the two had seen, had heard, had even uttered. But uttering, hearing and seeing were not their vocation. Sounds and visions seeking uttering vessels had caught them by surprise, possessed them briefly, then flown from their stricken minds. After they had spoken the three and the two fell almost entirely mute. Some thought they had no remembrance at all of the heavy utterances they had made. The most sagacious judged they had glimpsed truths that had stunned them to silence amid all the lying sounds and sights of surrounding life. Their utterances were at first not easy to understand, but it has come down that none of them were ridiculed. They did not suffer the fate of the suspicious ones, they who, speaking warnings not from any fundamental fear for the whole but from their own inner fear of generosity, had been laughed to scorn.

Anoa was not the first, not the second, not the third to speak. Hers, however, was a different, fuller utterance.

The vision of disintegration had been a stranger knocking on the doors of the first three for a mere day's welcome and had thence disappeared. The sounds of impending fate had shaken the earskins of the latter two with a passing message and had as swiftly vanished—whither, the hearers of a moment, shaking their ears like cats astounded, had no power to tell. With Anoa the vision found sufficient stay. The sounds came clear, lasted for repetition, and made error impossible. Anoa's utterance was not a shrieking fear ignorant of causes, oblivious of results, but a whole, clear utterance holding back neither blame for the two thousand seasons of destruction nor the promise of the way discoverable again at the end of the many seasons of our exile.

And Anoa, she was not even the first to bear that name. Among the most secret remembrances imprisoned in the memory of communicators one—so short it maddens the ear stretching to hear more—tells of a priestess Anoa, she who brought the wrath of patriarchs on her head long before the beginning of the fertile time by uttering a curse against any man, any woman who would press another human being into her service. This Anoa also cursed the takers of services proffered out of inculcated respect. It was said she was possessed by a spirit hating all servitude, so fierce in its hatred it was known to cause those it possessed to strangle those—so many now—whose joy it was to force the weaker into tools of their pleasure and their laziness, into creatures dependent upon their users. It has come down that the same spirit possessed the women of the desert white men's harem, possessed Sekela, possessed Azania, possessed all the women who slew our predatory tormentors. It was that spirit Anoa breathed.

21

Her life followed the urging of that soul, one among the guardians of the way.

At the time she spoke she was not of an age to have gained wisdom from experience. She had not lived enough. She had not had time to move patiently from one hilltop down the next valley up the adjoining hillside to the sounds and visions possible at the top then down again and on. But an intensity of hearing, a clarity of vision and a sharpness of feeling marked her character even in childhood, the time when most knowledge sprang from play. Thoughts seized her, and young as she was her seriousness itself imposed a silence around her no matter where she was. This intensity marked her; it did not close her off from others of her age. From the smallest sensations entering her, like riversoil she put out more, made more things audible, made more things visible out of what had entered her than others had an art to do.

At the time of her training, when it was thought she too could be led into choosing mother chores, she foresaw the intended separation, spurned it and asked to be trained with her brothers in the hunt. Rejected, she lost all interest in sustaining life, refused food, would touch no water till she was admitted to the training of her age. She confounded the plan to give her only trifling instruction by herself extending every hunting principle given her. She had a will to try out every stratagem to see what changes would be necessary under what conditions, what changes in the paths of the hunt for what different, larger, swifter or slyer animals.

22

Then when Anoa was possessor of the art of hunting she further discomfited her teachers by reminding them aggressive hunting was against our way, that the proper use of hunting skills should be for halting the aged lion seeking human prey in its dangerous impotence, for stopping the wild hog prowling about the growing farm, for teaching the sidelong hyena to keep its distance, not for wanton pleasure.

*skills not for wanton pleasure.*

That such talk of the way should arise at the time at all was a surprise, and not to the elders alone. That such knowledge of our way should have reached one so young with help from no older mentor, that the child Anoa could of herself have caught floating intimations of the way and in her mind have woven them into such coherent utterance, that was a wonder. That her knowledge should be of a kind so hidden and—after the elders had finished shaking their heads—found to be so true yet in such danger of being forgotten, that filled the elders with chagrin. The spirit of Anoa seemed to have moved from peak to peak, so light it had no need of mentors to reach the hilltops of the soul, from there floating to other, higher peaks.

She was slender as a fale stalk, and suppler. From her forehead to her feet her body was of a deep, even blackness that could cause the chance looker to wonder how it was that even the surface of a person's skin could speak of depths. Her grace was easy in the dance. In the work of every initiation she was skilled enough to have chosen to be a fundi. Men not commonly known for their lechery grew itchy-eyed looking at her. Her voice was torture to the

23

greedy ear. In her twenty-fifth season there were askers for her in marriage. Anoa knew her soul was shaped for other things. It was not that she was scornful of the wife's, of the mother's life. Her ears heard other voices, other thoughts visited her spirit.

It was in a season of rains that Anoa began her utterance—another season of good, prompt rain, opportune to every need, rain of a kind to lull the mind away from the thought itself of disasters, floods, droughts, anything but the pleasant, easy sufficiency of the time. That season was Anoa's thirty-ninth.

All were astonished not by what she said alone but also by the way her utterance was made, for she spoke in two voices—twin, but clearly discernible one from the other. The first, a harassed voice shrieking itself to hoarseness, uttered a terrifying catalog of deaths—deaths of the body, deaths of the spirit; deaths of single, lost ones, deaths of groups snared in some killing pursuit; deaths of nations, the threatened death of our people. That voice uttered fiery extinction, destruction among ashes and white, voracious conflagrations. It spoke of bodies driven to exhaustion for no purpose of their own, it spoke of souls stranded away from all the waters of the spirit fit to give them life. That voice told of saltwater washing over thousands upon thousands of our dead. In its uttering this voice was exactly like the briefer three and the curt two before Anoa spoke—except in its greater frequency.

From the same prophetic throat came the second voice. It was calmer, so calm it sounded to be talking not of matters of our life and death but of something like a change in the taste of the day's water, or of a slight variation noticed in the shape of grains of salt. For every shrieking horror the first voice had given sound to, this other voice gave calm causes, indicated effects, and never tired of iterating the hope at the issue of all disasters: the rediscovery and the following again of our way, the way.

Of the two thousand seasons of destruction what was it the first voice of Anoa said? This:

"Turn from this generosity of fools. The giving that is split from receiving is no generosity but hatred of the giving self, a preparation for the self's destruction. Turn.

"Return to the way, the way of reciprocity. This head-long generosity too proud to think of returns, it will be your destruction. Turn.

"But our voice is not harsh enough for your hearing. You are hastening into destruction so fast its flavour, its very name, will be sweetness to you, to your children, to so many generations of our people hurtling down the whiteness of destruction's slope. Two thousand seasons: a thousand you will spend descending into abysses that would stop your heart and break your mind merely to contemplate. The climb away from there will be just as heavy. For that alone can you be glad your doors have been so closed, your faculties are now so blunted. You will need them blunter still, to make less perceptible the descent of a thousand seasons. Two thousand seasons: a thousand dry, a thousand moist.

"One thousand seasons with the deepest of the destroyers'

25

holes behind, beneath you calling, taking many of you even to the last day on which we, people of the way again, reach the lip and leave our destroyers forever behind."

And then the second voice, the voice of causes:

"There is one cause—all else are branches: you have lost the way. You have forgotten the way of our life, the living way. Your ears have stopped themselves to the voice of reciprocity. You yourselves have become a spring blindly flowing, knowing nothing of its imminent exhaustion, ignorant of replenishing reciprocity.

"Reciprocity, that is the way you have forgotten, the giving, the receiving, the living alternation of the way. The offerers, those givers who do not receive, they are mere victims. That is what in the heedless generosity of your blinding abundance you have turned yourselves into.

"Ah, but this is wasted breath. Your doors are closed. You will not open them to hear the destroyer hiss before his fangs are buried in your eye. You do not see this, but not far off, ah, so near, already so near, another race is stalking, hungry for victims, thirstier than the desert it calls home.

"That race, it is a race of takers seeking offerers, predators hunting prey. It knows no giving, knows no receiving. It is a race that takes, imposes itself, and its victims make offerings to it.

"Slavery—do you know what that is? Ah, you will know it. Two thousand seasons, a thousand going into it, a second thousand crawling maimed from it, will teach you everything about enslavement, the destruction of souls,

26

the killing of bodies, the infusion of violence into every breath, every drop, every morsel of your sustaining air, your water, your food. Till you come again upon the way.

"Reciprocity. Not merely taking, not merely offering. Giving, but only to those from whom we receive in equal measure. Receiving, but only from those to whom we give in reciprocal measure. How easy, how just, the way. Yet how easily, how utterly you have forgotten it. You have forgotten that justice is not ease.

"Harsh and unjust was the time of men, and justly ended. An unproductive time it was, uncreative, a time which buried reciprocity and confused the way with crazy, power-thirsty roads. It was well for that time to end. Its correction should have been reciprocity, not this. Because the present path creates not harshness but a soft abundance, your minds are crammed with kapok and you too now confuse the way with thoughtless ease.

"Know this again. The way is not the rule of men. The way is never women ruling men. The way is reciprocity. The way is not barrenness. Nor is the way this heedless fecundity. The way is not blind productivity. The way is creation knowing its purpose, wise in the withholding of itself from snares, from destroyers.

"In your abandoned abundance how forgetful you have grown. This overflow of yours, its fruit will be bleak-eyed exhaustion, staring poverty. Fools again, you will think to repair faults stemming from your loss of the way by straying even farther from the way.

"You too will know the temptation to become takers.

27

Some among you will succeed too well. Their souls voided out of them, they will join the white destroyers but only in the way of dogs joining hunters. The rest, all of you, your children, their children, their children after them and generations after them again and again, all will be victims till the way is found again, till the return to our way, the way."

The utterance was impossible to refute. We had indeed strayed far from the way but thought no harm could come of mistakes made in such generosity. The prophecy first unsettled sleepy souls, but then we found ways to pass all Anoa had said under an apprehensive silence. How difficult it is to change habits already entered into.

Concerning the hollow-eyed beggars seeking refuge from their desert people's cruelties, concerning the easy hospitality with which we welcomed them there was still no change. But among the beggars themselves there were changes. More of them came. Cured and fed, they thought us fools and said so, then acted on their thinking to try and cheat us of things we had. In the fertile time we laughed at this, laughed because we could afford to part with what the white beggars from the desert so coveted, laughed because we had strayed so far from the way it was the paltry quantity of the thing coveted that drew our gaze, not the heinous nature of predation itself.

We did not have long to wait. We did not have to wait at all for the beginning of the unfolding of the truth of Anoa's utterance. The truth was unravelling itself even as she spoke. Under the calm surfaces of the fertile time a

28

giddy disequilibrium swallowed all lasting balance. Control became an exile. As for the guidance of the way, it was far—distant as the bones of the first ancestors.

# 2

# the ostentatious

*people who have forgotten the way*

# cripples

The predators, their first appearance among us was that of beggars. Haggard they came, betrayed and lonely in their hunger of soul and body. We pitied them, for is it not a part of the way that the stranger shall be given sustenance and helped along his road? But the way is not a partial remembrance only. How was it forgotten then that it is also a part of the way, inseparable from every other part, that the guest who turns contemptuous is a guest no longer but a parasite? How was it forgotten the hosts who spread a welcome for parasites prepare their own destruction?

None among our rememberers have ever sought to claim the first predatory attack could not have been foreseen. True, the attackers had come beggars. But time had passed. The wounds the beggars had come trailing on their bodies,

30

the wounds afflicting their remnant spirits we had healed for them. Strong under our healing they turned parasites yet still in the ease of our hospitality we did not even think to throw them out. They grew yet stronger, and in the fullness of their strength turned sudden predators against an easy host. Thirty days of unrelenting massacre brought them the fruit they sought: the power of new masters over their old hosts.

Fear was the mother of the predators' first empire over us. The constant threat of murder in the course of time cowed all but the most determined of our men, those who chose the lonely life of hunters in the grasslands. Our women the predators from the desert turned into playthings for their decayed pleasure. And our women, they endured, acquiesced in the predators' orgies so uncomplainingly that in time a profound confidence drew the predators to them.

Came a Rhamadan, the predators' season of hypocritical self-denial. Followed the time they call the Idd, time of the new moon of their new year. After a month of public piety and abstention the predators again threw themselves into their accustomed orgies of food, of drugs and of sex. Of these orgies we remember the greatest, and for those particular predators the last.

That night was a dark night, for in truth the moon was not really out. The predators in their haste to begin their orgy cheated their god himself.

Our women gave the predators an overflowing measure of joy, filled them with such exquisite happiness their

31

senses grew overloaded and pleasure turned them dumb, insensate. Outside stood the askaris, zombis kept to guard the predators, destroyers of our people.

This night the askaris' minds held nothing of the apprehension of revolt. Their masters had given them the strictest orders on no account to interrupt the revelry within their monstrous palace. The askaris had no intention to disobey their masters. They too felt something of the predators' appreciation for the beauty of our women, for at frequent intervals in the course of the great feast, as in the course of others before, our women sent the askaris loving gifts of food taken from the abundance within the palace: a dozen dripping lambs freshly taken from their frying fat, spiced hollow yams, seven whole cows turned two days and nights over slow fires, with only the liver, heart, the kidneys, brains and thigh meat taken from each beast. Of drink the askaris received an even greater sufficiency, for a little was all that was needed to make the predators themselves stupid with happiness uncontainable. But even more than food and drink that night our women in their kindness filled the askaris with their favourite stupefiant, the oversweet dawa drug. In the course of the mature night therefore not one askari was sure whether the noises in the air came from the palace—the town itself, forgetting distance, was too cowed this season for any noise—or from the lurid dance of the dawa in their blood, within their brains. At any rate they had their instructions not to disturb their masters' the predators' revelry.

Noises made by the predators from the desert in their

bouts of manic happiness had always been strange to us. This night of nights the noises they made were stranger still. Outside the palace many an askari knew momentary panic wondering if the grunts, the howls, if these shrieks puncturing the air with such accelerating frequency were truly cries of beings possessed with nothing different from joy.

Inside the palace our women, themselves eating little, touching no drink but water—at which abstention the Arab predators laughed frequently and long—plied the bloat-eyed revelers also with swollen quantities of the tastiest, spiciest food. Great was the pleasure of these lucky Arab predators as with extended tongue they vied to see who could with the greatest ease scoop out buttered dates stuck cunningly into the genitals of our women lined up for just this their pleasant competition. From the same fragrant vessels they preferred the eating of other delicious food: meatballs still warm off the fire, their heat making our women squirm with a sensuousness all the more inflammatory to the predators' desire. The dawa drug itself the predators licked lovingly from the youngest virgin genitals—licked with a furious appetite. Eunuchs they had brought with them played them their strange, nerve-eating music, sending the predators into trances without bottom. This was the time when a corrosive lust for our women possessed them and in a concerted movement the predators each sought sexual entry into the same genitals they had so recently eaten food and licked their dawa from. Our women watched them, watched them with

33

care and noticed that this languid lust of the happy predators was a lust unsupported by any potency. For in truth at that time the predators did not even know where on their bodies their own genitals were—so deeply had excess food and the wild madness of the dawa invaded their blood, their brains. Our women watched the predators in their fumbling ecstasy. Hau! Many, so many of the predators from the desert died that beautiful night of blackness. Who asks to hear the mention of the predators' names? Who would hear again the cursed names of the predator chieftains? With which stinking name shall we begin?

Hussein, twin brother of Hassan the Syphilitic. Hussein had long since given up the attempt to find a way for his phallus into any woman's genitals. His tongue was always his truest pathfinder. So after moving with the others in the forgetfulness of a momentary genital enthusiasm he had returned to eating buttered dates into his bursting paunch, buttered dates mined from three women's holes in turn. By the third round the circuit was making Hussein dizzy. The third woman therefore held Hussein's head in a tender caress. The second in a gesture full of love stuck a smooth, solid, well-honed knife into Hussein's neck, in a soft space between the cowries of his spine. The first woman stroked the disjointed head with affection, pressing it firmly down so the first hoarse cry from the throat came out a muffled sound of happy lechery. Then the first woman raised the head gently, to give the warm blood way in its quiet flowing from the predator's open mouth. On Hussein's face in the soft, dark light of the palace the three women

34

discerned a kind of smile of surprise. That devout Muslim accomplished one miracle even as he died: he swallowed the ninth date of his three circuits before he went to embrace his slave-owner god. He did not allow his blood to wash it away.

Faisal: He, the only one this night, had insisted on having his favourite askari with him inside the palace this night. Not, indeed, for the askari's normal duties of defense against justice armed, but for reasons even sweeter to the predator's lechery. Most of the night Faisal had spent happily licking his young askari with not one thought of females. But at the climax of the dawa's work on his brain he too from some deep bottom in his being felt like a man and yelled the desire was upon him. His shout was peremptory. What he wanted above all else was a black, black woman there and then.

Faisal sang that night. Laughing he sang. The words, what were they but a demented Arab praise song to black bodies? The lyrics were a confession Faisal wished to make, having lost control of the last remnants of his will, a confession that all his religion's stories of odalisks and little white virgins were fantasies for weak, crippled minds with little of the power of imagination, and no knowledge at all of real truth. Faisal beckoned to the black woman of his dreams. Beautiful as a walking dream Azania went to the Arab Faisal and he screamed his incredulous delight at her being real. Azania welcomed the predator Faisal, welcomed him with exquisitely knowing caresses, prepared him for love and then took him in spite of all his fumbling,

35

took him into herself and moved under him with a smooth grace that gave him his first ecstasy with a female. But Faisal, it had not been his intention to orgate into Azania all by himself. He wanted his young askari in him—from behind—while Azania welcomed him inside herself, so that he would himself be firmly clasped between his lower and his higher joys. So the scream that forced its way out of Faisal's throat during his first ecstasy was not Azania's name but the young askari's. This was not the first, not the thirtieth, not the thousandth time that the zombi had heard his name shouted with such loud desire. He strode forward at the urgent call and in a moment was naked upon his master's back, plowing the predator's open arsehole while the master tried to keep his forgetful penis in Azania. Then the joy of having his askari mount him overwhelmed all Faisal's senses. For long moments he lay insensate, hardly breathing. By degrees he lost all semblance of his former grip on Azania's body. And Azania herself, she slowly, lovingly helped him slide off her, so gently she did not disturb him or the askari pumping manseed into his Arab master. Azania did not have to use the dagger she had hidden in the cushions to which the predator Faisal was now clinging. The young askari had brought a sharp war spear with him even to this feast—great is the force of habit. Azania took the spear and pushed it with the energy of seasons and seasons of hatred shown only as love, pushed it hard through the askari's right side, so hard it went through him into the Arab panting beneath, threading him also in his right. The two, the predator and his askari, were

36

thus fused together when the agony of death usurped their sweeter pain.

Mohammed, the sheikh Mohammed, brother of Shaq'buht: Each woman, so commanded, stroked the licking tongue, the neck, the back of Mohammed's head. Sekela, she stroked the expectant tongue with a thin, sharp knife. The tongue, curled around its latest morsel of spiced meat, dropped just in front of Mohammed's mouth. Too amazed to feel the still imminent pain, the Arab was staring dumbfounded at his severed tongue when a sharper knife held in Nywele's hands slid deep into his neck and was jerked sideways to the left, sideways to the right. Mohammed died with his forehead stuck to the floor, like every good man of his enslavers' faith.

Hassan: Hassan had lived under a terrifying anxiety all his life: the fear that he might chance to live through one day and leave some new carnal pleasure unexamined. This night of nights he ordered six women to prepare themselves for him. They did. When the dawa he had eaten reached his brain what Hassan wanted was one woman, fat and greased with perfumed unctions, under his body for his penis. A second woman—Hassan was not particular as to her size, or indeed as to the size of any of the five apart from the favourite under him—sat in front of his head to one side of the fat one, and welcomed Hassan's tongue and teeth sucking at her genitals. The third and the fourth women, they sat to the left and right of his body. Their instructions were to take his fingers groping in their womanparts—or his thumbs if that was his fancy at any moment—and rhythmically to contract and relax their parts around them for his pleasure throughout the night. The fifth and the sixth were given a similar occupation, except instead of fingers and thumbs they received Hassan's toes—famous toes, for who did not know their overgrown nails were separated from the bulbous flesh a third of their ample length by sacred dirt?

This is how Hassan died: at the height of his oblivious joy a seventh woman unknown to him but known to the other six brought a horn holed at its small end as well as the large, and inserted the small end into the Arab's rectum. Hassan was overjoyed. A torrent of thanks and praises was pouring out of his mouth, directed toward the slaveowner benefactor god who had so thoughtfully provided such exquisite means to the completion of his pleasure when he felt something extra reach the lining in his rectum. It was honey, mixed with lamp oil, the mixture heated past boiling. Hassan's unforeseen benefactress poured an overflowing measure of the sweet liquid into his arse. To the end the six other women did not deny him one little scratch of pleasure. Hassan screamed, but this night of nights screams did not alarm listeners. For it was Hassan's habit—it was their habit, all these predators from the desert—to scream with immense conviction whenever he approached an orgasm; the greater joy, the louder noise. Outside the askaris heard him. If they thought anything at all of it, it was that this must be for Hassan a night of pleasure better than any he had ever known, a lucky night.

How many died quieter deaths that night with daggers

38

stuck into their throats? How many tried to vomit poison, and found it had already tied their stomachs and the sinews of their throats rigid with swift action? Thirty there rolled in the agony of murderers finally trapped by their executors; here another thirty lay forever silent in their blood. Over there lay thirty more covered in the final glory of their vomit; another thirty swam to face their slave-owning god—swam in a viscous paste of shit and their own slimy urine. Near the end seven predators burned together, sewed into sheets of cloth upon which they had stretched their bodies in the expectation of unwonted entertainment. Gut meant for making music tightened in the hands of our women round the necks of predators and strangled them. But who craves more mention of their filthy names?

Of our women fifteen died that night, murdered by stupefied askaris. How, why did these liberating women die?

Outside the palace the askaris, drugged with the dawa as they were, still in the end began to have their doubts concerning the nature of the sounds coming from within the palace. Yet they could do nothing—strict were their instructions, keen their fear of the predators' vindictiveness.

The yells and screams from within the palace may not have been unusual except in their intensity this night, but after they had all died down the silence was decidedly uncanny. The askaris were used to the larger noises of the predators' climaxes subsiding into smaller snorts and groans, the normal, easy noises of the predators' most peaceful rest. But now this silence was eerie. Singly at first, and cir-cumspectly, a few askaris ventured past the palace walls, peered trembling into the hollow dimness within. One, struck finally by truth's immensity, howled his alarm and brought the other zombis rushing into the dark interior of the palace. The askaris saw their masters not in repose after pleasure but in death's final quiet.

Conditioned to their work of killing, the askaris at once began an assault upon our women. Now the wailing of the women brought every body running from the town. Even the hunters came desperate from their secrecy in the grasslands bringing bows and arrows. The oldest women, coming from the nearest houses, were first to arrive. The very oldest—Nandi was her name—threw herself in the path of the slaughtering zombis. She was the grandmother of the killers' leader, and so her sudden appearance there in all that blood, naked in her hurry, for a moment caused the askaris to halt. Nandi looked around the palace yard, saw the women trying to defend themselves, a couple of their bodies already past defense, and the askaris ready to leap again at them.

"But for whom are you fighting still?" Nandi asked the askaris. She saw her grandson. "Son of my daughter, whose work are you doing? Look. Those who turned you killer, where are they? Look at them. That should have been your work: killing your people's killers, destroying your people's destroyers. You did not do it, the work of your life. Instead you chose the work of walking corpses, killing your own people. What could we say to you? We knew your masters. They would have screamed at you to kill us all, and you would have obeyed them. But look now.

There your masters lie. You can give them your obedience no more. They have been sent past its use. For whom then are you still killing your people? Son of my daughter, for whom?"

The askari zombi leader did not answer. On his face a look of terror, hate, despair, loss, a look as of one plunged unprepared into vertiginous motion. A shout followed, in the predators' language, Arabic. Then the zombis rushed again. First their leader killed his grandmother Nandi. Twelve more fell that night. It was the arrival of the hunters from the grasslands that brought the carnage to a stop. The hunters' fortune was good this auspicious night. The hunters made no speeches, but struck immediately, destroying the most desperate of the zombis turned into wild, ineffective fighters by too much dawa in their brain. The remaining askaris, more than half, the hunters working together with the smiths disarmed.

A time of pain followed, a time of attempts to understand the things that had happened. Painful was the groping after lost reciprocity. Fertile had been the rule of women, but its fruit had been a forgetfulness of our own defense. The rule of men—of any desire for that the recent cascade of disasters had cured us. We thought to find new paths to the ancient, abandoned way of reciprocity, the way ignorant of women ruling men, knowing nothing of men dominating women. But we were dazed still. Our thoughts were not yet keen enough to cut the roots of schism. Against the inner causes helping our destruction, against the uncreative splitting of our people, against the turning of one half against its twin, against all this we had lost all sure defense.

Here too lay the beginning of our long bafflement at the heavy phenomenon of the slave forever conditioned against himself, against our people. With such never will there be any possibility of creation, never will new communities of the way be born within their presence. Such contain even in times of liberation's sweetest possibility an undying nostalgia for the worst times of the oppressors' domination over us, the times of suffering for the shattered community, because for such those are times of ease, times of prestige, times of privilege. To such the possibility itself of our liberation is a threat. Their lives in times of such possibility are long nightmares about their personal, precipitate descent from privilege. The events of our hope are to them real terrors. In their drugged moments of forgetfulness they dream of days when they were elevated slaves, not ordinary persons holding their own lives, their own futures together with our people. In liberation's time the torpid forgetfulness brought to them by drugs alternates with a waking existence of catatonic despair.

How were we then to know what to do with these zombis? We left them in peace—a generosity we lived to regret. Some the luckier predators took with them in their escape back to the desert that had vomited them against us. Most never came back. But a few returned—a return heavy with disaster. Among the returners one, perhaps two, saw in what had happened to their lives a terrible nightmare. These sought a healing reinsertion among the people they had betrayed, hard as that was. But others without the honesty of heart to admit they had been used for evil purposes instead pretended their trips abroad had been an initiation into something so great it set them above the rest of us. A few came claiming to have been the beneficiaries of wonderful kindnesses. On closer scrutiny these turned out to have been ill-used as servants in predators' homes, yet now after their arrival their intention was to veil over their despair by giving their particular enslavement a legendary glory. They were ignored. Among them the heaviest was a man who came back old and blind, his soul filled with bizarre mumblings about the predators' prophet, he whose creed centered on the strange necessity for everyone to be a slave. This man, Abdallah was his name. He brought his wild message to us, shrieking dementedly: turn slaves, or perish! Others there were like him, though with neither his insistence nor his zeal. We ignored them all. But the zombis, those whose brains still craved a master, listened to him. Listening, their wilted zombi hearts were once more filled in anticipation with the blood of victims, blood of our people. Abdallah in time gathered a band of these perennial slaves around himself, charged them with a fanatical reinterpretation of everything around them. Then he unleashed them against us. Heavy, heavy is our remembrance, long our dispersal from our way, the way. But memory now flies faster than the utterers' tongue and it is time to heed the quiet call, the call to return.

To return: the roots of schism grew in neglected soil. Who would have thought in times of the way or even in the fertile time, who would have thought the infirmity of individual cripples could ever carry danger against our entire people? Infirmity then was a felt diminution not merely of the single stricken self, but of the whole. What need then had any cripple for dreams of vengeance? But the change that began with the turning of our leaders into single peacocks strutting against each other's splendour broke the individual cripple's connectedness and threw him impotent against the shrunken group at home, the invidious family resentful of any loss of strength.

Why after that should the cripple acquiesce in silent suffering? Why, when ostentation had become the disease devouring a people, should not the most infirm in self-protection embrace the new contagion with the most triumphant eagerness? What wonder that we spawned Bokasa, Togbui, Budu, Senho and a brood of other cripples rivalling even the brilliant sun of day in garish ostentation?

There were others, a perfect complement to these ostentatious cripples. These were the askaris. But how shall we explain their disease? Let sleep and death again give us an image. The mind: that is the soul's conciliator with the body, the guide to keep the awakened body and the soul together. In sleep, in death, body and soul are apart. The body may fall victim to attack. The body may fall victim to an alien conqueror. The mind can also suffer attack, the mind can also fall to conquest. A mind attacked and conquered is guided easily away from the paths of its own soul. The body is then cut off from its spirit as in sleep, yet still instinct with the conqueror's imposed commands, a soulless thing, but active. In this state of souldeath the body blindly, sleepily obeys the conqueror. Such a body is set to persist in such obedience even if its conqueror be a distance of days and days away, a time of seasons separate. Such are zombis. And among us such were the askaris.

Apart from the ostentatious cripples and the parasitic elders around them, people torn between a soured happiness at the oppressor's overthrow and chagrin that the methods and pleasures of their conquerors could not simply have gravitated to their own enjoyment, there were a few among us so lost in soul, men who found slavery so perfect for their spirit, the condition of having their people reduced to rubble by an alien power and themselves patronized, condescended to, protected—amid the insecurity of the general ruin—by the same power crushing their people so sweet to their minds, that after the revolt of the women they lost their peace of mind and could only hope to retrieve it by following the retreating remnants of their masters. These lost souls went across the desert, chanting alien prayers like demented men.

One fantastic quality they never lost: fidelity to those who spat on them. It was this quality that preserved them among their white masters in the desert till after forty seasons they were ready to return against us. They came back with minds somersaulting in the potency of religious madness, bursting with a zeal to impose on their people the slavery their conquerors had first forced upon them—

45

selves. For these people's destruction was for the predators not an end in itself but a trial. After its success the victims had one aim: to help destroy their people, forcing the yet undestroyed surroundings into unison with their lost selves.

It is not that we did not see them. The cynical among us despised them openly, called them the white desert-men's dogs and treated them accordingly. But among us the sentimental were many, and they pitied them. What none of us had any way of knowing till it was too late was that they were also part of the prophecy unto us. For by themselves they were most pathetic. Yes, by themselves they were most pathetic.

But they were not by themselves. The first attack of the predators from the desert had produced among us another breed of hangers-on. At any time these would have been lazy, aimless ones, the kind of people whose indolence is not the wisdom of a weakened body seeking rest but a matter of their innate character, the set of their minds being committedly away from any useful work.

The predators from the desert, the white men, were not long in discovering in themselves a particular affinity for these creatures. The predators had a special use for them, and their souls—souls a healthy dog would have vomited out of his body—their souls were ready to accept such use. That use was this: the predators consistently reduced these men first to beasts, then to things—beasts they could command, things they could manipulate, all in the increase of their power over us.

To reduce them to beasts the predators starved their minds. The predators lowered in number and in seriousness the matters that could cause these hangers-on to think, till in the end there was nothing at all they cared to exercise their minds on.

To reduce them to things the predators fed their bodies, indulging their crassest physical wants promptly, over-flowingly. The predators fed them huge meals of meat and drink and added abundant *dagga* for their smoking. The predators supplied them with women and watched their copulation as another kind of sport. Such was the askaris' life. From morning till sleep they were either at some sport, eating, drinking, copulating, smoking or defecating.

Their bodies having thus been used to draw them into a state of mindless physical strength, habit sufficed to turn the state itself into a purpose for these aimless creatures. The new-found end of their lives was how to keep from doing anything different from the hollow cycle of shitting, smoking, fucking, drinking, eating, playing.

The white predators, the desert-men whose presence among us had elevated these slugs into such ease, needed protection from us their victims. Every season, every month, often every week and sometimes every day, those among us not made to be animals for others, things in the hands of our enemies, were trying ways to end our humiliation. Those with courage were finding ways to attack the attackers, ways to destroy the destroyers.

It was the askaris' violent job to kill off all caught trying to end our oppression. In this the mindless ones were truly expert. To punish women caught plotting our freedom they had a way of suspending their victims' bodies naked upon stakes, stooped with the thighs apart, then goading horses trained for the purpose to copulate with them. The bloody victims were left hanging a day and a night, a warning to others.

The askari zombis knew how to drive needles under fingernails of those suspected of harboring secret thoughts of our liberation, depending on the pain to loosen strong, unwilling tongues. On those they desired to silence forever it was the sepow they used. They preferred it rusty, so that no matter how hard the torturer pushed it, it would not pierce flesh cleanly but tear its way in with the utmost difficulty. They drove the short arrow into the left cheek, rammed its three barbs through the tongue and pushed it out through the right cheek till the leading barb emerged. The sepow was never removed—how would that have been done? Each victim, yet another warning unto us, was left to wander among us till his death.

Among us some in spite of the plethora of warnings laughed at the white predators from the desert. On such the askaris performed their most restrained operation. They cut away the skin of their victim's upper lip and gave the wretch his freedom with the smiling injunction: "Continue laughing!"

Hau! There have been so many mutilated wandering among us, living witnesses to our impotence, a testimony to the oppressors' power to destroy us if we did not learn like dogs to love our own oppression.

48

The askaris' tasks were violent, brief, and safe. For them there was no danger in all this killing. We were a disarmed people. Our destroyers, those who had disarmed us, had armed them.

Still, there were times when the predators' listening ears could catch none of our living sounds till in surprise they were assaulted by the beautiful music of revolt. Then the askaris knew fear again. Then they killed not just for pleasure but also for their useless lives.

After each uprising a wailing period intervened, a quiet time for the oppressors till our wounds were no longer raw. These were the times when the vigilance of the askaris brought them praise from our killers, their masters. And the things to put their minds to sleep, the things to flatter their bodies, the things to help their masters turn them into animals and things, these things increased.

The askaris did their blood work well. After a hundred seasons we were so reduced, so abject had we become, that the destroyers feared no revolt, lost all suspicion of our humanity, could discern nothing of our destiny. After another hundred seasons the destroyers from the desert thought we were born to slavery, not merely fallen into these pits through their greed and our own unwise generosity. For us it was a time of bowing and smiling in the face of the thing we hated. For the destroyers it was a time of ceaseless self-gratulation, incessant feasting, an unending round of entertainments enjoyed at our expense, a childish euphoria created on our backs.

After the revolt of the women in the harem and the

overthrow of the destroyers that it brought, the dis-
combobulation of the askaris was immense. Their masters
executed by an avenging people, the few of them who
through some unlucky accident happened to have been
absent from their last celebration having fled in panic back
across the stony desert—sandy womb fit to vomit only
such creatures—surrounded by a betrayed people each with
our specific slaughtered to remember and avenge, the askaris
found themselves in a universe with no supporting place
under their feet. They had been trained to commit crimes
in defense of the predators. The predators were no longer
here.

But how profoundly the conquest had changed us.
How far it had driven us from our self, how much farther
it had pushed us from our way, the way. We had grown
more than a little accustomed to being a people entirely
disarmed, the only armed ones among us being the portion
willing to be used against us. Now the askaris were shorn
of their creature comforts, the clothes of their bloodwork
taken from them and burned with other rubbish, their
weapons broken. Some fell to relatives of those they had
murdered in their servile days of power. But—pointless
indeed has been all our generosity in our exile from the way
—many, too many of the askaris were spared.

Of those spared half destroyed themselves. Fear and
anxiety that some still-hidden crime of theirs might be
discovered yet, led them first into madness then to
preemptive suicide. Their survivors, shunned by a people
with too raw a memory of blood unjustly spilt, became a

50

band apart. In sullen silences they nursed a stubborn nostalgia for the greasy days of their crimes, unwilling, unable to turn human again, their souls forever set against us their people, their spirits far, irretrievably far from the way, with every breath travelling farther. A death of the spirit was their life: catatonia, a pale suspicion of every living thing, an inability to release from its secrecy even one of their real desires.

We thought the generations would change them. We thought as we healed ourselves from the wounds inflicted by them and their masters, and freed our tongues again to speak to those growing of times closer to the way, to speak in remembrance of those who even in the recent heavy time, refusing to give up their arms and be turned into conquered things, chose to live the roaming life of hunters in the grasslands hunting not only animals but the oppressors also and their askaris, and found an early death at the end of the liberator's road; we thought because of the change we had wrought they too in coming generations would cease transmitting their foolish, destructive dreams to their children, and allow them to grow again together with us. We were too generous in our thoughts.

The disappointed askaris cultivated secret wishes of destruction against us. These wishes they passed on to the first, the second and the third generation. Children walked among us believing secretly there had been an age of giants and doers of great deeds now gone, and that these doers of great deeds had been their fathers' fathers. They heard secret, nostalgic tales of a time when a brave man had no need to do the careful, steady work of planting, watching, harvesting, but could in one sudden, brilliant flash of violent energy capture from others all the riches he craved, then like a python lie lazy through the length of coming seasons, consuming his victim profit. Ah, that such unthinking ways should have power to lure so many people of our blood, we of the way itself. See, around us now, all the hurrying revelers running in directions just as bizarre, just as horrible, just as destructive.

When the white predators from the desert came a second time they found a brood of men ready to be tools of their purpose. This time again the predators came with force—to break our bodies. This time they came with guile also—a religion to smash the feeblest minds among us, then turn them into tools against us all. The white men from the desert had made a discovery precious to predators and destroyers: the capture of the mind and the body both is a slavery far more lasting, far more secure than the conquest of bodies alone.

# 3

# the predators

In this the second onslaught of the white predators from the desert was more cunning than the first: it did not depend upon force alone but grafted itself on to divisions already in existence among us, manifest, beginning to aggravate themselves. It was a division between rulers and the ruled, a division we had had good reason till then to think not too important, it being a division between creators and their creatures, our people and their chosen caretakers.

In the aftermath of the women's revolt against the first destroyers from the desert the force of recent habit had proved stronger than the maimed sense of justice. Chosen caretakers somehow came to do things after the manner of the overthrown destroyers. That these things were done by our own people blinded us, in those unthinking days when we had scarcely had time to savour liberation, blinded us to the more important fact that these things were being done not in our way, that they were things

53

being done against us, against our way.

Hear this for the sound of it. The men, and among them especially the elders, had seen the way the destroyers used women, turning them into things for their use, turning them into animals for their pleasure. The men had seen this, seen and taken note. Though in the heat of our oppression we had all—women and men—been dirtied with the ash of the oppressors' contempt, now that the women had wrought the destroyers' overthrow the men began to see in the breach the white men left behind a hole altogether worth their filling.

A long quarrel began, circling around the rightness of male against female succession. The quarrel did not involve the people themselves. To us it seemed childish, except that it was not about mere succession, but also about some new-found necessity to make all positions, even those of experts, hereditary.

The way itself is not ambiguous about the work of experts and the place of caretakers. These are not positions of consumption but productive agencies requiring care and the patient use of skills exactly learnt. These were not positions generally sought after by self-seekers. They were conferred on people who had proved their worth with no red-eyed straining to push themselves into haughty situations. Now monstrous desires had taken refuge behind arguments revolving about these positions.

The quarrel was never in a true sense settled—our people had no interest in it. Of the disputants one side would get tired, the other side would take advantage of the drop in its

54

opponent's vigilance (and of our people's constant indifference) to impose itself until the next change came. In this way the work of caretakers, the settling of sour disputes, the receiving of strangers devolved now upon the clan of the leopard, now on that of the dupon tree.

In the three hundredth season after Anoa spoke the most bloody complication springing from this quarrel arose. Pentsir of the leopards had been caretaker seven seasons, indifferent seasons, indifferent caretaking. When he died the elders—in this they did not stray from the way— asked the people if they would accept Kumi of the dupon clan as a new caretaker. The people, not caring overmuch, did not say no. Kumi became another caretaker.

Now Pentsir had been blood relative to Dwemo, he who had been among the caretakers before him; Kumi was not. On Kumi's nomination the long quarrel heated up again. The elders from the leopard clan argued that since both Dwemo and Pentsir had been caretakers it was an insult to their memory and to their clan to take the vacant position away from their clan. The elders of the leopard clan added another special reason. They said the art of caretaking could best be learned in that period by those closest to actual caretakers, by which in this case they meant members of their clan. In conclusion they proposed the elders swallow their first decision and accept their man Edusei.

The elders gathered together pointed out there was no insult to the memory of any of the leopard dead; that any person who had earned respect through work could be selected caretaker; that Dwemo himself had been thus chosen; that Pentsir when it came to his turn had won acceptance by a single voice because it was thought his calmness of disposition would be a perfect quality for the time, not because he was a member of this clan or that.

The arguers among the leopards grew quiet, but plainer than their taciturnity was their dissatisfaction. Their reasons had met defeat in open argument; their passions did not cease boiling in their covert anger. They conceived themselves humiliated. Their candidate Edusei, haughty with ambition, saw himself so abused, so foully deprived of a situation he considered his, that he took himself quite away from any participation in the work of our people, sat daily brooding by himself, and spent the energy of his mind contemplating a spiteful emigration with his clan.

That Edusei did not in the end migrate was due to the influence of one man, a willing slave of the predators returned after long seasons journeying across the desert in his masters' train. This man claimed some power to make potent medicines and charms using words spoken by the predators' god. His own name and the name of his family he had forgotten. He called himself after the predators' fashion, Abdallah, a name he said signified he was a slave—slave of a slave-owning god.

Our breath taken by the ridiculousness of the man's name, recoiling in revulsion at the abject state of his soul, we yet saw in his presence no terrible threat. And of his actions we were less than half aware till their putrid fruit burst against our face.

This is what the slave of a slave-master god accomplished

against us: Going to the sulking Edusei in his loneliness he with the craven shrewdness of a hyena poured into his ears music sweetest to a frustrated, isolated man.

"Your suffering is unjust," this Abdallah told Edusei. "Your value will be recognised. You will be recompensed. But how can this just restitution begin when you let your understanding itself run away from knowledge of your true worth? Realize yourself. How, you ask?

"Put yourself completely at the service of him whose road is the one sure road away from the way of your people who despise you. Your people—don't you see it yet?—they walk in darkness. They are blind. Further: they are cursed, they who have rejected you, you who will be blessed among all the servants of our master Allah. They have rejected you and your mind is filled with despair. They would be happy to see you depart, a stranger courting ruin in alien parts. Do not obey their will. Do not leave them. Stay here. Learn. Listen to the master's word. It alone will bring you peace. It alone will fill your days with blessedness. Learn, accept, and wait, you who have been chosen."

Edusei, now that a new hope had come to him, waited as only those filled with the sweet patience of hope know how to wait. No longer a recluse, he became hyperactive, a man possessed by that explosive spirit, vengeance. He drove his family to prodigious work, hunted like a famished lion himself and brought together a group of men to work with him, not in the manner prescribed by the way— each participant an equal working together with all others for the welfare of the whole—but along a road as far from our way, the way, as it is possible for human beings to go: Edusei's group worked together but did not benefit together. The group worked for the single profit of Edusei. In this and other ways he began building up a power to rival the caretakers. That his road was wrong we knew. That it was such a direct treat to our way, the way, we did not trouble our minds to think then. Ah, blind tolerance for the worm of death. Ah, foolish generosity.

Edusei worked on the bodies of his followers. Abdallah concerned himself with their minds. Many he changed to the white predators' religion by telling them there was no wrong, only good, in things they had wanted but had found no road among us to reach: the pushing of our women into pits of the most horrible contempt; the raising of askaris and like mindless creatures into created places of honour and respect. In such ways the shrewd Abdallah brought together the sour despair of Edusei and the askaris' long disappointment. In the alchemy of the desert white predators' religion he turned these bitter frustrations into a bloody hope. To the converted craving blood he gave one firm promise: they would be fighting for their god, that same slave-owning god he himself called his master, Allah.

The rest we know. Other Abdallahs we had never heard of worked elsewhere upon the minds of other men crippled with a feeling they had been wronged. Among us at its culmination the quarrel over succession merged into holy war. All the preceding bitterness turned the conflict

58

into a war of ways and roads: the strangers and their followers among us fighting to destroy the way of a whole people in a war of ways, a war of gods to those whose minds still need the world explained in fables concerning gods.

Nor was Edusei himself the cause of the worst trouble, for in this we were away on the edge somewhere, far from the worst events in the centre of the swollen empire. Where these events took place—the name of that place would scald our tongue—another cripple king rose to power trampling on the spilt entrails of seven rival brothers. In the aftermath of that first victory, in gratitude to his mentors and helpers, also predators from the desert, also believers in a slave-owning god, this cripple king embarked on a holy war against all the people neighbouring his. It was to him men like Edusei went to offer service. In him the askaris found a new fulfilment.

We fought, amazed at first that such brutal ferocity could be conjured up in support of such foolish reasoning, such an imbecile religion. We supposed in a little time the absurdity of the new faith itself would work its disintegration, thinking as we did that even the converted would have to begin using their brains again, that even the most ferocious adherents would have to wake from their stupid zeal like drunkards penitent. But from this poison there was to be no such rapid waking.

We held back our anger to see if the predators' violence would cease. Our restraint sent them into accesses of manic slaughter. We resisted. They grew terrified. Nothing could calm their panic but the destruction of all possibilities of revolt among us. Then in the fourth season of this continuous holocaust the horrible realization assailed us at length: the time long before prophesied in Anoa's utterance, the two thousand seasons of destruction, were already upon us.

Paralysed, fascinated in death's palpable presence, hypnotized by the heavy-lidded slaughterers' eyes, contemplating extinction, wondering about survival, we considered the paths still open. The first, the path of resistance to save our people, we would have tried. But our people were no longer of one heart. The division had already come within. It would be impossible to save a people fighting against itself. Other paths we considered and found impossible.

We were left with one: let the crazed have their devouring new religion. Let the weary consent to slavery. We, remainder of the slaughter of our people, our minds made up not to weary of seeking the way again, not to tire of searching for the way even after losing it, we would move again, move after so many thousand seasons of forgetfulness of danger, after so many thousand seasons in which our distances breathed peace, thousands of seasons when movement was about the desire for something to be found at the destination, not fear of destruction at the point of departure. We would move again.

Now the sound of Anoa's prophecy rang clearly in our ears. We were ready to go. Of the journey ahead we knew nothing save that Anoa had foreseen it, warned us of it. We would have her in our mind. Her spirit would be our guide on the way.

We had been forced to think of multiform death: death of the body for all whose bodies resisted oppression; death of the body also for those whose minds resisted, for any way different from the predatory conquerors' road was to them diseased, unholy, dangerous. We with our way were all condemned, our very colour turned into the predators' name for evil.

Those who killed their own minds, trusted the killers and crawled along their road were spared in body. The weary chose this road, preferring an abject peace to a troubled future. Strong was the temptation to join the peaceful conquered and thus end a sure time of troubles.

But there were those among us still mindful of the way, and they asked a question: what would be the purpose, what the aim of such acceptance? Examining the paths laid open before us we saw the prospect of our extinction as a people whichever way we looked. For what else would we be under a religion imposed on us by force but a people with a soul extinct?

Our way, the way, is not a random path. Our way begins from coherent understanding. It is a way that aims at preserving knowledge of who we are, knowledge of the best way we have found to relate each to each, each to all, ourselves to other peoples, all to our surroundings. If our individual lives have a worthwhile aim, that aim should be a purpose inseparable from the way.

The conquerors offering to spare our individual lives in return for our acceptance of their destruction of our knowledge of the way, these conquerors presume to bribe us with part of something stolen from ourselves, presume to bribe us into accepting our own death.

Our way is reciprocity. The way is wholeness. Our way knows no oppression. The way destroys oppression. Our way is hospitable to guests. The way repels destroyers. Our way produces before it consumes. The way produces far more than it consumes. Our way creates. The way destroys only destruction.

Absurd then for us to continue here merely for the zombi purpose of existing, things to be used to serve the conquerors' alien purposes. Here was no offer of life but the infliction of that deepest death from which there would be no regeneration. Here was the death of water flowing to the desert.

And what was the proffered destination, what was the new religion anyway? With the predators' devotees, servants of a servant-using god, force is goodness. Fraud they call intelligence. Their road flies off opposite reciprocity. In their communion there is no respect, for to them woman is a thing, a thing deflated to fill each strutting, mediocre man with a spurious, weightless sense of worth. With their surroundings they know but one manner of relationship, the use of violence. Against other peoples they recommend to each other the practice of robbery, cheating, at best a smiling dishonesty. Among them the sphere of respect is so shrunken they themselves have become sharp-clawed desert beasts, preying against all.

They plant nothing. They know but one harvest: rape.

The work of nature they leave to others: the careful planting, the patient nurturing. It is their vocation to fling themselves upon the cultivator and his fruit, to kill the one, to carry off the other. Robbery with force: that is the predators' road, that is the white destroyers' road.

The thoughts raised by the times and the troubles they brought then were restless thoughts. They were doubts which in their generosity of soul our ancestors could not reduce to certainty. Faced with a people whose manifest purpose in life is to destroy life, we, people of the way, people of creation, where lies our fidelity? Must we remain upon the land we have come to call home, and there have the destroyers drag us each day farther from the way that is our way? Or leave the land and go seeking unknown soil in order to be true to the way? Before the journey to Anoa these thoughts exercised our minds and the conclusion they brought was this: the land is good, but the land is a means to finding the way of our life, the land is not the way itself. If the necessity is for the land or the way to be lost, better then the land.

There was no ease to that conclusion's coming. Women and men from all the clans, most notably from the clans of the duiker and the parrot—sweet speakers when they find it worth their while to speak, and of courage to speak their minds even against a tide of powerful voices—spoke long and persuasively, telling us stunned into utter silence by their truths that a people in flight is already a people destroyed; asking us whether in our minds it would not indeed be better to change the nature that brought us conquerors as our guests, to learn a fitting ferocity and fight to keep our land even if the fighting degraded us into soultwins of the desert predators, the white men?

Those for moving had more voices on their side than those who would stay even if staying meant our becoming predators like our attackers. No other paths seemed visible, for in that time all suffered from the hazing over of the way, all ears were blocked to the true vocation of the way.

Four seasons we looked, four seasons listened. Seeing the way the acceptors of the new religion lived, it was clear we would become a community shattered into hustling zombis, our separate energies laboring to support, to comfort parasitic, predatory alien conquerors.

Already we had seen the work of continued fighting where we were. Those among us who had accepted the new religion being pitted against those who had not, the result was the same extinction of our people, the same destruction of our way. Better then not to turn the resistant fraction against the zealous, hypnotized fraction, the fraction rejecting slavery against those accepting servitude. Better not to have the accepting fraction used by the killer to erode us irretrievably, mutually reducing ourselves till attrition made us not a people any more but individual grains of sand, loose desert sand, porous, incoherent, barren. Better then to leave.

The decision for motion once arrived at, the need for secrecy was great, its fulfilment made almost impossible by the need, equally great, to make swift and certain preparations for this movement of thousands of thousands.

Secretly, while still paying taxes to the predator, we stored our grain. Four seasons we needed to hide a sufficient store for a journey whose length we were uncertain of, four seasons of the strictest discipline in which no one among us indulged himself with more food than he needed, yet no one was allowed to debilitate himself with over-zealous abstinence. In the strenuous times ahead ill-health would have destroyed us just as surely as the predator's greed.

The selfish we eased from our midst. We curbed the impetuous among us who wanted—following the too-generous, unthought-out promptings of their hearts—to set themselves impossible tasks at work and in saving grain.

The time of waiting found other good use. We found our legs again, took every chance to learn something we had practically forgotten in the softness of the fertile time, swift motion. In every possible thing we found reasons to walk again. The labour we were forced to do fetching and building for the predators, the new festivals the destroyers brought with them, the exigencies of their puerile enter-tainments, all this we used as pretexts for giving our limbs back their strength.

Never have we been a people of the swollen centre. We have been a people living away from the tumult of growing kingdoms and empires, closer to the sources than to the rushing rivers of the swiftly passing day. So at the moment of choice there was no prolonged hesitation once the paths open to us had first been cleared in secret conversation. Better to leave all familiar things, everything to which our growing consciousness had become rooted, every material thing made to give comfort to the flesh or to remind our souls of those gone before. Better to leave everything behind and go seeking unknown places where our spirits would still have room to move. Better than to stay here in bodies emptied of our spirits, with alien, hate-filled spirits forced into them. For how were we, a people of friendship, a people of reciprocity, people of the way, how were we to accept a road of life constructed by a god of hate, god of unreasoning violence, a childish god who promises each of his heavy-lidded dotard slave followers virgins for his final, unending lechery?

The ripe time came. We began our movement. A portion remained behind to close the predators' eyes, to keep our motion from being noticed too early, and after that to delay interception, and to prevent our movement being stopped.

The time chosen was wise. In the fullness of their victory the conquerors, secure, had already begun bickering over the size of spoils. This was also the moonless time they called a time of fasting, a time of no true fasting but a hypocritical abstinence till dusk, then at night a greedy debauchery of food and drink—so assured had the destroyers become of our docility and of their safety.

The order of our going was agreed among the clans. We journeyed fast, each clan leaving enough people to continue the tasks given it, but only in areas visible to the predators in their easy somnolence. In this way the conquerors' suspicion slept till our main body had long been gone. Then those we had left behind, sworn to protect us, pretending immense amazement at our disappearance, inventing long catalogues of belongings of theirs we had stolen on our march, offered a third of their number to lead a numerous force of askaris after us.

They led the askaris along the most direct route to the first forests—we ourselves had taken a more circuitous route—weakened them daily by mixing their food with entrail-loosening poisons in place of their accustomed dream-inducing drugs, and on the way were joined secretly by the remainder of those we had left behind, armed with all the hidden weapons we had not taken with the main body.

Together one night—but why halt our remembrance here to make that good night live again?—they destroyed the askari army, setting one ferocious zombi against the other under the moonless sky. Our pleople had prepared themselves for the coming confusion by choosing a cry of recognition, the call of the black vulture. Afterwards those who had been directly in the fight adopted the vulture as their double.

Let the ignorant laugh at such identification. We listen to their mindless laughter, see their brainless faces. Of the vulture what is it they know? That bird that lives off carrion but never kills a living thing that has not first attacked it, that bird is also of the way.

The ordinary route, not of escape but of simple departure, lay across the river Kwarra, past the younger twin town Ilalani, two days' journey before the treelands and then

67

three more days—five if the travellers were many and had to keep to the speed of those past maturity and those still immature—to the base of the mountains before the great forests. Season after season our people had gone down these paths from the river to the mountains. Of the clans living in all that space each was now in some way relative to us.

Among those we had left behind by far the greater part were true, but even among them there were traitors. It would not occur to these, soulless bodies who would prevent our departure by informing their masters of our intended direction, to think we could have gone another route. As for the normal paths, all knew none would be crazed enough to go as a people to the desert; a disturbed soul now and then, but not a people seeking life.

At the time of departure we had announced with thoughtful indiscretion our path would lie opposite the desert, across the plains, up the mountainsides, then down again into the forests. That indeed was the way we started, keeping the place of the falling sun to our right, to our left the place of its coming out. We went at dusk. Enough light came from the falling sun to make the first steps rapid, easy. The country was known to us. It was also clear, open.

Night came quickly, more abruptly than on the river's other side. We continued a third of the distance we had come, then in the darkness there had to be a halt. We changed direction. Turning to the fallen sun, we searched for the seven children and the ancient woman, found them and moved steadily, slowly toward them. A third of a third of our fighters volunteered to go more slowly and to move straight down, positioning themselves to lure the attention of any askaris following us. In addition to their food they took an excess of filth, the kind of debris a travelling multitude is bound to leave: shards from broken vessels, leaves from food consumed, and other waste. All this they scattered along their path, discreetly so it would not appear a trap, so it would appear our escaping people had taken reasonable pains to guard against discovery but had simply been unable to reconcile the need for speed with the need to cover up our path, the need for leaving nothing behind.

As for the main group, it took the greatest care not to leave any trace at all. Not even defecation was allowed till we had crossed the Baka pool, wide, shallow daughter of the Kwarra, leaving no footprints behind.

Soon enough the enslavers started their pursuit. The traitors among those we left behind had done their job too well. The askaris marched swiftly, zombis scenting blood. They were not well armed, for they were expecting to slaughter a rabble of unprepared fugitives, not to fight a forewarned people bent on regaining our way. Our watchers in the rear did not reveal themselves but let the askaris march in deep. Where the ordinary road divides itself between Kedian, Fulani and Gao, our fighters watched the askaris split into three groups as, trusting signs deliberately left for them, they calculated they were almost upon us but were not sure which route we had chosen at the trivia.

Then our fighters took counsel. They would strike first at the weakest band of askaris, swiftly, before the other two became aware. Then they would disappear, watch, and strike again at the smallest group exposed to them.

In their counsel our fighters had gone farther than reality would require. The first assault on the askaris was so sudden, the zombis so surprised, that of those left alive half ran off amazed without their weapons. The other half prepared places for the night and lay down to get some rest. They needed it. They left guards at five places, starpoints of their camp. Because of the darkness of the night, the recent attack they had had no time to understand, and the terrifying cries of our men, their nerves were bad. Our fighters decided their wisest field of battle would be the askari camp itself.

The askari guards on the side leading back home were the least afraid, the most relaxed, and so the sleepiest. In groups of three fighters to each guard we overpowered them, their little whimpers of surprise unheard amid the chorus of our vulture cries. They had lit low, red fires in the centre of their camp for warmth. When our fighters began their work among the sleepers the light of the fires was not enough in the confusion of the general frenzy to help the askaris recognize each other. It was enough simply for each embattled zombi to discern a panicky neighbour, to apprehend danger in the struggling form and to start defending himself in desperate fratricide. The following day real vultures hovered where the askari camp had been, hovered and peacefully descended.

70

Whether the lucky remainder of the askaris did not dare go back to tell their masters of their failure for fear of punishment, whether they went back but told fantastic tales of monsters waylaying them, of jinns helping us the devil's children, killing them, preventing them from even knowing where to turn in our pursuit, we have no certain knowledge. The pursuit was not retaken.

What we do know is that after the success of our escape the white predators executed another terrible slaughter among those who chose to stay. The relatives of all who had spurned oppression were burned to ashes. Children not yet born burst out alive in that fire, then scalded with the hissing liquid of their mothers' wombs regained oblivion. All were burned and the ashes scattered in the river, to make sure—so the principal priest of the white predators explained it to the weary tremblers—to make sure the spirit of rebellion had not even the vestige of a home left among those remaining, to make sure the un-challenged reign of Allah, slave-owning god of slaves, could now begin.

As for the main portion, for three days we went with the sun before we came upon the first large group of people. We had taken counsel never on this journey to take aggressive initiatives. If we came across any people we would ask them for food if they wished to trade, drink and shelter if they were willing to give us these, and guidance if they felt persuaded to help us on our way. If they refused us we would ask to cross their land the quickest route, and if they denied us even that we would skirt it and moving

71

as fast as possible try to reach places inhabited by less shrivelled souls.

We had no trouble with the people of the first place we came to. They would have offered us food but their harvests for four seasons had been bad and now they had barely enough planting seed for the coming season. Something else had befallen them. Men from over there—they pointed in the direction of the desert wastes—had attacked them, killed several in each family, robbed them of their supplies leaving only the plantseed buried in secret places, taken many among them captive and gone like white lightning back into the dry sands. Water these afflicted people had, and of that they gave us plentifully.

We washed in the river there, then told them our news, why we were leaving, though of our hoped-for destination we had nothing to say. We made it clear to them that from their description those who had attacked them and made them destitute were kin to those who had attacked us also and tried to make us all slaves, though not yet as numerous. We warned them the predators would come again in greater numbers to attack and to enslave them unless they could find methods to defend themselves—a huge task, since they would be attacked internally first through schisms of the spirit, then externally through predatory force—or prepare to move to less accessible land.

They thanked us for our news, but that was all. They seemed a good people, like a people of the way also—their language we understood with little difficulty—but they were numbed with calamity, unable to decide to break

72

the habits of sedentary ages. We thanked them, left them something of our own travelling supplies and set off the next day. They gave us guides to help us along the part of our route known to them.

To the next town it was more than eight days. Not that in the intervening space there had never been habitations, but these were no more. Two days from the gentle people we started counting villages destroyed, burned completely by some vengeful horde. We counted twelve.

That eighth day we came to a large town, larger than where we had stopped among the gentle people. But here only the physical place was left, and of that merely the charred husk. We sent a careful group to draw closer and examine the place. There was not one living creature there. Death had visited this place, and time had passed over it. There were no corpses, only skeletons. From these too the bones were being removed—by which night creature we could find no indication.

In the houses all things useable had been taken away, all things except heavy household stones and mortars. Some houses toward the back of the town bore still persisting signs of a desperate struggle. In the centre stood a huge baobab, leafless, all its branches dead.

Here was desolation so complete it weakened all our spirits and set some to wailing loudly, saying there could never be a home for us anywhere since there was death behind us and death also before. It seemed indeed our path would lead to more disaster, not a home.

Next morning on our way from the town we found two

hollow-eyed maniacs. They fell on us so suddenly and with such fury they killed one man among us and wounded four, yet their weapons were mere sharpened sticks and stones. The deadliness was in the desperate wrath with which they attacked us. These men were filled with an overpowering hate. It seemed if they continued alive at all it was solely to express that violence. They killed the first among us to see them, then wounded four who had hurried there to help him, before we could arrive to subdue them.

After a stubborn silence they talked, a language hard to understand. With deranged, fantastic interjections of pain they told us of attackers who had pillaged everything, killed men, enslaved the rest and transported them across the desert, leaving no survivors except the two themselves.

The killers from the desert were white; that the two survivors knew. But so shattered were their minds, at the peak of their suffering they grew sure we were ourselves the killers, and we had to have strong people hold them to keep them from trying more homicide. Bound, they trembled with the fury of their impotence, defied us to kill them, begged us to kill them, before again subsiding into their bottomless silence.

We took them with us, bound for our safety. But they died before the third day. The first died without warning, his blood escaping through every aperture. Among us the experts of the healing art knew there was no remedy for him. The second looked at his dead companion silent, lost, and would touch nothing, neither food nor drink. It was not of hunger that he died, however. Neither was it of

thirst. A fit of trembling came upon him in the cool of
night: first a fevered shivering, then a trepidation more
intense, his body like a baby's shaken by an angry man.
We buried him beside the path, a day from the companion
of his misery.

Surrounded by the work of death we halted again for
counsel. It was time to travel down away from the zone
of destruction, away from the desert, killer of our hope,
from where other predators could come against us any
time.

Turning left we moved along a new route. After eight
days we saw no more destroyed villages. But the communities we passed among were hostile, living in fortified
places on hilltops. How they hated strangers! They refused
to give us any help. Nothing would they trade. Whenever
they caught us vulnerable, themselves in an impregnable
position, they assaulted us.

We fled them, fled their inhospitable land. When we
reached the mountain foothills we found a people less
stricken with suspicion. These traded freely, though for
every thing they drove a bargain without mercy.

The decision was taken to cross over the mountains at
the next good pass, then journey back on the other side
of the mountain range to a meeting with those we had
left to protect our escape, in so far as there would be any
left—we imagined then they had fared far worse than they
had. In most of our minds they had chosen nothing less
momentous than unavoidable self-sacrifice.

The crossing over was long but not hard. After the

mountains we reached strange territory—land of an unwonted fertility, some stretches muddy with too much water, and, most pleasant surprise, an abundance of drinking water everywhere. Slowly the new place enticed us into changing recent habits. Once more we could delight tired bodies with the freshness of water every noon and every dusk. We took lighter and lighter loads of water on our days' journeys, till finally we allowed the idea to come to us that we did not need to carry water at all. Within any day's march in this place we crossed numbers of little streams and one substantial river at least.

Habitations we did not come across with any great frequency. There were not many dwellers on this side. Those we found seemed to know farming but not to practise it with any serious care. A shy people with an easy train of life, they preferred, it was clear, to keep some distance between themselves and such a large body of people as we were.

When we had gone as many days' journey behind the mountain range as we had gone before it we began to move in a more scattered way. We built a line of villages each talking to the next, built them easy to defend, able to survive for seasons, for a long time if necessary. Together they made a net of safety awaiting those we had left to protect our escape. If there were any left they could not fail to pass this way. We had another reason for building there: we had enough grain for a season but the next season would be bad unless we planted and had good harvests.

It was here we learned to set traps for the elephant and use his meat and hide. Pathfinders went down and up: down to see where we could best pass on our continued journey, upward in the hope of meeting those we had left behind if any there were left, and to learn what new threat would be coming from the desert. From the upward direction first there was nothing but occasional new groups of harassed refugees, dazed casualties wandering aimlessly beneath the mountains, stragglers who had realized too late that even the voiding of their souls would not save them from the murderous greed of their Muslim overlords. These we left alone when they came to us. We had no need to swell our numbers with people with no sure sense of who they were, people who could only desire to be themselves again after their masters' hot greed had made it impossible for them to betray themselves.

We were a people in motion still, but now we moved more slowly. Because the place we had come to was secure we decided not to abandon the mountainsides till we had found other, forward places as secure, as well provisioned naturally, and as defensible.

Small groups went ahead of us looking for new land. Where they found others already settled they asked permission, so that in our passage we worked alongside our hosts. In this way did a chain of granaries and friendships grow along which our people passed each season, halting at each place long enough not to break the flowing of our life but never definitely settling down.

Our hosts failed to understand why we had to go; we

warned them of the terror we had left behind. Some told us there was no better place ahead, that farther down we would find only frightening forests, strange sudden sly beasts, treacherous rushing waters and a maddening abundance of encumbering vegetation. Others talked of a land cursed with an unimaginable wetness, all mud so thick nothing could survive in it, all useful plants there being overwhelmed with giant reeds and poisonous weeds. Two women told us we would come to a place they could not describe except to say it was a horrible place, for it would be neither land nor water. We heard the warnings of our hosts. We gave them ours again, then we moved on.

A hundred seasons we spent in this slow flowing. In our minds the terrors of the immediate past grew not so pressingly terrible. Fewer among us woke up in the middle of their sleep screaming against the murders we had suffered. A new generation had grown to produce children, and on the surface these children did not come bearing scars. Our wounds were covered over by new growth.

Over a hundred seasons of this slow, peaceful passage. Then our farthest pathfinders came back telling of abrupt changes in the character of the places we would be coming to. They told of implacably hostile people, users of the terrible poison arrow, sitting fiercely in our path on both sides—coming as well as falling—of an immense, salty bogland. On the side of the sun's coming one group of our pathfinders had been killed; on the side of the sun's falling two, with every indication in addition that there would be more killing if we pressed forward in either direction.

Again we took thought. We knew nothing of the numbers of these people, only of their hostility. Unless we had it inside us to start on a road of killing and being killed whose end we could not judge there were only two paths open to us: we could stay where we had come, or we should cross the bog.

Those for staying were fewer than those whose thoughts were for our going on. The latter pointed out that the range of mountains was no insuperable barrier, and that the predators we had fled were rapacious white beasts. Once they heard of the goodness of the land beyond the mountain range they would be sure to descend on it with all their greed. Better then to put between ourselves and the predators all the barriers possible. Better to move on. Better to cross the bog.

Not only that. Here in this new place we were guests and in no position to put down roots going straight down like a people on land of our own. Here we would have to enter someone else's house, follow someone else's path. These people, true, were friendly, but had they too not in a way lost purpose, lost their way? In so far as we aspired after purpose, in so far as we wanted to remain a people of the way, and even if we lost the way hoped to find it again, we should not become one with the purposeless.

We prepared ourselves for that journey. Pathfinders went as far as they could go, simulating the pace of the whole people. They took increasing bundles of food and drink. Each group of pathfinders started back when half its supplies were gone. One group, two women and two men, at last came back with news of a habitable place beyond the bog.

Now also there began an ominous striving for power among our hosts, a kind of struggle familiar to us except for one horrid twist—one side was eager to enlist our support in the internecine conflict and the other side seemed happy at the prospect of blaming everything on us, and talked unknowingly of sending to the enemy we had fled for help against their opponents. We were ready for continued journeying.

We planned the movement to the edge of the bog: first a small group to prepare the way, then a larger, then a larger. Behind us we left a few in case a temporary return became necessary. At each point we took care to send on sufficient supplies at the head: water, food, healing medicine. Together with these things went masters of all our necessary crafts.

The pathfinders had told us what to expect. We were still amazed. The hostility of dwellers beside the bog forced us to hasten the crossing. We hesitated a third of a season asking news of the bog from such as we chanced to find singly or in small groups, and they were few indeed in this place. We asked how the bog was, how long it would take to cross it, which was the best and the quickest way across, what we could expect to find after the crossing. Answers, where there were any, were sullen, curt. Terrible, we were told the bog was. We asked for details.

We got none.

"Have none of you gone into it?"

"Some have."

"How then was it?"

"They did not say."

"How? They did not choose to speak?"

"They could not."

"They did not return?"

"They did not."

Before the crossing, returned pathfinders urged the making of long, strong ropes to carry with us. Those in the lead carried tall stakes sharpened at one end to test the firmness of underlying ground before we moved over it. For long stretches, often for days, we waded in watery mud reaching up to an adult's crotch. Children were carried, old people supported or also carried. Some among us died when land that had looked firm, felt firm to the first passers of a sudden slipped from under them with no help near, the ropes too far for them to hold. Twice a massive chunk of harder mud sank with everyone on it, and there the ropes could not even begin to be of help to anyone.

The pathfinders had located firm ground in an immense, looping half circle, islands in the mud. We planned our journey from one to the other of these islands, rested, then moved on. It was a slow journey. We had not learned to ignore the sucking leech. Small crocodiles, wilder than the larger, snapped at us trapped in their mud. With the water snakes they killed each day a number of our people. The farther we journeyed the worse the terrors awaiting us. Each day we supposed we had seen the worst. Every next day gave us reason to regret the passing of the previous day. Discouraged, some were for a desperate turning back. The pathfinders themselves, having to coax a weary people to make greater efforts every disappointing day, feeling a deepening guilt for all the deaths and diseases of the bog in spite of understanding words from the most steadfast among us, unable to answer despairing questioners pleading to know if we had not yet come at least half the way, the pathfinders themselves lost heart.

On the largest of the islands some were so tired they refused to move. We had to move. The water we had brought with us was running low. Food was getting finished. Any stop for rest meant a dangerous depletion. As long as we were on our way food occupied a low place in our minds. But the stops for rest were times of famished gorging, and consequent resentment of discipline imposed by those with tougher entrails and a longer view.

Contemplating all that suffering and perdition Ndile, most sensitive of souls among the pathfinders and one of the four who had in fact reached the end of the bog, in the grip of an unrelenting fever proclaimed he was responsible for our terrible plight, that he had led us along paths he knew nothing about, and that he had no remembrance at all of any way out of the bog. In different stages of dejection, weakness and disease other pathfinders came to him. The three he had travelled with, two women and a man, reminded him they had gone together to the end of this horrid nightmare and there seen land, seen beautiful land, good land. But the delirious Ndile, long past hope, was certain all their words were about a mere deceptive dream cutting derisively across our unending nightmare. Nothing in this world seemed ever to have been real to him, nothing save death. Upon those who had come to him thinking to reassure him his fevered insistence that all here was a fantastic nightmare had an uncanny effect. They lost their assurance and took on his doubt. It was soon clear to all that the delirium of doubt had gained them too.

It was at this time that a crowd of men, themselves fevered beyond patience, each the loser of beloved relatives and friends around whom the meaning of life had had a tendency to weave itself, hearing misty reports that one of the pathfinders had confessed to fraud and that the others were even now emerging from some guilty secret they had shared, in a frenzy rushed at the gathered pathfinders demanding red-eyed truth.

The pathfinders were in the grip of a merciless anxiety. They could give no prompt answers. They could give no answer at all. In the emptiness left by their silence the voice of the dying pathfinder rose unchallenged, shrieking its wild, incoherent message.

"We have tricked you into death. Look. Now it comes. You will not escape it!"

Greater than the amazement of the other pathfinders was the anger of the crowd surrounding them. None knew what to believe, where to find a seed of hope. Each new word rising from the throat of the dying man brought a horrible addition to the general anxiety, to the sense of desolation inescapable, till all found the tension no longer supportable, and it broke.

First the three companion pathfinders, waking from the paralysis of their minds, laid hands on the dying man. It was their intention not to frighten him but to shake him into a different world from the ashen place his soul had entered, to bring to him the unreality of every one of his words. The man was close to death already. Some higher fear filled him and he let out one long scream of agony: "They are killing me!"

The three pathfinders holding him took a firmer hold on him—the dying man was shaking so—but his screaming grew louder. The outer crowd now pressed in baffled, uncertain what to do. They reached the delirious pathfinder at the exact moment of his death.

There was no doubt in the mind of the crowd concerning the event that had just taken place. The pathfinder had been throttled by his companions to keep their guilty, heinous secret, they were sure. Impatient of explanations and delays, each heavy with remembrance of beloved ones left dead along the way, they seized the remaining pathfinders and tore them limb from limb. Two girls tried to help the pathfinders: Noliwe and Ningome were their names. As for the victims themselves they were dazed, incredulous, powerless to stop any of the things happening with such speed. The slaughter of the three pathfinders enlarged the crowd, which then envisioned for itself the task of destroying all the other pathfinders, calling them all privy to the secret of the dead. The killing of the three therefore grew into a massacre swallowing all thirty pathfinders—a shameful rage.

In the aftermath of all that blood it was a little time before we found calmer days again. The knowledge there was no one left to guide us forward, as also the knowledge we would surely perish completely if we attempted going back, produced in all a profound consternation. The most vacillating evinced a readiness to give up every hope and die there in the mud. Each night was rent with nightmares fetching their origins from every disaster that had befallen us, the most remote mixing with horrors only just undergone. More than the number of pathfinders murdered died spastic deaths in the fury of their helplessness at night.

Five days Ningome and Noliwe lay unconscious. The crowd had beaten them, but they had not died. On the sixth day they woke up serene, Noliwe a little after Ningome. Their voices sounded clearer than before. Their actions too had a sureness about them that no one remembered them for. They asked for water, and, in the weakness of their fresh waking, help to wash themselves. They remembered not to drink too much water, and they ate nothing at all at first. Then they spoke.

They spoke in vindication of the murdered pathfinders, said they were good people of the way but in their last days had been overwhelmed with doubt; not doubt as to what they had clearly seen—the end of our journey through the bog—but a doubt brought into their souls by sorrow, a sorrow hovering about the tremendous suffering we were going through to reach the destination they had seen and told us about. It was this suffering—so close, so cutting was their understanding of it—that had filled the pathfinders with such deathly despair, making them unable, unwilling even to defend themselves to preserve their lives when so many so innocent had died along the path they had found.

The land the pathfinders had seen, our destination, was real. The pathfinders had not lacked fidelity. All they had lacked was the hardness necessary to watch their people suffering on the necessary journey. On that journey we would move again.

There was no ceremony. Simply picking up their prepared bundles Noliwe and Ningome started on the way. They went wearily, but never once did they look back to see if the rest would follow. We followed.

It was a silent journey. No one had anything to say. There was not one left among us that did not have some bodily infirmity to nurse. In this general condition of pain there was no occasion for anyone to draw attention to his particular affliction.

Following the path Noliwe and Ningome had taken, we moved on slowly, steadily. Two more islands of firm land we passed, small islands. At the second, in spite of a devouring weariness preying on everyone Noliwe and Ningome did not stop, neither did they eat. They simply each took a draught of water and moved on again, their pace now quickening.

The soil did not grow firm in gradual stages. The soft mud ended abruptly. Real earth took its place. Noliwe and Ningome had made the transition without marking it in any special way, and we who followed them, we were too absorbed in our sleep-like walking at first to notice the change that had taken place. Only our stumbling bodies, unused now to such firmness, told our minds after a little time what had happened.

As for Ningome and Noliwe a new aim now possessed them. For after we had gathered together the wandering bits of our mind we saw ahead of us, not more than two days off, hills in the distance losing their leaf colour to the sky. These hills, they were of an even height, with no great gaps between them visible.

Noliwe and Ningome were impatient to move on but now exhaustion forced them also to take rest. Those who cared most for them fed them in their utter immobility. No sooner had they risen from their torpor than they pressed on. Not all of us went with them. Now that we had reached real land again the long exhaustion claimed most of us and we fell in a great sleep. After it we were possessed by a crazy appetite and a fiery thirst. We ate, drank, rested again, then wandered around in a daze looking at trees again as if they were things entirely strange to us, wondering at animals running on slender legs. The third day hunters beat the undergrowth around and caught live duikers unused to being hunted. To augment our supplies we smoked their meat. Then we followed those gone ahead. We found them stopped at the foot of the hills.

Night came. We rested. At dawn we got up for the climb. Some went scattered ahead to give us warning of danger or to let us know if they found human beings, but neither people nor danger did they find. The hills that had looked so gentle in the distance, in the climbing they were steep. Some among us were already saying under their tired breath that we had risen from the impossible only to head for the killing, when Noliwe and Ningome, rushing up a final crest, halted and called out to the despairing others. We clambered up forgetting all our tiredness and for the first time we saw this place, this portion of our people's land.

With what shall the utterers' tongue stricken with goodness, riven silent with the quiet force of beauty, with which mention shall the tongue of the utterers begin a song of praise whose perfect singers have yet to come?

And the time for the singing, whence shall the utterers, whence the listeners gather it when this remembrance is no easy celebration but a call to the terrifying work of creation's beginning? Quick should be the utterance of stricken tongues. This promise of a praise song will pass swiftly; we shall not halt the main remembrance long.

What could they think but that there must be immense truths in all the impossible dreams of our nights, those who saw you first, Anoa? Who saw mountains flung far to the falling, so far they in the end seduce the following eye and raise it skyward, whence the return to the source, to you. Descending slopes, unhurrying even at the long curve of the waterfalls, descending into the gentleness of land, of earth so good it is seldom visible itself, earth covered under your forests: who would have known,

88

coming from so near the desert, who would have known there was in this world such a variation, such a universe of green alone?

Water hanging clear, water too open to hide the veined rock underneath, water washing pebbles blue and smooth black, yellow like some everlasting offspring of the moon, water washing sand, water flowing to quiet meetings with the swift Esuba, to the broad, quiet Su Tsen, river washing you, Anoa, water washing you.

Land of the duiker, best of animals, attacking none, knowing ways to keep attackers distant, land that should have been perfect for the way, land that will yet be: your praisesong should be woven from the beauty of sounds found only in the future, a beauty springing in its wholeness when the way is found again, Anoa.

Exhaustion had eaten into Ningome. Both she and Noliwe had been going forward under the sheer impulsion of their obsession with reaching our destination. Once we arrived they lost reasons for living, did not care much to be a part of any of the things we were absorbed in from one moment to the next, and allowed the natural fatigue of their bodies to take over every part of their beings.

Ningome was the first to die. The survivor, Noliwe, made it her habit to sit each day looking at the river. One morning she climbed up the first hill overlooking the town near the river and stood there looking at the river till the sun came overhead. Then she came home pronouncing over and over again and with great clarity the exact words of Anoa's prophecy. In addition to the repetition of Anoa's utterance Noliwe brought heavy words from within her own far-hearing soul.

First Noliwe asked pardon for bringing a tired people not what they craved—restful news, soft music to each weary soul—but more thoughts to disturb minds already too long harassed. She claimed her utterance would be mere warning, not certain prophecy. Yet the urgency possessing her—it has come down so with every rememberer —had the strength of visions already seen, not mere foreboding.

Noliwe was solicitous to have all understand that she too remembered we were a people split, with the murderers' mark fresh upon our flesh and soul; that we were tired after flight from the future promised us by death's harbingers, the white predators from the desert; that we would need untroubled generations and generations to make new homes in this new home, think quietly on the sense of our escape from the recent death when the immediate panic of it was no more, renew the battered sense of who we are, who we intend to be; that we needed time to throw out the portions that welcomed rottenness into our people's soul, time to grow new parts to replace the lost. She was solicitous to have all understand her understanding: that for these our tasks we needed long and peaceful time, and that we had not yet begun to have such time. Then Noliwe said what she had to say.

The violence we had left behind—this is what she said— the fraud of the white predators from the desert, this was not all. The sand had brought us woe. Water, this same

90

living, flowing water of the river itself, water would bring worse deaths to us. We who had fallen victim to our own abundant generosity even in the drier lands close to the desert, now we had reached this new place that itself gave us surroundings answering the generosity within, the inner abundance we had found no way to curb. Such uncanny unison—the effortless flowing together of inner and surrounding generosity—would in time put to sleep even the wariest of minds, and it was not in our nature to beware our giving: a fatal, heedless generosity.

Noliwe poured no hatred on our giving. She did not want us turned against our own generosity. But against the unison and the oblivious peace promised by the abundance of our new surroundings her voice uttered a warning taut with urgency: a terrible destruction would be our welcome here if we let the peace of the place put us to sleep; if we forgot again the cause of our straying so far from the way, and then the result; if we thought we could merely laugh at the greed of ostentatious cripples and still survive its afterbirth.

In great disturbance of spirit, before she had put an end to all the words she had to say, Noliwe rushed again like a person called in urgency to the crest of the hill she had been standing on. There she sat and once more stared down at the dark, flowing line of the river. At the falling she came home speechless. She never spoke again, but sat each day looking down the river, gazing in the distance as if from where she sat she could see as far as the sea, the sea and everything that was to come from it against our people.

91

We came away from the desert's edge thinking we were escaping the causes of our disintegration. The causes running deepest were twin: among us had arisen a division between producers and the parasites. Chief among the parasites were the ostentatious cripples, men who for no other reason than the need to veil their own atrophy of spirit wanted to be raised higher than everybody else even if that raising was merely the pushing down of all of us. Then there was the complementary cause: the predators from without, white destroyers determined on our annihilation, who found in the parasites among us and their leaders the ostentatious cripples perfect instruments for use against us, perfect weapons for widening splits among us to the advantage of themselves.

We came away from the desert's edge thinking we were fleeing ruin, but its deepest causes we carried with us to new places. Within our bosom we still made room for the inadequate wanting stupid, noble privilege. We fed a disease killing us. The other, complementary disease, the blight without which the first would have remained mere irritation, that other plague came at us incredible, monstrous from the sea.

The thoughtful among us had thought in the new place to search again for the way whose beginning is reciprocity, whose continuation is reciprocity. But here in this new home wild and strange new arguments arose to stun the thoughtful into silence, to urge the thoughtless to the dance of triumph. For now men rose to cast blame upon the spirit of reciprocity itself for the suffering we had undergone, men capable of seeing some strange possibility of rebirth in the destruction of reciprocity itself. These men, they had seen in the destructive thrust of the desert whites against our people a fire to fascinate their souls. They praised the white predators' road, seeing in it the generator of a triumphant violence. On us they urged the desirability of that road, the road set irrevocably against reciprocity, the road set against our way, the way.

In the suppression of women first, in the reduction of all females to things—things for pleasure, things for use, things in the hands of men—these admirers of the white predators' road saw a potent source of strength for men. In the subjugation of producers to the parasites—amazing, senseless somersault—those fascinated with the white destroyers' road heard the promise of power unlimited. And at the peak of their enthusiasm they urged on us the setting up of a king from among the parasites to whom all— parasites, producers, women, children, in the condescension of the white destroyers' road—would be bound in un- thinking, unquestioning allegiance. In such arrangements the admirers saw the roots of the white predators' power. Along that road they urged our going.

To give their vision strength the admirers of the white predators' road exhorted us to think of fire and to accept the image that the power of the white beasts from the desert was a power much like fire. What better way to fight fire than with similar fire? The admirers asked who among us had any doubts that the white predators' road had made them fighters to be feared?

Among us the thoughtful tried to raise a voice but it was feeble, filled with doubt, while the admirers of the white predators' road looked close to bursting their neckveins with sheer conviction. To the first arguments they added other arguments. Was it not plain, they asked waiting for answers from no one, was it not plain that having lost such numbers of our people in the attacks of the white beasts from the desert and their askaris, having had so many more among us die in the terrors of our journey through the bogland, was it not plain that being so reduced we should strain every sinew to the increase of our numbers? And what better way to do this than to make of every female a childbearer as soon as her body showed it was ready, and for as long as her body continued to turn manseed to harvest? Was it not also plain that the raising of a multitude of children and the provision of a home for them would be work sufficient for all female energies? Should not then the men be given exclusive rights to settle matters beyond the maintenance of bodies in particular homes, and given powers to make their judgments effective?

The admirers of the white predators' road were determined. Opposition to their desires would have brought another split to torture us. The thoughtful among us were defeated in their soul. The admirers of the white predators' road had their way. Overwhelmed, the women in their astonishment accepted the place of childbearing bodies, in their soul wondering why the ability to do such necessary work should bring as its reward such vindictive slavery at the hands of men.

94

Some in rebellion against the motion away from reciprocity refused the childbearing, homekeeping destiny. From time to vatic time before they too disappeared they would warn against the fatal fascination, telling of a better way, a way to generate potency from reciprocity itself. They too had arguments for their refusal: they would not consent to the production of mere zombi bodies in a community doomed—for they knew doom awaited any group forgetful of reciprocity—to fall prey to enslavers among ourselves and then to enslavers rushing against us from strange places. The refusers would bear no children fated to be slaves. Around them they pointed to the children, pronounced them all destined to be slaves as long as we were so heedless of reciprocity, so contemptuous of our way, the way.

But these prophetesses also, the time absorbed them ineffective like water dripping onto hot, endless sand. Those among them with a hearing too strong to be ignored were suppressed at once. Their bodies sometimes floated naked down the river in the beauty of an early morning, their genitals mutilated for the warning of docile multitudes. The weaker ones were given fondling treatment. For their individual female selves a small place was reserved among men so that it was usual to find one at a time even within the new male army itself, a mascot, or a simple honorary male. In the fullness of time these retired, to take on in the remainder of their lives the public character of barren women, stock for silent, easy laughter, living argument for the frivolity of their own best dreams.

No. Of the seeds of our disintegration we left none behind. We had fled, our hope being that new places, new circumstances might bring us back to reciprocity, might bring us closer to our way, the way. In the new place reciprocity found new murderers. The way was lost in the fascination with the white heat of easy roads to power. Among us new ostentatious cripples—the more dangerous because theirs were no visible, physical infirmities but deep inadequacies of the soul—were finding ways to turn the whole community into a lifeless thing, their crutch.

From beyond our new home it was not too long before news came rushing from the future. The coming experts of the thirtieth generation came back from the shore telling us white men from the sea had arrived at Edina, ten days off, searching for a king among the people, bringing gifts for the special enjoyment of that king, and asking him for land. For these first white men from the sea, like other white destroyers of our remembrance they too said they were searching for a hospitable place, they too said they were searching for a home.

That in the fullness of our continuing generosity we again laughed at the new ostentatious cripples and treated them like children needing to be humoured, that was another sign of the distance we had strayed from the way. In the unfolding of our destruction the presence of these ostentatious cripples has had a most terrifying effect. For it is not only that they have deformed our community so thoroughly that they have left it broken, unable to hold together, and therefore incapable together of resisting the greed of invaders. Worse, to complement this weakening of our community it has been the work of these glittering cripples to call upon our heads by their ostentatious invocations the same white predators, the same white destroyers most apt, most eager to profit from our schisms. Have we forgotten the stupid pilgrimage of the one surnamed—o, ridiculous pomp—The Golden: he who went across the desert from his swollen capital twenty days' journey from where we lived; he who went with slaves and servants hauling gold to astonish eyes in the desert?

Have we already forgotten how swiftly the astonishment he aimed in his foolishness to generate turned to that flaming greed that brought us pillage clothed in the idiocy of religion? We have among us even now humans with a reputation for wisdom in the knowledge of our people who yet remember that journey of an imbecile as if its gigantic wastage meant some unspoken glory for our people. The aftermath of that moron journey was the desert white men's attack on us. In the further aftermath of that stupid crossing other white men, their eyes burning with uncontainable gluttony, came roaming the sea, searching to find a road to the source of all the wealth the ostentatious traveller had displayed hundreds and hundreds of seasons back.

Closer to the desert—memory cannot have made dotard fools of all our rememberers—the ostentatious cripples' infirmities were more often physical, clear to every sight. Happening upon such a creature with a body twisted by some infirmity of birth the unwarned recoiled instinctively,

97

placed an isolating distance between themselves and the disadvantaged body. This distance first imposed by others' revulsion the cripple, intent on survival in spite of every thing, himself adopted, turning the wounding retreat of the whole in body to his own defense.

Here, with more of the cripples crippled not in their bodies but in their souls, a similar distancing made the disadvantaged crave vengeance against the unmutilated. For there are a kind of cripples on whom the unconnected eye can find no withered faculty. With these too the distancing is there, a distancing not physical, but spiritual. It is the feelings that recoil, the nerves that turn back into themselves. That the recoiling is not overt and physical does not make the hurt of distance less. The crippled soul can be contained in a body surrounded, touched, pressed in upon by a thousand other bodies. Still, between those other contained souls and the crippled one there is no touching. Each healthy soul prefers to hover at a height that is its own, some soaring into dizzying spaces, most floating at their easy, normal level. All leave the cripple crawling on the ground.

Only the most sensitive, the empathetic, turn away initially, reflect on what they have done, see themselves placed in the cripple's position, then having understood, return to the cripple not needing the distances between. But among us the truly empathetic have been few since the beginning of our exile from the way. Among a people hustling into doom the feelingless are kings, and the thoughtless always follow kings. The vast ranges of mediocrity have room only for those trained in indifference. Those capable of joy in the hurt of others grow many, and the normally mediocre find in the true cripple's disadvantage cause not for empathy but for gratulation of the different, distant self. First they turn off in horror. Then, happy in their difference, if they return they return to attack, to harass, to persecute the cripple.

The cripple regrets the disappearance of the first distance, imposed by others' shrinking, now remembered as useful insulation for himself. The cripple dreams of such a distance, no longer merely a defensive distance but a distance to turn the contempt of others into contempt against others. This kind of cripple, his deficiencies are inner. But an inner reparation lies beyond his long despair. The external, the superficial, the manipulable: on such he must depend in his ambition to distinguish himself. The world of tinsel, the superficies, comes as perfect clothing to cover the cripple's deformity from recoiling sight. In the fullness of the ostentatious cripples' dreams the spirit of community is raped by worshippers of impressive trash.

So among us the ostentatious cripples turned the honoured position of caretakers into plumage for their infirm selves. Which shall we now choose to remember of the many idiocies our tolerance has supported? Shall we remember Ziblim the heavy one, heavy not like a living elephant but like infirm mud, he who wanted every new bride's hymen as his boasting prize, but turned the tears of women into laughter when they found this massive would-be king had not the blood in him for entering the widest open door?

Or shall our remembrance be of Jezebu, he who for the solace of his shrivelled soul wanted all coming into his presence crawling on their knees? Or of Bulukutu, he who gave himself a thousand grandiose, empty names of praise yet died forgotten except in the memories of laughing rememberers? We should not stay too long with them. Let us make haste to move beyond them and their stinking memory. The smallest arrowpoint they occupy in our thoughts is too much space. But for the terrors flowing from their presence in our midst we should be glad to forget them all—completely, easily. Let us then make haste.

For a cascade of infamy this is: the names and doings of those who from struggling to usurp undeserved positions as caretakers, in the course of generations imposed themselves on a people too weary of strife to think of halting them. Let us finish speedily with their mention. The memory of these names is corrosive. Its poison sears our lips. Odunton, Bentum, Oko, Krobo, Jebi, Jonto, Sumui, Oburum, Ituri, Dube, Mununkum, Esibir, Bonto, Peturi, Topre, Tutu, Bonsu, and lately Koranche.

Who among them was the worst would be fitting argument for puerile fools or dotards feeling time heavy on their heads, not for rememberers. The quietest king, the gentlest leader of the mystified, is criminal beyond the exercise of any comparison.

Bentum had his followers seize land. For the first time among us one man tried to turn land into something cut apart and owned. It was asked what next the greedy would think to own—the air? An unknown avenger of the people sent him hurrying to face the wrath of ancestors, but that was not the end of the greed of kings.

Krobo had the grasping spirit of Bentum. It was not land alone he craved, but humans also as his tools to work the land. One youth he had pressed into labouring for him felled him with iron sharpened days and days on raw stones by the farthest stream. With the still bleeding weapon of his vengeance the labourer cut out his own tongue and came again among the wondering people mute forever. Whether he had killed the king alone or breathed in the spirit of some larger group he no longer had the means to tell. Silently the watching people tried to stop his bleeding death while all agreed the king had been allowed to live too harmfully long.

Jonto came among us with a spirit caught straight from the white predators from the desert. Destruction was his pleasure. In his gentlest moods he was a bloody lecher. From the unprompted craving of his soul he had a special enclosure built. In it he shut up not only selected animals but also virgins—girls as well as boys—chosen for his insatiate urge.

It was his never-finished craving for newer abominations that ended him. He loved particularly the tender arseholes of boys not yet in their thirtieth season. Some he had oiled for ingress but in his happiest moods he dispensed with oil, preferring as lubricant the natural blood of each child's bleeding anus as he forced his entry.

In the course of an exhilarating orgy an accident befell him: the palm wine he loved almost as well as the children

101

relaxed him beyond the fondest of his dreams. A poison had been mixed with his drink. The women responsible for serving him the drink, on perceiving he was dead, all of them wept with such striking sincerity, so loud and for so many days on end, that it would have been unholy to have stopped them for the purpose of asking them if any knew which way the poison had come into the gourd.

Ituri was the first king to go mad with jealous fear of his own servants. A hundred he made slaves outright, had them castrated and, contemplating their subsequent swelling, gave them a laughing apellation, elephants. His peace of mind restored, he again made them the bathers and pomaders of his women.

In Esibir's time the experts of the weaving art found new ways to give cloth colours different from the ancient blue of the sky at dusk. They found the yellow of a fowl's eye, greens of the forest, red clearer than noontime blood. Of the experts one was ambitious, the kind of fundi whose skill is an excellence merely of the physical hand, not a beauty and a goodness entering also his mind and heart. Some experts there are who have lost all intimation of the way. This particular fundi— no rememberer has thought his name worth remembering—seeking the cheap, empty praise that comes from the mouth of kings, by himself went secretly to the king with a shiny present, the new cloth.

The king Esibir was entranced. Just as secretly, he asked the fundi if he had woven this magic cloth all by himself. Anticipating untold wealth and endless honours for himself the fundi nodded, just nodded yes, for the earth has ears.

As secretly the king asked the fundi if he had made any more of the cloth. The fundi shook his head: not yet. Just as secretly Esibir the king had the fundi's eyes put out. No other man, if the king Esibir had his way, no other man would ever wear cloth to rival his. Till Esibir's death the unblinded masters of the weaving art made their new cloth secretly. For them also, and not for them only, Esibir's funeral was a happy festival.

Topre lived with fears singular even for a king. Anxious to have all the blood in the veins of his heirs flow from his own family, unable—in this he was most wise, most realistic —to believe that any woman would choose to remain faithful to himself, he would copulate with none but his only sister, older by ten seasons.

Tutu, first son of that copulation, was an idiot; not, like his mother, astounded into imbecility by Topre's heated insistence, but in his own right a pure, congenital fool.

After Tutu there was Bonsu, his stupidities so monstrous and so well known it would be wasted breath repeating them. And then there came Koranche.

Koranche of all the children of his time was slowest. It was his habit to stay wherever he was left from morning till evening and sit staring straight ahead of his body. He could not smile. The only expression he had was a constant dull, flat, ever-staring look from which diviners themselves would have been defeated trying to draw a meaning. He could not cry like other children. If he fell— something he did often enough, though how he did it from such immobile postures was always a mystery—if he fell

103

and banged his head against a stone he lay quite still, silent the time it takes a person to swallow his moisture seven times. Then only would Koranche decide to begin to cry. And then he cried with a constricted, explosive violence quite astounding to all hearers.

This slowness, it came to be a distinguishing mark upon everything Koranche did. He reached ten seasons before he could accept weaning from the suckling breast. To discourage him every bitter herb known not to kill was smeared around his mother's nipples and, after his mother's milk gave out, around the nipples of women who had lost their children or had milk to spare. Koranche would recoil momentarily after tasting the bitterness prepared for him, stare just once directly at the source of his milk, then return to suckling just as if the taste of sour juice was also acceptable to him. Then in his tenth season he suddenly spurned the milk of recent mothers, theretofore his only food. That season he would vomit at the mere sight of a woman's naked breasts.

He walked in his thirteenth season. As far as any healer could tell there was nothing wrong with any sinew in his limbs. As for talking Koranche waited till his seventeenth season to begin it, and then every speech of his was a cataract of words shot out after unbelievably long periods of silent, internal struggle. This was not stammering, unless we wish to take it into our minds to give lightning and any little stone-spark the same name.

Uneasy at his slowness his mother and his father took him to the healer and diviner with the greatest reputation among

104

us. The healer knew Koranche's father, knew of his vindictive temper when in any way he was displeased. He took a long, deliberate look at Koranche and at the end of it pronounced there was nothing wrong with him which a healer could correct. The father reminded the healer of the child's entirely extraordinary slowness in everything, and then asked him for a more meaningful prognostication. The healer looked from child to mother, from mother to child, from child to father, from father to child again. Then he looked down at the floor.

"This child," the healer said at length, "his slowness can only mean one of two things. Either he will grow to be a fool among fools," the healer raised his eyes from off the floor to look up at the prince's father's face, taking good care to smile as he did so in a friendly sort of way, and proceeded quickly, "or he will be a sage."

"Which do you think, yourself?" the king asked the healer, a bit impatiently.

"It is too early yet," replied the healer, and nothing could induce him to add another word.

After that visit to the healer and diviner the king would watch his staring son, shake his head and softly murmur to himself: "How he stares like a fool." To which it was the habit of his wife to answer if she happened to be near enough: "Like a sage he stares, my little Koranche. The healer himself said it, like a sage."

In his twentieth season Koranche was pushed into beginning the first initiation, the season of games and dances of protection. His companions were children in their tenth

105

season. Even so in everything they did the smaller children left Koranche far behind. Repetition did not help him; he seemed destined to stay last in any group. Some of the teaching masters, sympathetic beyond the limits of their duty, tried unknown ways to teach him common disciplines. They failed. One fundi, teacher of the smiths, and expert also in the giving of quick, accurate judgments, simply refused to waste days trying to teach such a dead spirit. In truth that fundi was not in his impatience cruel. Koranche did not have it in any of his bones to excel in any way at the doing of any thing.

Yet Koranche did have one formidable gift: a genius for obliterating the proofs of other people's superiority to him. He did not care to push himself to excellence in any craft. That he was inferior to others in capacity he seemed to accept in all equanimity. On one point alone he found it worthwhile to assert himself: that others should not go unmolested in the practice and the enjoyment of their skill. In finding means to destroy the efforts of people more skilful than himself he now and then displayed a truly uncanny talent.

The first clear demonstration Koranche gave of this quality was at the end of the sixth initiation. The masters of the carving art had taught the children of that season all that skill alone could teach. The season's beginning experts in the iron-shaping art made adzes for the young carvers. The woodcutters brought them selected trunks of good, black wood, kusibiri brought from quietest, darkest forest shades, and the masters of the carving art instructed the children

106

to make each for his beloved and himself masks for the dances of the season's celebration of craftsmanship attained.

Beautiful beyond imagination were the masks the children made that season, each male mask a pithy proverb, each loved one's mask a song of love. But Koranche's trunk remained a heavy piece of wood throughout. There was no spirit in his being whose flowing could direct his hand and then the adze to bring out any beauty, any truth trapped in the wood to answer whatever there was in his soul.

Koranche alone was untroubled by his failure to carve the kusibiri wood. He seemed entirely unaware that there was anything amiss. He continued with great placidity now and then stroking the wood with his adze, staring all the while at the masks the younger children around him were busy finishing.

A week before the dance of celebration all other masks were ready. In the second grove the children built their hut and in it placed all their masks together. Koranche added his piece of wood to the rest, then went home with everybody else. Unlike the others he did not stay at home. That same night he took a palm-wine tapper's brand from his father's courtyard and walked directly to the second grove. There he set fire to the hut of masks. The night was moonless. The light from the burning hut brought people running to the second grove. There was nothing anyone could do to save the masks. They saw Koranche standing apart from the flames, staring steadily at the conflagration.

In the art of hunting too there seemed to be nothing at all he could learn. Worse, he was a danger to his companions

107

during every hunting exercise. His arrows never hit an animal, but to human flesh they found their way from time to time. Koranche was therefore left behind when the children of that hunting season went out on their first real expedition. He did not seem aware, much less perturbed, about what had happened. Placidly he went by himself along the path leading to the higher ford on the first side stream. A wandering stranger, one who made his living charming snakes for the entertainment of crowds on market days, lived along that path. Koranche begged him, for he knew him, for the loan of an untrained adder. The stranger was a gentle, loving soul. He granted Koranche his request but warned him to be careful to keep the snake away from human beings.

Koranche thanked the gentle stranger, went back to the hunting hut, looked for Beyin's mat—Beyin who was the highest skilled among the hunters entering mastery—slid the serpent still sleeping into it, rolled it up again, then took his position just outside the hunting hut, waiting patiently.

The hunting party returned. They distributed the meat they had brought, sent the older people theirs and kept their own in the hut for the coming feast. That done they went down to the first river to bathe. Koranche was still sitting in the same position when they returned. The hunters sat near him, told stories of their day's work, cooked meat around their fires, and late in the night got ready to go to sleep.

Beyin had had a better hunting day than even his great skill had led everyone to expect. His soul was high that night.

He did not unroll his mat the ordinary way but raised it high above his head and in playful violence flung it hard against the floor. Angered beyond endurance the serpent rushed out of his comfort. The first thing on his road, an antelope's carcase left in the cool night breeze near the door, he sank his fangs into. Just then the swift Beyin picked up a heavy club and smashed the serpent's head. When Koranche saw the adder dead in the hands of his intended victim he heaved a short sigh and went home.

On Koranche's accession to the throne—his father one night burst his stomach with overeating and died before the next sun's coming—an event took place that blasted what there was of his slow mind and plunged him into an interior despair more leaden than any he had ever known.

There was a woman. Idawa was her name. There are not many born with every generation of whom it may be said they have a beauty needing no counterpointing blemish to make its wonder clear. The best moulded face may lead the admiring eye in the end down to a pair of lumpen legs. The slenderest neck may sit incongruous on a bloated bosom. Idawa had a beauty with no such disappointment in it. Seen from a distance her shape in motion told the looker here was co-ordination free, unforced. From the hair on her head to the last of her toes there was nothing wasted in her shaping. And her colour: that must have come uninterfered with from night's own blackness.

Men may crave closeness to such physical beauty and still be forgiven even if their loved one has no suspicion of an answering beauty in her soul. But Idawa's surface beauty, perfect as it was, was nothing beside her other, profounder beauties: the beauty of her heart, the way she was with people, the way she was with everything she came in contact with; and the beauty of her mind, the clarity with which she moved past the lying surfaces people held in front of themselves, past the lying surfaces of the things of this world set against our way, to reach judgments holding to essences, free from the superficies.

For the best of reasons the men of her time each wished at some point that Idawa would consent to share her days with him. Most soon enough brought their affections closer to what was possible and left more tenacious wills to continue hankering after her.

The king Koranche was one of those who found it impossible to deflect their affections from Idawa. Everything a king could do to show himself to advantage before a woman he loved Koranche did in the hope of pleasing Idawa. Idawa was unimpressed. She went on with her life as if she did not hear, did not even see the king courting her attention.

Koranche sought help first from poisoners, then from healers, and after that even from the hangers-on at court. He had the great drums themselves beaten together with the iron gong. When the people assembled his oldest spokesman proclaimed there was to be a new dance at the very next full moon, a dance at which the king would pick the woman of his heart.

The week before the full moon Idawa on her own initiative proclaimed her love for Ngubane, one among the

110

younger experts of the farming art, and asked to marry him. Ngubane was a quiet man. Great was his astonishment at Idawa's boldness, but greater far was his joy at his own unhoped-for good fortune. Ngubane married Idawa.

The king heard the news. He sent seven separate messengers seven separate times to ascertain first from Idawa and then from Ngubane if the news was really true. The messengers did not deceive the king.

The season after that Ngubane the farmer died. The king's official announcer beat the lesser iron gong and told the children assembled to go home with this news: Ngubane the farming fundi had fallen to a beast. Beast unnamed, strange beast, strangest of beasts indeed, that severed the dead man's genitals, stuffed them in his throat and threw the body in the river weighted with a rock, beast suspecting little that the mutilated body would float upward so soon, beast not thinking the creatures of the river could ever want to eat through string before touching flesh thrown down to them.

Blood was to prove no solace to the king. The rejection he had suffered at Idawa's hands pushed his spirit into a comfortless hole in which, alone with himself, he searched in vain for ways to run from his inner emptiness—something he had not had to wrestle with as long as he kept his life to external pomp sufficient to cover him in the eyes of the world, and therefore in his own. The multitudes he was not frightened of. It was not their habit to see through his protective social pomp and call it empty. And the few whose hearing, whose vision could penetrate its hollowness

111

could not shout loud enough to be heard against the general noise of acquiescence. Therefore the king's sense of who he was, of his importance as a person, was never before threatened in any profound way after his accession to the throne.

But now, at a time when he had thought himself moving on a path along which failure would be impossible—using the given glory of the social scene in a personal pursuit— here was Idawa, a woman not only able to see through this social glory and see it as mere flimsy artifice, but also of the heedless courage to articulate her vision in the rejection of a king.

Idawa had confronted the king with his inferiority. The event depressed the king. In searing flashes he found at first impossible to control he was forced to see himself the way Idawa must see him: an empty, strutting fool, suffered to strut this way only because of thin social conventions.

The king, in order to preserve his sanity and to survive, learned to push the woman Idawa's viewpoint out of his mind from time to time. Whenever he could do this he regained with gratitude his own point of view. His profound inferiority he recognised it would be madness to try and do anything about. It was a part of him. To denounce it he would have to denounce himself. An impossibility.

It was all the more important for him to strengthen the social conventions that made it possible for him to veil his inferiority with given power; to live at a social level higher than his own qualities would make possible if there were reciprocity, if all in our society started from the same

112

point, none set above the other from the start. To the king then these became things of the utmost significance: the developments that had projected his type into their ascendancy. These developments, maintained, entrenched, should make it possible first for him and then for his offspring to be protected against the just consequences of their own hollowness.

The king decided his heir would never repeat his own early life, never be obliged to join the groups of initiation. His heir should have a special place apart.

The king felt happier, more satisfied, every time he thought of so many people willing to accept the social facade as reality. He had heard from his family how their ascendancy had been attained. At important points he felt momentarily terrified at the flimsiness of the edifice, a structure resting neither on moral power nor on real material power, but mainly on mystification. After each such fright the king would return to consideration of the enormous, the infinite capacity of the people to be mystified, to be served the surface only and to be satisfied with it. Then he felt no threat to his security, for he was reassured it rested on solid, heavy, lasting matter—a people's gullibility.

The presence of a woman like Idawa was therefore particularly unnerving. Whenever he thought of her the king felt overpowered by a kind of heat. Hot air, it seemed to him, was trapped in the back of his head, along his spine. The thought nagged him: how horrible things would be if she were not alone, if there were thirty, a hundred, a

113

thousand, thirty thousand of her kind.

In his worst nightmares the king imagined himself caught in a whole society of unimpressed eyes, sceptical ears, staring, listening, undeceivable. If ever the society became that way it would be impossible for him to remain king. Such people would think a king a clown, refuse to support him, refuse to respect him, and ridicule the socially ordained rituals of reverence. He would have to suffer comparison with people like the experts, people who without a shred of artificial social respect to bolster their importance yet managed to command an overflowing share of effortless respect; people like Ngubane the farmer, Ngubane the dead; people, above all, like the outcast Isanusi.

What was it about these people that made him feel so helpless comparing himself to them? They were the opposite of himself, they who needed no artifices of social respect, they who did not need any stratagem to divert people's respect to themselves, these people interested, season after season, only in the perfection of their fundi's art, and in the uses of that perfected craftsmanship.

It was hard trying to find ways to attack the masters. On account of their discipline, of the concentration they applied to their work, all knew them as excellent in what they did. Yet this was not an excellence they were known to try and use to set themselves above other people—it seemed to be one important rule of theirs that any such attempted abuse was bound to destroy the fundi's skill itself. The level of their living was always far below the ostentation they should have found possible. Others without their qualities

114

pretended, others without their means borrowed in order to impress who would be impressed. These masters, they did not seek to impress anyone, and it was impossible to impress them with anything but the quality of good work.

The king's mind was troubled by an unsolicited image: these people can walk naked and not be ashamed. Words invaded his head: they give more than they receive. I, the king, I only know how to take. They are full vessels overflowing. I am empty. In place of a bottom I have a hole.

The uninvited words burned the king's mind with rage. He thought again of the way Idawa must see him, how her contempt would never change. In spite of everything the lucky social pomp could do to hide his emptiness the one woman he wanted more than any other, the person who would reaffirm for him his manhood, that person felt for him nothing but contempt.

Anger against Idawa never stayed long attached to her shape in Koranche's mind. Another feeling crossed it out. It was not love but a devouring greed to possess this perfect being who had fled his reach. The anger turned to thoughts of the dead Ngubane. The king felt happy at the thought of Ngubane's destruction, and gratitude filled his heart when he contemplated the social power that had made it possible. Now life became clear again in his mind: a conflict between the unjustly intelligent, the experts with their skill and their intelligence on the one hand, and on the other hand those born mediocre, those inferior through no fault of their own, the hollow ones, the stupid ones, the uncreative ones. Lucky arrangement indeed, that power in the present world

115

was placed at the disposal of the latter. Lucky that the talented were usually too preoccupied with their craftsmanship to bother to master those other crafts useful for destroying people better than oneself, those roads without which the unintelligent would be so surely, so cruelly lost. Lucky chance for kings, that power was pitted against intelligence. Lucky chance, that talent was suppressible by power.

It was in Koranche's time as king that the children of our age grew up. It was also in his time—disastrous time—that the white destroyers came from the sea.

# 4

# the destroyers

We had thought, from seeing the waters of Anoa—water suspended bubbling at the lip of its forest fountain, water falling like long, translucent threads airing in the wind before the masters of the weaving art take them for their use, water flowing, rushing, water slowed down behind new obstacles, water patiently rising till it overflows what can never stop it, water calm, immobile like the sky in a season starved of rain—we had thought, from seeing Anoa's waters, from hearing their thirty different sounds, that there was nothing of beauty in water we had yet to see, no sound of its music we had not yet heard. But the last of our open initiations took us to the coastland. There we saw in the same water we thought we knew so well a different beauty.

Down the river our rowing was easy. The songs we had learned from our first initiation to the seventh, these songs now flowed from us with added meaning, their smoothness answering the river's even flow. In that harmony our rowing was no hard exertion. Near the sealine the fundi guiding us told us it was time to change our songs.

Songs we had learned just that last season, songs we had learned to sing but had yet to understand, replaced the earlier songs of our growing. Their rhythms were more disturbed, their tempo far more shaken than the earlier songs. Singing, rowing, we came upon the river's seamouth and for the first time knew the meaning of the recent changes in our initiation.

Where the river met the sea its easy flow gave way to a wild turbulence. The seawater came in long, curling waves to a meeting with the darker water from the land. In both waters there was a forward motion, so at the place of their meeting there was no quiet mixing but a violent upward surge from clashing waves. A wall of water stretched unbroken the whole length of the rivermouth and beyond. Here in the moving, constant barrier formed from the meeting of the waters there was a tremendous beauty. At times the massive spray rose higher than any wawa tree.

Within us the spectacle elicited a mixture of fright and admiration. We rowed toward the turbulence, to the end of our open initiation. The fundi of the rowing art, our guide, repeated his instructions to us as we drew up to the wall of water. His voice was calm. Now and then something sardonic mixed itself with his more serious words. That was his manner always. He told us nothing to fill us with a false enthusiasm. He told us of the danger, of the violence of the waves. He warned us not to pit ourselves directly against the power of the waves—for that would only exhaust

118

our strength—but to watch the water's rise and fall and to rise and fall with it, conserving strength.

"This canoe, the raging water will overturn it," he said. "Do not allow fear to madden you. If you do not try to force it you know the canoe will float up again on its own. That is its nature. Take it, work it along gently, patiently till you find yourselves free on the other side of these waves. Right the canoe. Then will be the time for releasing the twins of your lost oars."

The canoe was thrown like kapok in the air when we hit the water wall but no part of it was broken, and of the oars we had tied to it not one came loose, though all we held in our hands we lost to the waves. The fundi had instructed us it would be better just to let them go. In the moment of our separation from the canoe we saw the wisdom of his words. One of us, Tano, in blind desperation tried to hold on to his oar. The rushing waters twisted it in his hands, turning it into a flailing weapon that smashed into the two people nearest him before another wave tore the thing out of his reluctant hands.

Of the barrier's crossing itself we shall say nothing here. This is not the time for any soft-eyed remembrance of initiations. The crossing seaward and the easier crossing on the way back home after we had turned with the sun and rowed to Poano where we stayed with the fishers our sisters and our brothers till the next full moon, these crossings were important ways to raise our courage, to reduce those things that might still have the power to awe us. But in the past— so recent the past—an even greater importance had attached

119

to our people's knowledge of the water barrier.

Now the words of Noliwe's prophecy, daughter of Anoa's ancient utterance, were to us mere sounds no longer. We had been to Poano, seen the white destroyers from the sea already settled there, more settled than among us at Anoa, living in the strong stone houses they had had built for themselves, and the people of the place standing helpless, some forced to help the white men build more houses of heavy stone, not comprehending what medicine the white destroyers had used so to poison their king's mind.

We had been to Poano and this time heard what happened at Edina and at Enchi, ten days' rowing into the falling sun. At Enchi too, we heard, the white destroyers had come from the sea thirty seasons earlier asking to be shown a king. The people laughed and indicated to the white destroyers they had enough respect for their souls not to need a king. The white destroyers asked for land. The people told them land was not a thing to be possessed. If they wanted food they could farm. If they wanted shelter they would always be welcome as guests. But as to owning land that was a request even babies would laugh at. The white destroyers went back silent to their ship. At night they brought it closer to Enchi and from it sent hot balls of iron flying through the air to destroy their hosts. Before the coming of the next full moon the white destroyers from the sea had killed half the people of the town and built a stone house for themselves on the hill closest to the sea.

All this we heard. We heard also of the attempts of other white destroyers to reach other places here. We heard how

120

they had reached Simpa, Anago, Bomey and Ahwei, but how they came to Anoa—ah, disastrous coming—we had not heard till after the last open initiation, and even then we heard but a portion, and for a season the rest remained a mystery to us, till Isanusi opened our closed ears.

The white destroyers had reached Simpa, Anago, Bomey and Ahwei, but had long failed to penetrate the beauty of Anoa because the wall of water broke every single one of their big ships that tried to come. For Koranche, then newly a king, the failure of the white destroyers to reach Anoa was cause for chagrin. He had been to Poano, visited the king there, Atobra, seven times since the coming of the white destroyers to Poano, seen how the selfish power of Atobra had grown against his people in the vivid glare of the white destroyers' presence, and his rotten soul cried out for the coming of the white destroyers to Anoa also. It was he and his parasites who told great boasting tales of immense wealth contained in Anoa, and taunted the white destroyers they found at Atobra's court with their continuing impotence before the barrier made by the river with the sea.

There is nothing white men will not do to satisfy their greed. Ten seasons did not lapse after the height of Koranche's boasting before a ship of the white destroyers from the sea, one built with some special strength for breaking through the water wall, broke the barrier and came to lie heavy, full of menace, down the river less than an arrow's flying distance from our home.

The things that happened after the coming of the white

destroyers have all been heavy, monstrous things. At the time these things were happening our understanding was still infant. And most of the events took place in such a way, at such times and in such places that their meaning was hidden from our knowledge until we ourselves had had our souls forced into the heaviest knowledge of the world the white destroyers came to make.

At the time itself what we knew was this: the white strangers emerged from their ship and came to land. They were looking for the king, but Koranche came to meet them on the bank himself and took them home. The morning after this the drums were beaten for a meeting in the centre of the town, an open one. A spokesman, an older spokesman—not Isanusi, the sweetest speaker and the most truthful of them all, he who on any such important occasion should have come to speak—told us the white strangers had come wanting to be our friends, to give us goods they had brought in return for ours, and to tell us of a wonderful creature they called god, a creature superior, so the white destroyers said, to our remembrance of the way.

Here a woman of the duiker clan, no great speaker but of a sudden filled to overflowing with the spirit of truth, rose to interrupt the aged spokesman of the king. This woman—Akole was her name—said we the people were tired of lies, and that the lies we had just heard that day were more dangerous than all the previous lies together. She said it was true enough the whites were strangers here, but we had already heard of them and their deeds were known to us—deeds of thieves, deeds of killers all of them.

122

Akole reminded us we all knew the white men from the sea were homeless brigands and soulless too, men roaming the seas till they came upon a people they could exterminate, whose lands they could rob, whose spirits they could scatter into an endless, barren emptiness. Monsters they were, and even if we did not have in us the courage of truth to execute them outright as punishment for their crimes against all people of the way we should at least have the wisdom not to welcome them among ourselves.

All listening were stunned: the people by the truth of this quiet woman's words, the king and his flatterers by the bitterness of seeing their fondest dreams of power in danger of disintegration. The old spokesman rose, leaned like some wise man on his staff and silenced the woman with an oath. The people murmured their disappointment, for when Akole had spoken it was as if the people had been waiting all day for just such a voice.

First the spokesman spoke in whispers to the king, next to others of the flatterers. Then he turned to tell the people the meeting had come to an end. The king Koranche needed time for heavier thought. One voice, uncalled, unknown, rose at the tail of the spokesman's and asked the piercing question: "What more is there to think about?" There was no answer. The king sat staring like a rabbit charmed. His hangers-on pretended they had all lost their ears that moment.

The night following that day was dark, propitious. In the darkest of that night, from up where the experts of the spear, the arrow and the bow have their homes, fires flew

123

silent through the night and found the white destroyers' ship, setting it aflame. In a panic the white destroyers went back down the river.

Next morning no drums were beaten, not even gongs. There was no open meeting held to announce what heavier thoughts the king had had that night. Neither was a meeting held the next day, nor the next. Three full moons shone and disappeared. Still nothing happened. And ourselves, we were still too young to hear the whispers of the time.

The peace of the fifth night after the fourth full moon's disappearance was shattered by noises louder than any we had ever heard, save the noise of thunder. All woke up running to see what catastrophe had reached us. In the night they saw flames bursting on the river, then they heard sounds like smaller thunderclaps. In the town itself a different sound came from the upper part, up where the experts of the spear, the arrow and the bow have their homes. The sounds were of people dying, of houses burning, of earth breaking up under burning iron. Crowds went there wishing to help and were destroyed together with the greater part of those living there.

The day following the massacre was placid. Where the fires had burst in the night, upon the river there lay the white men's ship, in its old place but carrying new iron pointed at the town. No one doubted these were the bringers of death.

The dead were buried quickly. Their flesh was found lacerated, their entrails blown open to the sun and therefore quick to rot, and there were many to be buried.

In the town people made ready new weapons, new thoughts of protection. There was fear in our minds, but also a determination to destroy the destroyers, those who had come to wipe out so many in just one night.

From the king and his hangers-on there was nothing but an astounding silence. More astounding was what the king did when the sun calmed down a little from its height. With his retinue of flatterers, dressed as if they were going to ask for some special bride, the king went walking to the riverside and waited with the patience of a fearful servant for the white destroyers to come to land.

The white destroyers came. The first wore clothes with pieces of metal shining all along his front, and cords and other nameless things tied around his arms. In addition he carried a short stick. He walked as if his bones had nothing soft between them. The second wore similar clothes but he carried less metal. The third wore a robe unlike the clothes of all the others. It was long, covering him almost completely so that in his movement he was just a red head carrying itself forward above folds of white cloth. Fourth came another in a dress not unlike the clothes of the first two, but with no shiny metal at all on him except his weapons, of which he carried two, a long one on his shoulder and a smaller one in a pocket by his side. There was a fifth, dressed somewhat like the fourth, carrying nothing. Beside the five white destroyers there were eight black men with long weapons and they wore clothes of a fantastic kind, not like the white destroyers', yet not like any of ours. These men, though black like us, walked stiffly like the first two white men, as if in their bodies too nothing soft separated bone from bone. It was they who had rowed the wide boat in which the white men came to land.

There on the bank the king greeted the white men as if they were lost brothers of his now found again. There were words between them, soft words passed from the king to the white destroyers and from them to him through one among the fantastic-looking black men. After the words the king climbed into the white destroyers' boat together with two of his flatterers and with the white destroyers and their black men they all went back to the ship.

Long was their stay on board that ship. Another morning came before they arrived back on land. This time they came in two vessels. With them came eight more of the fantastic-looking black men. In addition they brought strange objects: first a mirror such as it was said the king of Poano, Atobra, had had given him two seasons back; then barrels, from one of which the king no sooner than he touched land asked for a drink, after taking which he did a minute, grotesque dance of joy; then rolls of cloth, some red as daytime blood, some a deep blue close to the colours of the most ancient of our cloths. There were other things impossible to give a name to or to describe, except that they all shone fiercely in the sun.

Men from the palace took the shiny things, the cloth and the barrels of new drink, and disappeared behind the king's walls. The gates were closed against the people's vision. For two days the only coming and going there was was between the palace and the white destroyers' ship, a long exchange of

126

gifts and visits.

Inside the town the most determined continued their preparations for the expected conflict with the white destroyers. Others, having seen the king's behaviour and his welcome for the whites, wondered what new disaster had come to pursue our people.

The third day early in the morning the great drums were beaten. The people assembled and were a little heartened to see the speaker this time would be Isanusi himself, best spokesman, of whom it was said truth was his food. Isanusi looked tired, like a man who had spent days and nights without sleep, with no comfort for a punished body and no rest for a mind wrestling with heavy matters. Isanusi walked to the centre of the public place, greeted the people with respect but as briefly as he could, and began at once:

"I have been unwilling to speak at all. The king persuaded me I would be betraying our people if I held back my voice at such a time. I will not betray our people.

"It is about the white men. You have seen them. They have brought to the king and his courtiers greetings and presents. Those also you have seen. And they have brought requests which the king bids me lay open to you for your thinking on. The king wishes you to know beforehand that as far as he himself is concerned—and that goes for his courtiers too—his heart responds kindly to all the white men's wishes, and he is of a mind to grant them. Of the white men's killing of our people the king bade me say nothing. I was bidden to speak to you only of the white men's wishes.

"The first wish of the white men is this: they have heard of our land, of the beauty of the mountains and the plains' fertility here, and of the metals our earth contains—iron in abundance, gold, silver, and our pure, red copper. These metals it is the white men's wish to take away from us, to take it to their home beyond the sea. In return they promise to give the king and his courtiers shiny things, entertainment for their eyes. They would have us break up the mountains, take out what is good in them to give them, leaving ourselves here the waste sand."

The people assembled murmured their astonishment, but they respected the custom forbidding any interruption at a time like this. As for the king he was still in his palace with his guests the white men.

"This is the white men's second wish," Isanusi continued. "They have been told of the forests here and of the grass-lands; of the birds and animals we have roaming the land. It is the white men's wish to have us help them kill these birds and these animals. They do not want their flesh for food. The elephants they say they want destroyed but only for their tusks. There is a hunter among the white men, and a trader. These two say tusks can be sold for riches. Leopards they want dead for their hides. As for our gazelles, they would kill them to use their heads for decoration.

"You have heard me. The white men, guests of the king, would have us destroy our mountains, then our animals, and give them what is of use to themselves, leaving here the offal. In return they would reward the king with gifts, the king together with his courtiers.

"There is a third wish the white men have made. Land they want from us, but not the way guests ask the use of land. The white men want land cut off from other land and set apart for them, as if land could ever be a thing belonging to any but the people as a whole. On this their cut-off land they would like to have crops grow. But the white men are not accustomed to doing their own planting and it is not in their minds to get accustomed here. They would have the king give them men to work the land—I use their language, for they think the king owns men he can give away to others—so that to speak truth ours would be the planting and the caring, theirs the harvest and its profit. In return they would reward the king and his courtiers with more gifts.

"Listen to their fourth wish. The white men say they have heard we have many people here—too many, they say— and that our women's fertility is reported a wonder among them. It is their wish to take numbers of our people away from us. They say these numbers would in the new places beyond the sea work on land as fertile as ours here . . ."

Here a groan of utter incredulity rose from the people assembled. Isanusi held his words, waiting for the sound of distress to die down, but it rose higher. So he spoke again.

"Those who would still know the reason of the white men's coming, let them listen. The white men have come here wishing to buy humans, to buy women among us, to buy men among us, to buy children among us and take them to unknown lands. In return they will reward the king and his courtiers with gifts."

129

One among the king's flatterers turned ashen at these words, took back escaping breath, then rose in a hurry.

"Stay, Otumfur," Isanusi turned and called to the hurrying man. "Stay and hear the end. I am almost there. Then we can go together to the king and I will help you tell him what it is I have told the people. Stay."

That flatterer, thus caught in Isanusi's honesty, mumbled inaudible words to himself and came back to his seat. Isanusi turned again and continued.

"Hear now the last wish of the white men. They have a road they follow, and something called a god they worship —not the living spirit there is in everything but a creature separate, raised above all surrounding things, to hear them speak of it rather like a bloated king. It is the white men's wish to take us from our way—ah, we ourselves are so far already from our way—to move us on to their road; to void us of our soul and put their spirit, the worship of their creature god, in us. For this they do not think it will be necessary to reward the king and his courtiers. They say it will be reward enough when we have lost our way completely, lost even our names; when you will call your brother not Olu but John, not Kofi but Paul; and our sisters will no longer be Ama, Naita, Idawa and Ningome but creatures called Cecilia, Esther, Mary, Elizabeth and Christina.

"Hear now the end. The white men wish us to destroy our mountains, leaving ourselves wastes of barren sand. The white men wish us to wipe out our animals, leaving ourselves carcases rotting into white skeletons. The white

130

men want us to take human beings, our sisters and our sons, and turn them into labouring things. The white men want us to take human beings, our daughters and our brothers, and turn them into slaves. The white men want us to obliterate our remembrance of our way, the way, and in its place to follow their road, road of destruction, road of a stupid, childish god."

Isanusi brought down his staff of office. The people did not have to hold their words any longer. Isanusi found Otumfur and with the other flatterers they went to the king.

That same day before the sun had left its height the great drums were beaten a second time and the people summoned to another meeting in the open place. This time Isanusi did not speak. He did not appear at all. In his place it was Otumfur who spoke, telling the unbelieving assembly words the king had bid him say: that Isanusi had that morning betrayed his king and lied to the people; that the white men had come as friends, not as destroyers; that for everything the white men took from us they would bring us goods of great benefit; that the white men's road was a wise road it would profit our souls to follow. Otumfur also—raising high the spokesman's staff—told the people the king and his elders had decided to punish Isanusi for his infidelity to them; that Isanusi would be an outcast till the end of his days; that no woman, no man, no child was to give him help in any way, not a drop of water, not a grain of food, for Isanusi had gone mad and like a rabid beast attacked the honour of his king.

The morning after, those already past their last initiation— we were not even close to our first then—marched to the palace intending to tell the king the white destroyers must go. Inside the palace the king and his flatterers were still conversing and drinking the new drink with the white men. The white men had told their guards what to do if men came menacing the tranquility within the palace.

The guards' weapons barked long that morning. There was no counting the numbers of our people who died then. Their corpses were left around the palace for three days— a warning to all who still had the spirit to pit themselves against the king's friendship with the white destroyers.

# 5

# the dance of love

All this was before the time when we of our age began our initiations—for us a beautiful time, time of friendship, time of learning, when in the blindness of childhood we knew only of our own growing powers but of the weakening, the destruction of the power of our people we were completely ignorant.

Before everything came the games of childhood, games and dances we loved for themselves. In fuller growth afterwards we discovered sharp, sweet surprises hidden in each to help us at every succeeding level in our quest after the fundi's mastery.

We moved first to the skills of protection. Here almost all reached the beginnings of the fundi's mastery. The teachers told us before the dances of recapitulation and rest: "You are welcome to deepen yourselves here if it is in you to make yourselves experts in the arts of protection. Whatever your decision, go learn the skills taught by other teachers. If you come back we shall be glad to go forward with you

133

in your deepening. May your going be good."

We came to the skills of farming. A fourth of us, the largest portion in any season, chose that level for their self-deepening. We came to the skills of hunting. Not many chose to deepen themselves here, though a seventh of our number reached the skills for beginning experts.

We moved through the seasons of fishing and rowing, seasons of building, of carving, of working leather, of turning metal, of molding clay, of weaving cloth, seasons of the healing arts, each season with its riddles, its proverbs and its songs, its dances—pleasant seasons in which skills already learned found constant deepening.

At the last initiation beyond all the open initiations there were twenty left of us, girls and boys who had reached skill enough to have chosen deepening at any level but had gone beyond, every season, not having found the one vocation strong enough to draw our souls to it. The teaching masters gathered together looked at us and smiled, a certain smile. There was so much we could not understand those days.

The teachers told us quietly that the way of experts had become a tricky way. They told us it would always be fatal to our arts to misuse the skills we had learned. The skills themselves were mere light shells, needing to be filled out with substance coming from our souls. They warned us never to turn these skills to the service of things separate from the way. This would be the most difficult thing, for we would learn, they told us, that no fundi could work effectively when torn away from power, and yet power in these times lived far, immeasurably far from the way.

This distance from the seats of power to the way, this distance now separating our way from power usurped against our people and our way, this distance would be the measure of the fundi's pain. They told us there was no life sweeter than that of the fundi in the bosom of his people if his people knew their way. But the life of a fundi whose people have lost their way is pain. All the excellence of such a fundi's craft is turned to trash. His skills are useless in the face of his people's destruction, and it is easy as slipping on a riverstone to see his craftsmanship actually turned like a weapon against his people.

There was so much of this talk of ways, of our way, the way, we did not then understand.

Then the masters began to speak in riddles deliberately pitched beyond our age, riddles easy to remember for their sound, hard to understand for their meaning. They talked of the imminence of an initiation beyond all initiations, and we could only listen in our ignorance.

We asked them questions. Some they answered, including one we all wanted answered, about the abandoned ship. When we had been to Poano, after we had crossed the barrier and gone beyond Poano itself, we had seen the white ship abandoned within sight of land, there in the shallow sea. We had asked about it. The fundi of the rowing art had said the time had not yet come to talk of that.

Now an older man told us it was believed the white man in command of that ship, beset by the avenging spirits of thousands he had already destroyed—this was a carrier of slaves to their doom—ran abruptly mad, lost the skill he had misused so long and ran the ship with demented fury in the irresistible direction forced on him by the avenging spirits of his victims. His ship, its strength broken, was trapped where the waves, meeting higher seaground, break into surf, continuing their forward motion with great speed but little depth till the last fingers of foam tire out, able to go no farther on the heated sand.

"What happened to those still on the ship?" Such questions we asked but at the time no one knew any answers.

"You will hear words from people," the older fundi said, "but they are sounds not coming from any real events. They come from the teller's particular imagination, no more knowing than your own."

A thousand varying things happened before our soul was open to absorb their meaning. The veils of the first initiation, the second initiation and the third, all these veils hid parts of the truth from us. It was not till the veil of the final initiation had been torn—a terrible tearing—that understanding broke in on our violated soul. Then it was that uncomprehended stories, senseless fragments, joined other pieces from which they had been forced apart and the truth of our lives was whole—a terrible wholeness.

But this we learned then: that we came from drier places, wide open spaces where eyes can see across fields like seeing across seawater. Trees cut your vision, but they are few, solitary, almost strangers in the place. This place, our present home, is more abundant. The soil here is softer, the rain incomparably more generous. Here the rainmaker

136

is a foolish joke. But it was not the abundance of the place that pulled us. It was something in our people we would not allow to get destroyed. We would rather move from scenes of our ancestors, from places and from things animated with their memory, than let the spirit of those same ancestors, the spirit of those yet to come, the spirit of all our people, be destroyed. We moved.

What we sought was darkness: the darkness of forests, darkness to let broken things grow whole again, darkness, origin of life. Behind us we thought we had forever left the white abomination: violence in its pure state, hatred unmixed.

"Change, or we will kill you," the first white predators, those from the desert, had said. "Believe in our road; abandon your way. Forget your ancestors; forget your posterity. Forget who your people are; forget your very selves and we will let your bodies live."

Yes, we were told to kill our soul so our bodies might live. Into these forsaken bodies alien, fictitious souls were to be poured to do the bidding, do the work of others. Slavery was shown us—held up to us—as the beautiful road, the right road of our lives. Among us the destroyers raised from human refuse ludicrous prophets preaching acceptance of slavery, love of pain inflicted upon us, love of destruction directed against us. Half our people—more, the will of men is weak in times like this—weary of fighting for the spirit's life against a bloody, crazy enemy, bent before the predators, stayed, emptied their bodies of their own souls, and took into themselves alien spirits, destroyed,

137

destructive minds. The other half—less, the will of human beings is weak in times like this—left land, trees, stones, all the things that had filled their lives with recognition, taking only the spirit of a people with them on their way. Beyond mountains and boglands we sought the safety of these forests and these grasslands that are now our home.

Now too we began to understand descent. We thought of descent of the body, blood line running through mothers, life's creators here. We thought of descent of the spirit, descent of skills passing through experts to novices; descent of the mind, the mental line through teachers, passers on of knowledge about paths, knowledge about the way along which the people in body will be kept together with the people in spirit, the body of our people with our soul.

Then we went into the forests, our minds still filled with prohibitions, with fables of gods and spirits. The undetermined stayed bound within these prohibitions created only to measure growth. Those among us with the will to grow discarded each prohibition as readily as we found there was no more sense in it. The circle of our craft, the circle of our friendship grew closer, and our affection deeper. In the riddles we found strings not to tie the mind but to guide the seeker, provided the search was serious. So in the forests we found a carefully created way of growth where, following our urge to reach the height of the fundi's art we came at length to a greater understanding of our soul—our gift along the way.

Then began that initiation beyond initiations of which the fundis had spoken. We whose dedication had not yet

138

been drawn to any of the particular arts, we were left to float to the knowledge of a craftsmanship of the soul, the vocation of those who used to be the soulguide of our people, the rememberers of the way, but who had for seasons and seasons, hundreds and hundreds of seasons now, become outcasts—the power of the people having fallen into hands animated by rotten souls, hustlers who if they have skills will use them not for healing, not for keeping our people's body and our people's soul together but for killing, for splitting the soul and keeping it a thing apart from zombi bodies.

There were twenty of us: eleven girls growing into women, nine boys growing into men. In the natural growth of our friendship, in the pursuit of our vocation we wandered against the force of all unexplainable prohibitions into the forbidden grove, the grove of sources, intent not on destroying but on seeking.

It was on this search that unsuspecting we found Isanusi in the grove and knew him finally not for a madman but for a fundi whose art went beyond any skill of the body, whose mastery reached the consciousness itself of our people; he whose greatest desire, whose vocation it was to keep the knowledge of our way, the way, from destruction; to bring it back to an oblivious people, all else failing, at least as remembrance; he whose highest hope it was to live the way as purpose, the way as the purpose of our people.

Isanusi was not disturbed, though it was a great surprise to him that so many of us had come in this one season of

139

initiation where in the past each generation had given barely one. He asked us if truly all of us had reached the skills of the beginning fundi yet still desired to move on at every level. We told him it was so. He smiled. We did not know then what a testing time our presence would create for him; how much he had yearned for an end to his fundamental loneliness, how we brought with us the promise of its ending and the beginning of things closer to his spirit, closer to our way, closer to the way.

But because of what we had yet to know he would be forced to wait, to risk our complete disappearance and his plunge back into the destructive loneliness of his soul, because we had yet to know.

He tried even then to tell us. He said words about what had happened to our people, gave us warnings to beware the surface of things, to stay clear of the hypocrites of power if we could not ourselves destroy them.

We did not understand him. Had we understood then we would not have left him, we would have stayed there in the secret grove with him, and there begun the search for paths leading to our way, the way. We did not understand him though his words themselves called for respect, and so uncomprehending we listened. Then we took our leave of him.

The long preparation for womanhood, the preparation for manhood, both had come to an end. Energies we had never had to use, strengths we had not thought we possessed, had risen in us for the tasks of the final open initiation. Now it was time to find rest for these energies. The time of love had come. The last, the greatest dance of all our youth, would mark the passage into adulthood.

The dance of love is a dance of choice also. It has always been the custom at this festival that the growing women of the age, if they are already of a mind to do so, choose the growing men they wish to share their lives with.

Concerning most of the choices of our season we were already sure. It is not easy to hide any kind of love, and young love loathes disguise. There were still twenty of that age, eleven female, nine male, whose particular preferences we could not predict. It was not that there was a dearth of affection among us. On the contrary, among the twenty there was so much unforced affection, of a quality so intense, that it was clear this would be no pairing love but something greater, embracing all our group. That the last great dance would be the pairing dance itself, that raised a quiet, suspended interest in all the season's youth. There was a waiting to see how a group that seemed to live beyond the need of pairing would weave itself into the purpose of the dance.

There was just one remaining matter for anxiety. The king, before the completion of preparations for the dance of love, had called for the mother, the father and the uncles of Abena, one among the eleven girls, and asked them if any youth had set his mind on her. Abena had a mind that had filled every fundi teacher's mind with joy. But it was not her mind, it was simply the beauty of her body that made the king wish to set her apart for his son.

For Koranche the king had a son. This son, Bentum was

his name, name chosen after another of our disastrous kings. Bentum was also of our age, but we did not grow up knowing him. It was known the king Koranche had suffered in his childhood from the necessity of dragging his feeble wits and lethargic body in the initiations after children younger than himself. When then his son Bentum reached the age of the first initiation the king decided it would be better for future kings to have an upbringing entirely different from others of their age. The king sent the boy to the coast, to Poano where he arranged for his raising in the largest of the white destroyers' stone places. It was said here the white destroyers raised the boy to be their servant, but—so far have we fallen in our exile from the way—even the service of white men seemed honour enough to the king Koranche.

Twelve seasons later Bentum was sent beyond the seas with some white traders to their country, a cold place where his soul, so we have heard, was voided out of him at once, an alien language forced into his throat, and a name to make dogs bark in derision was given him: Bradford George. That was not the end. Before it was time for him to return to Poano to the big stone place there the white men thrust on him a wife—ah, cruel ruse. In this the white men did their victim most grievous injury, for they chose for his companionship a creature more than twenty seasons past the poor prince's age, a dry, white woman more than half deaf, blind in one eye, with a body so dead it was whispered here she never could feel her husband enter her, and would not know what to do with him in any case.

The king Koranche asked Abena's people if their child was taken. They replied this was one of the children more concerned to be a fundi than to be taken for a wife. She had not been taken. The king asked no more.

For the final dance, the dance of love, the dance of choice, the king announced a sudden change in paths.

This has always been the dance of selection. Three circles dance: the girls of the season within, the pairs of the last adult generation next, then without the boys of the season. Between any two dancers in the second circle there is the space of a single dancing step, one swift beat and no more. The dancers in the centre make their choices one by one. But to reach her choice in the outer circle each growing girl has to dance with skill enough to cut through the middle circle untouched by any member of the older pairs, so reaching the welcome of the male outer circle, dancing still. Once there she is entirely free to dance to the lover of her choice.

The middle circle is easier to breach in the beginning of the dance. Close to the dance's end it moves closer to the shrunken core and its tightness makes it so that only with the greatest skill can any dancer break through it. It is a small part of the way to let the shakiest dancers be choicemakers first. The dancer most known for her grace and skill—in our time this was Abena, she also who was most desired— is last to be closed within the tightened middle circle.

This was the sudden change in paths the day of the dance of love: it was the king's wish that the girl left last within the middle circle should choose not a dancer from among

143

ourselves, but a special guest of honour he the king was bringing us. We did not have to wait to find out who this special creature was: the prince Bentum, renamed Bradford George, voided of his soul, had fled his white cripple of a wife and come home looking for beauty and goodness to sacrifice to his murdered soul.

The announcement produced a high-nerved eagerness in all the females in the inner circle. At other times they would have strained from pride alone to come as near the end as possible. Now they competed to pierce the middle circle first, avoiding the unbeloved prince.

The king Koranche and his courtiers came. The people who desired to watch the dance of love had gathered already in the centre of the town. The dance began. The prince sat in the very centre of the dance, where according to the way only the dancers ought to be, his clothes a bloody red and glistening with bits of metal even in the soft light of the moon.

Efua broke through the middle circle first. Anxiety robbed her dancing of its beauty, but her fortune this night was good and she was not stopped. She chose Mofolo, an unsurprising choice.

Subira danced her way out next and found Birago waiting, a happy choice.

Esiama danced to Bampo. Maanan chose Igun and caused Mungai a bitter disappointment. Ekua chose Konadu. Ronke chose Ayodele. Rukia went to Oko—why break our ears with all the names, all the choices?

Abena did not vie with the other girls to seize the easy

chance. That had never been her way.

And then there were eleven girls left and the dance became a thing of swift surprises. For in place of the one girl who should have leapt in readiness to breach the middle circle ten girls jumped as if the spirit animating them had turned them all into one individual person. They danced like one. The dancers of the middle circle were still digesting their surprise when, as swiftly as the ten had begun, each found her exact simultaneous space and danced out triumphant to the circle of the boys—a wonder taking breath.

The ten did not divide their choice. When they reached the outer circle they were content to dance together near the nine of us, those, like themselves, still seeking our final vocation. There had been no separate choices at all. The ten had chosen the nine together, a most unusual choice, selection filled with a nameless beauty.

Abena as yet had found no liberating space. She danced, alone in the centre of the middle circle. Close to her the sitting prince looked up at her and grinned like a rodent in repose. The king now ordered the dance stopped a while and bade his faithful dotard Otumfur make another speech. Otumfur told us to remember the prince had also had his initiation, an initiation greater than any, that he had been to the white men's land; that this made him almost the equal of white men, and it was therefore only fitting that the best of our women should become the companion of his days. That said, Otumfur sat. The king motioned, smiling, for the continuation of the dance.

Abena danced. She danced to make the beholding heart

145

ache with desire for closeness to such grace, such fluid beauty. She danced long, and her dancing was a dance of trances, dance of the soul in thought. Her body itself, that moved little. It turned round the redness of the seated prince there in the centre, and it seemed as if it was all her intention to dance her best and then to succumb to this prince chosen for her. But when the silence of admiration was deepest in its descent upon those watching her—dancers, watchers, even the prince with the ridiculous name—Abena cut a step unexpected in its speed and without one halt she slipped untouched past the dancers of the middle circle, and she came to us. We did not wait.

The dance of love takes the dancers always to the forest. The remembrance says the first such dance was no dance but the hot flight of forbidden lovers from their elders' bloody anger. It is a small part of the way for the chosen to fly with their beloved, seeking the safety of the forests till the anger of the thwarted elders turns to wisdom.

Willing messengers, secretly connecting the lovers with what they have fled, bring food and news to soften the hardness of forest life: hardness that joins real lovers together, hardness that destroys the foolishness of mere infatuation.

The pairs found the places of their secrecy not far from the town Anoa. They looked at us with warnings and invitations in their eyes when instead of staying with them we pressed on into unfrequented parts. From the third grove onward there was no one else with us. We looked behind us to make sure. There was no cause for anxiety. The others were far behind, eager to begin savouring the happiness of their pairing. They had called to us telling us we could still break into pairs and stay near them. We laughed with them but ran on. We ran through the third grove and the fourth. Under the slender alari trees we stopped for rest. All of us had come: Pili and Ndlela, Suma and Kwesi, Manda and Ude, Tawia and Dovi, Ankoanda and Sobo, Liamba and Mokili, Kenia and Lini, Makaa and Ashale, Ona and Kamara, then Naita, then Abena.

We climbed up the tall alari trunks. Where at the top the branches grew slenderest we leaned on them and made them bend till they brought us to other branches high above the ground. A hundred and thirty branches bent separately with the succeeding weight of each of us and brought us with no visible trace of our passage to the river's hidden arm. Past the waterfall feeding the river we ran till near the spring of Noliwe and Ningome the silence of the place entered us and we stopped running, stopped talking.

At the spring, where last we had found Isanusi, we searched for him but he was not to be found. We rested, then worked to build ourselves a place to stay. Food we found and gathered, not in abundance but sufficient.

The second day Abena asked a question that had been on all our minds. What were we going to do? It was not her opinion we should return. It seemed impossible to her that the king would ever acquiesce in her refusal and ours to do his will. She was for our finding entirely new directions, though what these directions were she could not say, simply declaring herself ready to think with everyone of us. The

147

truth of her words, added to our own unreadiness, unsettled us. Ndlela asked Abena where she thought these entirely new directions could lie. Abena repeated she did not know for certain, but said if we were all willing to think and to search, it would be joy to her to search and think with all. That night we did not sleep well.

We woke up to find Isanusi standing close by our place. We asked where he had been. He laughed and said dwellers in the grove had to take care of their secrecy. He had not known if we would all return after the dance of love.

"You did not break into pairs, then?" he asked, seeing all of us emerge.

"We came together."

He looked at us, a kind of longing look. He looked at Abena and said: "This could be a new day beginning." Abena had no reply for him.

"We came because of you," Ankoanda said.

"Not because of me," Isanusi answered. "But we must talk. You have sought the spring so young. And so many of you. Though," he shook his head, "if we had not strayed so far from the way twenty would be too few, a number to laugh at."

The words were a puzzle to us, except perhaps to Abena. She seemed to have some unspoken understanding of Isanusi's thoughts.

"We have much to talk about," Isanusi said. "I came here older than you are now, though I was called the youngest of the spokesmen. The one I found here, as you have found me, was near death. It was not old age alone that had eaten

148

her life. She had been thrown out from among us in her time. Her crime was speaking truth offensive to the powerful, singing truth. That is the way it has been among us for too many generations. All thought she had been destroyed, but my time of despair also came and in my wandering my soul was drawn here and here I found her. She had been waiting for one like me, a little bitterly because the blindness of my soul made me slow in coming and she feared she would die with none of her knowledge, the deeper knowledge of the way, passed on—a fearful possibility.

"Some of what she told me I knew and you already know: of our origins, of our journeys till now. But much else has been hidden from you, some wrapped in riddles whose sounds you know but whose meaning you have yet to understand, some simply kept unrevealed to you. You have yet to learn we are not a people to nurture kings and courtiers—the parasites feeding on human souls. You have yet to understand these are recent excrescences among us. And you have yet to learn why we have found no paths to clean ourselves of them.

"You have been told of our migrations, but of their deeper causes you have till now been left in ignorance. You have not been told of the deformed souls among us turning into princes and kings, their minds too puny to understand that power is not something to be stolen from the whole for the individual self's consumption, their souls too shrivelled to understand reciprocity, too blind to see our way, the way.

"You have grown up seeing white men among us. Of their coming you have been taught none of the deeper

149

truths. Perhaps, too, of the destruction they have already wrought and are yet to bring, in your minds you suspect nothing. We have much to talk about, but we should not begin with heavy matters. Tell me first of the dance of love. How did it go with you?"

We told Isanusi our news of the pairing dance. The news pleased him, but at the end of it we said we would be going back to Anoa when we got news the king had seen the folly of his wishes, and Isanusi grew pensive. He asked if we still thought kings and leaders had wisdom enough to grasp their own folly, but he waited for no answer to his own question before he began again.

Such was Isanusi's conversation with us:

At the time the white destroyers broke through the wall of water and arrived from the sea the king Koranche had already shown he was greedy for power over our people, eager to wield a tyrannous power. But this was impotent greed and he had found no means to worsen the destruction of our people.

Then the white destroyers came: first a trader wanting to buy goods from us and sell us things. With him was a hunter who the next time he came to Anoa killed a woman pointed out by the drunken king to show the power of his gun. There was a third white destroyer: a missionary who wanted to replace all knowledge of our way with fables even our children laughed at then.

We told the white missionary we had such fables too, but kept them for the entertainment of those yet growing up—fables of gods and devils and a supreme being above

150

everything. We told him we knew soft minds needed such illusions, but that when any mind grew among us to adulthood it grew beyond these fables and came to understand that there is indeed a great force in the world, a force spiritual and able to shape the physical universe, but that that force is not something cut off, not something separate from ourselves. It is an energy in us, strongest in our working, breathing, thinking together as one people; weakest when we are scattered, confused, broken into individual, unconnected fragments.

Among the white destroyers there was no respect for anything we could say. They had come determined to see nothing, to listen to no one, bent solely on the satisfaction of their greed, of which we had ample news. But the king was infatuated with the white destroyers and would not heed the people's will, as quick in its expression as it was clear: to tell the white men to go. The white destroyers had brought the king gifts to entertain his crippled soul, together with a hot drink to burn his throat and further addle his brain with a grand, illusory happiness. It was this drink the first taste of which prompted the king to point to the unfortunate woman, first victim here of the white hunter.

Some among our people shot flaming arrows into the white men's ship one dark night. The ship withdrew down the river to the castle at Poano.

The king was angered. He tried all ruses to find out who had brought together the arrowmakers. But the king did not find an easy path. For what purpose was the search,

Isanusi had asked in the court. The king in the rashness of his anger was drawn into an admission he wanted to inflict a punishment upon the arrowmakers—wrongdoers, he called them.

Isanusi asked: "What wrong did they do, the arrow-makers? They drove away a pest. Was that the wrong they did?" The question drew an unforced "No!" from the court.

"Or was this not a pest?"

"A pest indeed," the others answered.

"These white men are not just pests," Isanusi said. "They are dangerous animals, they are destroyers, they are killers."

The court was murmuring its approval when the flatterer Otumfur, seizing the spokesman's staff, shut everybody up. Otumfur argued that in a matter of such importance the arrowmakers did wrong not to seek the king's permission first. Now what the court murmured was the confusion of its mind, and Otumfur pressed his advantage, casting grave insinuations about the danger in doing things behind the king's back.

Isanusi allowed Otumfur's words to reach their crest, and then he rose.

"Strange is the community," he said, his voice soft and slow, "in which the common good cannot be sought without permission. Three seasons have passed since a leopard came—you all remember—and devoured Kotu, son of Ikoku, fundi in the art of making drums. Sibiri, daughter of Kimia, on her own initiative took a goat and set a trap for the creature. Akpofure, the same who later

152

married Sibiri, killed the beast, losing his left hand doing it, and we all breathed again. Perhaps here my memory does me wrong. Set it right for me then: with whose permission did Sibiri and Akpofure rid us of the wild predator?"

There was silence in the court, chagrin on the face of the king's most faithful flatterer, Otumfur, and hatred in the staring eyeballs of the king. Otumfur boiled especially that one so much younger than he, younger than any of the spokesmen, could with so little effort so conquer him in reasoning and in eloquence.

Isanusi continued: "Among us no permission is necessary to do ourselves good. Permission is a question when a stranger comes among us and requests to settle. We ask about his character, the background he comes from, the desires he carries in his mind. If we are satisfied we embrace him. That is the way all those from Kankan, from Boma, from Gwelo and from Ankole came among us, to be a part of us so that their good would be our good.

"Now this other permission the white men have been pressing for, let us look at it. First, they do not want to be a part of us. Their good is not necessarily our good, then, since they are not of us and have no wish to be of us. They belong to a community we have yet to see, and the purpose of their presence here among us is to do that community good, not us.

"Have we forgotten the cause of our long wandering? Did we not learn near the desert how priests and warriors are twin destroyers, the priest attacking the victim mind, the warrior breaking bodies still inhabited by resisting wills?

153

We are not a trading people. We have always held parasites in contempt. We have seen traders and their work. They and their goods work on the will, steadily, constantly, supplementing the disintegrative work of soldiers and priests on bodies and minds. The traders are creators of unreasonable desires. Where the priest fails to make his victims willing slaves, and the soldier is impotent to make living slaves, his violence only producing dead bodies, the trader enslaves the will itself, and men are led to want their own enslavement, thinking it is only the pleasure of owning things they want.

"All honest people who have come to us have come because they sought to do themselves good among us, as part of our people, and they said so. These white men, they do not want to be a part of us. But here they have come claiming they have crossed the sea from wherever it is they come from just to do us good. They are pretenders. They are liars. We have asked them for nothing. We should not let them come among us. They have no desire to live with us. They will live against us. Do you not hear how they have started their sojourn among us with insults and with killing—or do you no longer recognize death? Do you not recognize insults when strangers come claiming they know what is good for us and we don't know it?"

The king tried subterfuge after lying subterfuge, but a decision was reached. The white men would not be permitted to return. They would have no permission to build their factory or their church, if they came again to ask.

The king was defeated for the time, but his greed was not in any way diminished. The king sent secret messages to Poano, to the white men. The white men answered the king secretly. Secretly the white men and the king exchanged gifts, tokens of their mutual esteem. In his messages the king indicated with rising insistence his longing for the fiery rum, keener than his desire for any of the other promised gifts. The white men answered they would be glad to give him all the rum he wanted as soon as his people changed their minds.

The king complained he could not fight his people's will. From the white missionary a message came. It said it was an incontrovertible teaching of the white religion that a king had a right, a duty in fact, to impose his will strongly on his people, for to the white men the king was always the head, the people merely the body. Replied the king: I do not have the strength. Said the white trader: We can help with that if you will be a faithful friend of ours, for that is what friends are for. The king said secretly: Yes, but let us act in secret. And the missionary spoke the final word in his message: Secrecy, yes, at the appropriate time. But sometimes you the head will have to make the heaviness of your authority felt, and felt openly. As for strength to do it, fear nothing as long as you keep faith with us, your friends. The strength of your friends is your strength also, as long as you take good care to keep our friendship.

Isanusi, hearing news of secret visits between the king and the white men, asked his questions in open court. The king lied, denied everything, and in court the prudent

155

began to suspect Isanusi of the disease of unreasonable suspicion. Not for long.

The white destroyers returned one sudden night and sent flaming iron flying into the exact area where the fundis of the spear, the arrow and the bow have always made their home, killing three hundred human beings in one night alone. In the morning a people disoriented by the violence of the night before saw two white flags flying in the undecided breeze. One flew on the white destroyers' ship, its twin above the palace of the king.

The white destroyers came to land. The king greeted them with affection. The king was taken aboard the white destroyers' ship. He returned with whole canoeloads of things, had them loaded on the bank on to the heads of his servants, and preceded them into his palace. These goods were announced as a gift, a present to the king and his court, and a prelude to negotiations, the white men having come to renew their request for permission to set up on our land a factory, a hunting station and a church.

By the time the king emerged from the dreams induced by the white destroyers' drink the moon had disappeared. He distributed the gifts to his hangers-on by firelight. Among the courtiers that night greed replaced the last remaining shred of wisdom.

Isanusi, unable any longer to contemplate the scene, walked out in disgust and despair. Among those he had counted as potential allies on the people's side—he had thought of five—three were at once won over to the king at the sight of presents supposedly sent specifically for them.

The remaining two were first drawn into confusion, then their will was reduced to nothing, so that though they still with their minds were able to perceive treachery in the king's behaviour they quite lost the ability to act on their perceptions. Their silence left the king free to claim his actions had the force of tradition behind them. Their inaction left Isanusi facing a choice of desperation: to fight a lone, and therefore doomed battle against the king with not a single ally and on the king's own ground, or to withdraw completely from the court, and therefore from the community under the power of the court, unless like the other courtiers he too changed his will and agreed to be bought.

For the king had tried friendly approaches to win Isanusi to his side. He had told him what the white men ultimately wanted: permission to mine the hills of Anoa for gold, and the court's agreement to the establishment of plantations for spices, in great demand in the white men's country. To get our people to labour in the mines and on the plantations the white destroyers wanted the king to fill our people's mind with tales of the goodness of labouring for whites.

The prophecy of Anoa, the warnings against servitude, prologue to the spokesman's oath he had taken, hit Isanusi's mind with a wounding sharpness. He remembered the vow to speak truth, the first formal vow and the last in the initiation of masters in the art of eloquence.

Isanusi walked through Anoa looking for solace in a place destroyed, his spirit heavy with the realization things

157

had gone far, had changed past rottenness. Where the arrowmakers lived Isanusi saw in the dark the form of the debris caused by the white destroyers' iron, and he saw the people at a general wake for the dead. Women recognising him came to ask him why the king had not come to join the preparations for battle against the white murderers. They asked what sense there was in the things they had seen: the procession of carriers taking things from the white destroyers' ship to the palace of the king. They asked Isanusi why instead of clarity there was so much confusion everywhere.

Isanusi had no answers to give. In his own spirit the turmoil was twin to the people's around him. He walked on through the night, a fugitive from realities he was still reluctant to understand, from questions he was impotent to answer.

A messenger came running after Isanusi, requesting him to return to the court. The king wanted to consult with him. Isanusi returned. The king said again there was a matter to be explained to the people, and only Isanusi had the eloquence to do the work of persuasion.

Isanusi asked: "What matter?"

Said the king: "You know, what happened with the white men."

Isanusi said: "I do not know what happened with the white men."

The king explained he wanted Isanusi to soothe the people's inflamed feelings. About the killing and the destruction the white men had brought, all the king said was the lesson was already clear. "What we now say to the people does not matter. We can even say it was a mistake the white men made. Let us say they had wanted to fire the guns to show me their respect, as indeed I have seen them do at Poano for Atobra. Let us tell the people something like the wind turning the hot iron balls the wrong way, eh, Isanusi?"

Isanusi made sure he had not heard wrong: that what the king wanted him to do was to use his gift of eloquence to mystify the people. Then Isanusi rejected the assignment, pleading incompetence.

The king urged him to reconsider, to accept. "The people respect you. They listen to you, Isanusi, and they believe what you say." The king promised Isanusi gifts, promised him more gifts, asked Isanusi what his heart desired, asked him what would give comfort to his tongue.

Isanusi considered the heinousness of all that had already happened, considered the terror of his own position, how he was being forced to fit into the strategies of destruction. And in his mind he conceived a plan. Isanusi undertook to speak to the people.

Isanusi spoke to the people. He spoke truth to the people and the truth raised a fury among the king and his hangers-on.

The king and his courtiers declared Isanusi mad and had him thrown out of the people's protection. Otumfur the flatterer was picked to do the work of deceit Isanusi had refused to do. His lying tongue, however, failed to persuade the people. When the people heard what the king's wishes

159

were the bravest among them went home to prepare their weapons. The following morning they converged upon the palace. Had they succeeded in the realization of what was in their heart and mind it was their intention to destroy the white destroyers and their ship also. But from the palace the white men's guns in the hands of zombi guards, the new askaris brought against us by the white destroyers from the sea, exterminated them.

Immediately following the break with the king Isanusi's spirit fell into a state of confusion and his mind knew utter despair. He saw the things happening and disgust grew in him, but all his love was in Anoa still. Every place here had important memories for him, even those places where painful things had happened. All such memories had acquired a sweetness now, the sweetness of the whole of life remembered where the navel lies buried. Bitterness itself to Isanusi was any contemplation of exile, so he made no preparations to leave Anoa. Declared a madman, he continued quietly to live in the place of his birth.

Most men at first, uncertain what next the king might do, knowing Koranche for a vindictive man and not wishing to be trapped in another blood quarrel of his making, forbade their sisters to give Isanusi food. The women said nothing against their brothers' careful warnings. At night and in other secret ways they brought Isanusi food and whatever else he needed.

A place to sleep? That too became easy for him. A woman, a widow known for the beauty of her mind, her will and her body, came to Isanusi openly by the river, and calling him by his name and his mother's name asked him to come to her house whenever he wanted to and to look upon it as his home. Isanusi thanked the woman Idawa.

Isanusi knew Idawa—who did not?—knew her and remembered her first defiance of the king Koranche. It was known Idawa had not simply in her younger days returned the king's presents of courtship but had actually insulted him with truth, saying she would never spread her thighs wide enough for any fat worm of a man to enter her. Further, she had said everybody knew a fat body was always the house of a rotten soul.

Truth it was before the ancestors the king was fat. All men laughed secretly at him. In our own tenth season we had heard him called He-whose-penis-is-hidden-from-himself. Idawa, who had at that time said openly what others would rather whisper, called Isanusi to her home.

Isanusi loved Idawa as she loved him. But his spirit found no rest in that single love. From one new moon to the next for two seasons Isanusi wandered alone without hope. Thinking of our people's arrival here, feeling the call against all prohibitions to go where Noliwe and Ningome themselves had gone in their search for the source, Isanusi wandered into the fifth grove and there found Ndola, aged, in despair, but still alive.

Ndola too in her time had been a fundi in the art of eloquence, a poet, a singer. She sang truth at a public ceremony when the king, at that time the moron Tutu, craved only pleasant songs of deceit. Ndola too had been declared insane—a salutary madness, for there is no need to destroy the mad physically. She had been left to fend for herself unhelped by any human being, and she had spent her life after that waiting in the grove for the arrival of another soul who could see the truth and act on it. What she knew, things that had been hidden even from Isanusi, she revealed in an anxious rush, and not many days after she had unburdened herself she died there in the grove.

Isanusi buried Ndola and went away from Anoa, went to the town Poano and for four seasons lived there. There he saw the victory of the white destroyers, the utter destruction of souls. He saw there was no fundi there who was not first of all a prostitute. Experts in the art of eloquence he saw bought to speak for thieves. Experts in the art of singing he saw bought to sing the praises not just of one parasite, the king, but also of any bloated passer who could pay their paltry price.

Four seasons Isanusi spent in the town Poano learning what the town could teach his soul. At the end of the fourth season he returned to Anoa, not to be a part of it, but to live unknown, an outcast in the grove.

All his thinking led him again and again to the realization there was nothing he could do against destruction as long as he remained alone, and yet he knew his loneliness was not a particular thing, that it was something that would go beyond the span of his single life, for the victims of destruction he had seen everywhere were in a daze, in their confusion not yet clear enough to have begun to think of what to do to fight destruction. All were hypnotized victims; most were fascinated by destruction's shiny dross;

162

all were numbed by its new pain. So much experience, such long destruction would be necessary before a greater realization came. Meanwhile Isanusi thought and thought, for the headlong progress of destruction raised in his mind an infinity of questions about what went wrong, where, when, how, why; about what people could do against destruction, how, where, and when.

Lonely he was, but he had been lonelier among crowds of men bound for destruction and not seeing it, only wanting more of it, because destruction had found ways to flatter and excite some superficial sense of theirs.

Isanusi told us it tired him unnecessarily to talk of his personal loneliness, and that it was a waste of our time. "The whites intend a lasting oppression of us," he said at the end of everything. He told us in the town Poano he had heard a white man, a missionary whose white greed was so subtle it looked forward to the ending of the open trade in human beings, to the beginning of a subtler destruction. This white missionary thought there would be far greater profit in keeping the victims of the trade here on our own land, having the kings and their courtiers use them to mine and grow whatever the whites need, then offering the product to the white destroyers, the kings and courtiers getting gifts in return. Isanusi said this white missionary would be busy finding ways to eternalize our slavery through using our leaders in a cleverer kind of oppression, harder to see as slavery, slavery disguised as freedom itself. "The whites intend a long oppression of us."

The town had deepened for Isanusi a heavy realization:

163

that the naturally decaying class of kings and courtiers—everything filthy among us—was now being deliberately supported and helped to multiply by the white destroyers from the sea for their own ends, a deliberate sickening of our people, since only from our disease could the white destroyers hope to get the things they had come looking for.

We listened to Isanusi, and vague realizations assailed our minds: that the world of friendship we had looked forward to living in before the final initiation, that world for which we had thought we were preparing ourselves, did not exist. Not only that. That world, the very seed, the mere possibility of it, the idea itself of it, was under determined attack from a people of a road completely opposed to it, and in the attack our world, our way, was yet the loser.

Our choices in the life we were ready to begin would not be many: we could fit into existing arrangements, abandoning our dreams of that better world, dreams of our way, the way. Or we could try to realize the way. That would mean fighting against the white road, the white people's system for destroying our way, the way.

We listened to Isanusi. We did not know then the knowledge contained in his words was immediate, urgent knowledge. We thought we would have time to absorb it, time to adjust to its meaning. We had none.

Isanusi tried to warn us but we misjudged him. We thought there was a distance between his words and reality, a space for us to manoeuvre in. There was none.

Isanusi told us the meaning had been taken, voided

164

out of all the official ceremonies of our initiation. He warned us to stay completely clear of the new arrangements, the positions which had already become mere jobs for parasites. "The way things have become, if you do not want to be parasites you need time in which to think of what else there is to be. And above time, courage to do what you conclude you ought to do, which is more difficult."

Those we sent from time to time to the second grove to bring us news of the town told us before the next new moon the king's anger had cooled, that the wisdom of the ancestors had entered his head, and he had decided there was no reason for resentment against Abena or against any of us. Further, the king wanted us to know he had thought of a sort of gift for us: the feast at initiation's end would this season be the first of its kind, entirely different from any there had ever been among our people. He had prevailed upon the white men his friends to call us aboard their ship. We were to be the first black people in the world to feast with the white strangers as their guests and to get gifts of appreciation from them at the ending of our youth.

So we made ready to go. Isanusi watched our happy preparations in silence. When he saw we were entirely ready he asked us why, with the exception of Abena, we were so eager to depart. What were we going to the feast to celebrate when the integral way of our ancestors had been so forgotten, when the feasting had become an end in itself, a senseless gorging? Or did we not see even the form of the feast had grown stupid? The ritual feast was now to take place on the white people's ship, vessel of destruction, merely because the king had had a whim. "If you knew who you were," Isanusi said, "you would accept no invitations from black men who call white people friends. Such unnatural friendships are fed by bloody interests. You will live to be their victim."

We respected Isanusi. But at times when he spoke his words merely glanced off the surface of our world's opacity. We did not know how to listen to him.

"Go then," he said, a man distracted. "If you survive you will know why you should not have gone. If you do not survive none of this will matter anyway."

The king was a jovial, laughing man when we saw him again. The entire planning of the pairing dance, he said, had been a deliberate joke to tease us into showing our true spirit, and we had done as well as he had thought we would. He called us his special children, the darkness in his eyes, and told us we were welcome to anything he could give. About the prince Bentum, renamed Bradford George, he did not choose to say much, save that he had returned in high spirits to the stone place on the coast where the whites his friends had important work for him and where he had left his wife.

The king laughed long at his own mention of the prince's white wife. He told us it would have been impossible anyway to give the prince a second wife since he was travelling on the white people's road—in this the king was true to his lost self; there was not one thought of our own paths to reciprocity on his mind. The king asked us what we thought of his offer to hold a feast for us on board the white men's ship. We indicated our agreement, except for Abena who in the presence of the king said nothing to contradict us, and afterward simply looked at us and could not help her tears.

The night of the feast the moon rose early. It rose above the earth's bending larger than a falling sun, the yellow of its light tinged with a soft red like washed blood on undyed cloth.

We danced at the palace till it was time to go, danced no fixed dance but a free dance changing as the drummers, the singers and the coaxers of the thirty-stringed cora felt the spirit of the evening change. Near the end Abena asked the drummers if they could beat rhythms for her. She asked for drums alone. The singers and the coaxers of instruments fell silent.

To the heavy, slow beat she had requested Abena did a dance like the dance of birth, the dance of awakening, but as if the birth she danced would be a reluctant birth, a possible abortion, even. For though Abena had more than enough time and supple skill in abundance she never carried the dance to its proper end. Always when the end came near, with an imperceptible change in her movement Abena returned to the beginning, to the slow, heavy, mournful steps of blindness ignorant of sight, the steps of flesh not yet inspired. She chose an arbitrary end when, staring fixedly at us, she shook like a person surprised in some sly trap, shook with a fury that seemed aimed at us in spite of her love and the impossibility of her desiring to cut herself adrift from us, and then abruptly she halted her unfinished dance.

167

A quiet breeze blew that night. The moon was high. The river under its light looked silvery like a fish unscaled. High up on the ship the white men raised a bright light to tell the king they were ready. We rowed to their ship in three canoes: ourselves, the king, and five of his courtiers.

On the side facing us the white ship cast a soft shadow. There we dropped our canoe stones and climbed up ropes lowered for us on to the white men's ship. The highest part, where we walked first, was bare except for rows of thick mats on the floor, each mat under its roof and walls of some thin white veil. One white destroyer, asked about the veils, said they kept insects and diseases away when the whites slept outside their rooms on the ship, something they did often because to them this place was unbearably hot. We sat a little away from the veils.

There was no dancing at this the white men's celebration, no singing, no expression from the soul. They seemed to think it was enough to eat and drink. Of their food we did not eat much. Our stomachs were not accustomed to its texture, and to our tongues its taste was strange. It was their drink that began our undoing.

At first we had not liked the white men's drink any more than we had liked their food. It lacked the throat-caressing friendliness of ahey, and in sweetness it fell far short of even fermented palm wine. Its taste was sharp, and in its journey down the throat it travelled like an angry enemy, scorching its way down. The king told us it was not the taste of it we should direct our minds to, nor should we mind the burning of our throats. He advised us to drink as much as we could take in at once, hardening our eyes against its taste, then wait for its effect.

We drank, all except Abena, Naita and Lini. Naita and Lini tried the drink, did not like it, and left it, saying they would rather sit through the night with dry throats than punish their bodies with such poison. Abena that night wanted nothing to do with food or drink. She seemed to suffer keenly from a kind of greed for our company, and the way she looked at us it was as if she had lost hope of seeing us again.

Soon enough the king, who had been the first to begin drinking, began to talk the language of a drunken man. He found all things extremely beautiful, like a fool to whom the presence of physical beauty in the world had just occurred, and on whose thoughts this new presence had intruded with such force as to push out any remembrance of ugliness. The night sky, the moon hanging in it, even the white destroyers' vessel he exclaimed about. At first we all thought his chattering foolish. But in a little time first one, then another among those of us who had drunk the rum joined the king in his newfound admiration of everything in the universe.

The whites were silent. Among us the taste of the drink was not a matter to worry any drinker any more. In the middle of our exclamations of delight two of the white destroyers went down into the belly of their ship. On their return they brought boxes in their arms. These they set before us for our examination.

169

Great and sincere was our admiration of every little object in those boxes, though of their uses we knew nothing. Equally great was the pleasure of the whites at seeing us so filled with admiration. Much of the contents of the boxes the king grew intensely curious about, and ended up wanting for himself. The whites obliged him, made presents of the objects to him. Other boxes were brought up, other little objects examined, other gifts solicited and given. But nothing drew such astonished admiration from us as the final, special gifts, the gifts brought up in the last of the boxes. Of these the white destroyers announced beforehand we could each have two: one for the hands, the other for the legs.

These gifts, what were they? They were precious jewels, the white men told us, bangles and anklets of a special kind. Perhaps we would want to wear them on extraordinary occasions, for unusual celebrations. Perhaps we would want to wear them for dances—here the white men shared a smile. We examined the things. Of a truth they shone more brilliantly in the light of the moon than we had ever thought metal jewels could shine. They were circles of white light, joined together by linked miniatures of themselves: smaller, somewhat less perfect circles, joining each two of the larger circles. The special jewels for the legs were the same, only bigger.

"But no one can wear them," laughed the king. "The circles, the circles. They are too small for wrists and ankles like ours. How can these my children get their jewels on?" He laughed, a happy, demented, high-pitched laugh.

170

"Watch!" one of the white destroyers answered him. "Let them stretch out their arms and also their legs, so!"

We did as we were requested to. The white destroyers, each taking two of the shiny things in his hands, moved among us opening each of the things with a movement we could not see clearly, slipping them on to our wrists and our ankles. They moved fast among us, the white destroyers. It did not take them long to have the shiny metal encircling the wrists and ankles of each of us except Lini, Naita and Abena, who refused to try the trinkets on. We took our time admiring the things. The king and his courtiers moved among us together with the white men, nodding, looking, smiling.

Liamba and Mokili tired of the trinkets first. They tried to slip them off and found them hard, unbending. They made gestures to the whites to help them. The white destroyers smiled. The king and his courtiers smiled too, like the white destroyers.

Naita and Lini went to Liamba, to help her. Abena knelt near Mokili and tried to free him. The whites called their huge askaris, and they came. First they went to Lini. They struggled with him till they overpowered him, then held him down for the white trader to slip the metal things on his wrists and his ankles. They ignored the blows of Naita and Abena till they had immobilized Lini. Then they turned to the two girls and did to them what they had done to the rest of us.

The king walked in front of us, staring. He looked completely sober. The manic look of the night was gone

171

from his eyes, and his voice was lower. Against the frantic efforts we made to break out of the imprisoning metal his voice came calmly.

"What is the matter, my children? How are you enjoying the feast we planned for you? For you alone we planned it, my children." The king talked on and on. He repeated his questions, turned from one to the other of us, peered into our faces like a man who knew us but wished now to deepen his knowledge. At Abena he stared the longest time. Tears formed in his eyes but they did not run down immediately. The girl stared back into his face, then spat straight at him. The king made no motion to draw back his head. He did not even try to wipe the spittle off his face. He continued to stare at Abena, then in an access of happiness his tears came down.

"Enjoy your feast, my children," the king said. "It is yours. It is in your honour, in celebration of your many-headed genius. This night we pay tribute to your intelligence, and to your courage too. This is your feast. Enjoy it."

In a sincere voice the king told the white destroyers he was tired. The white destroyers lowered one of their boats and their askaris rowed the king ashore, together with his courtiers. The white destroyers' askaris came back, climbed back on to the ship and hauled up their boat.

The ship moved silent down the river. In its wake the ripples were barely strong enough to disturb the three canoes left floating in the river's centre.

In silence we were taken down the river. Silence in

which we looked at the river banks slipping past yet missed their familiarity. We were not like people seeing familiar things the last time but like people seeing everything the first time. Moonlight was keen like a sharp knife, cold. The things it lit stood out in accusation against us, against our greed, against our blindness, against the ease with which we had let ourselves slide into doom. Inside there was the endless howling chagrin when we considered the many chances we had had for avoiding this perdition; also an irresistible feeling, first of shame so intense there was no containing it, shame that the promise of mere entertainment had been sufficient to bring us so unresisting, so eagerly to our own undoing. Again despair at the chances of refusal overlooked. All were stricken with this despair, all except Naita, Lini and Abena. Naita and Lini wept too, quietly. They were unsuccessful against a kind of resentment they had struggled to overcome, a resentment against us. They told us of this resentment. In their telling there was more regret, more love for us than hate. One, Liamba, asked them for forgiveness.

Abena had made no sound. She had not cried again, not even silently, after the feast had begun. She was like a person after initiation, a person who had decided to say an irrevocable farewell to things in her past, and was beyond regret. Hers now was an expression of the most steady attention, the look of one thinking, studying herself, us, everything.

"But you, Abena, how shall we ever deserve your forgiveness?" It was Kwesi's voice, but the question belonged to all of us.

"Why forgiveness?" asked Abena. Her sound was of true surprise.

"You could have saved yourself." Sobo said this.

Abena laughed. Laughter so unexpected here that we were startled, and two of us, Ude and Kenia, asked sharply: "Why do you laugh, Abena?"

"But I could not have saved myself."

"You did not want to come to this . . ."

"I did not want us to come."

"You came because of us."

"I came because of us, yes."

"That is what Sobo meant. You could have refused to come. You could have saved yourself."

"Saved myself apart from all of us?" Abena asked. Silence. "There is no self to save apart from all of us. What would I have done with my life, alone, like a beast of prey?"

She gave up talking and gazed at the twin hills of Takora sliding by in the hazed-over moonlight. She gazed into the water near the bank to the right, water rippling in the weak light with the motion of slow crocodiles. Could there have been so many crocodiles in this river when last we rowed down it? Then our canoes slid down knife paths in the water and the beasts scattered in sidelong panic and kept their distance from our oars. Now they were not scattering. The ship, massive though it was, pushed them to no panic. They coasted alongside it, leisurely, as if they had found it kin to themselves. Playfully they let the ship gain on them,

174

falling behind till a new family farther down converged on it.

Dawn came. A morning of fantastic brightness. The ship sought the deepest channel near the river's centre. Where that channel twists close to the bank on the falling side, pushed there by mud from the island of silk cotton trees, we saw duikers at the waterline seeking a drinking point. They found one. Three drank. The fourth had barely brought its head to the water when a snout broke the surface and caught the duiker by its lower jaw. The crocodile had surfaced briefly, then disappeared, dragging its victim reluctant into the killing water. A moment from that place a different crocodile lay restful on a rock projecting above the water. Its mouth was open. Above its head hovered two white birds, pickers after chewed meat left unswallowed by the earlier crocodile.

We had come this way before, so recently, and in the fullness of our energies. We knew this river upon which we now floated impotent, trapped, our spirits grown heavier than our bodies, our minds blanked out with the overwhelming reality of capture. These hands of ours now useless before us, caught in the white destroyers' shiny jewelry, on a different voyage they had been active, inspired with the energy of our youth, so alive they were potent to take the spirit's urge in the mind and turn it to motion animating even wood. Down the middle of the river we had rowed to that final open initiation that left us still with no suspicion of this impending beginning. Our destination then was child of our own desire, our speed the child of our

175

own effort. Remembering, we looked at our hands, looked at the white gifts upon our legs, then our eyes seeking rest found the Su Tsen running backwards from the ship. Our eyes were tired, dry, needing sleep but unable to embrace it.

After the height of day a seabird flew toward us. It came in a white streak directly above us, then hovered in sudden indecision. It flew back a piece of the way it had come, then shot downward against the water. The flier caught its prey and flew with it backward to the sea. We were not far from the water barrier. The ship went more slowly, then stopped altogether. Here we were given food and water; we were thirsty and hungry, but few could eat, though we all took in water.

The ship did not go all the way down the river to the water barrier. Not far from the island of silk cotton trees the white destroyers turned their ship away from the river's centre and up a sluggish arm of water more mixed with mud than the main stream itself. The place was not familiar. It was not that we had avoided it on purpose all the days of our growing up on the land. Simply, the place held no great promise of anything a seeker might want. But now in its diseased secrecy the white destroyers had found a fitting place for their purposes. Here was stagnant water choked with dead matter, animals floating bloated with here, there a remnant limb sticking in the air out of the water, dead palm trunks breeding grubs, too light to sink in this heavy water, too sodden with decay to float. All things here passed us by in a dragged-out dance of rotten things. Night had not yet come when the ship reached its destination. There was a widening in the river's arm where soft clay had been licked away by the water of ages to form a pool under a tongue of harder overhanging stone. The water here was deep.

The ship edged carefully up to the rock and stopped on touching it. Four askaris brought a broad plank from the far end of the ship and laid it sloping gently from the ship to the rock. They passed a rope through holes in the higher end of the plank and secured it to the ship. Then two of them walked down the plank, one holding another length of rope. When they reached the rock they shifted the plank till its end rested between two lumps of rock thickened at the top like huge, closed fists. The askaris passed the second rope through the lower holes in the plank and tied the ends to the projecting lumps.

One of the white destroyers and two askaris came to us. Bending before Ndlela the white destroyer unlocked the traps on his ankles. But he did not take them away. He motioned to the askaris. They hurried forward and, grabbing Ndlela by his feet, dragged him till his body smashed into Kenia's. The white destroyer unlocked the left circle of the trap on Kenia's ankles, turned the whole thing so that the open circle caught Ndlela's left ankle, and locked it. Sobo was dragged toward Ankoanda and locked together with her. Ashale was locked with Suma, Ude was locked with Ona, Dovi with Makaa, Lini with Naita, Kwesi with Abena, Kamara with Manda, Mokili with Tawia. Pili and Liamba they locked together last. We were pushed along the plank on to land again. Two askaris went in front of us, four walked beside us and two more followed a few steps behind. One of the askaris in the lead shot his gun deliberately into the air. Close by a gunshot answered, but the noise's source was invisible from where we were. This was deep forest still, though we knew we were not far from the sea and the air itself even here in this place of decay carried a salt savour.

The path the askaris led us down felt rock-hard underfoot. It seemed the projecting rock continued some distance into the forest in a twisting path. When we had lost sight of the rock and the river arm we reached an abrupt drop. The hard path gave way suddenly. In its place there was nothing but a depression. The descent down the depression's side was difficult. The path was not wide enough for two people and yet the way we were locked together we had no choice but to move abreast and squeeze our way along, struggling falling. Dovi fell once and brought Makaa hurtling down on top of him. Both twisted their ankles so painfully it was hard just to watch them along the rest of this journey. At the depression's bottom the path grew wider. It was hard rock again. We walked the length of one grown odum, then the path began to climb again, more steeply than the descent. Here steps had been notched into the rock. By holding on to the sides we avoided a disastrous rushing fall backward.

We reached the top with no further accident. The place we had come to was huge. The hill itself was circular, but on its top the place the destroyers had had built was of four walls enclosing two long double houses, one near the side wall to the right, the other built against the end wall,

178

with a great space before them. The house to the right was home to the destroyers living there. The other house held things below and had space above for the slaves of the place. At each corner of the walls a narrow building stood on which sat an askari with a gun.

We were sitting in the open space where we had been brought when the slaves kept in the place came back. They walked unbound, carrying wood and water together with food into the space to the left. Some lit fires and began cooking meals while others ground maize. One, a woman, washed clothes—white destroyers' clothes.

A single shot sounded in the quiet night. Another, from where we were, answered it. Two askaris carrying bright torches crossed the open space and went to the gate. There was a conversation. One askari hurried back and went to knock on the first door of the white destroyers' long house. A destroyer came out, crossed over to the gate, then returned in a while. Behind him was the askari who had fetched him, then an Arab in Muslim robes and a huge turban, two zombis with guns, and a line of people like ourselves, male, female, children, bound with ropes. Two more zombis with guns came in. Then the gate was closed. The predator went with the white destroyer into his room. The destroyer called an askari. The zombis conversed with their companions, the askaris, and from time to time walked round the seated captives to see if all was well. From the white destroyers' long house there was the sound of violent argument, then laughter. The predator and the destroyer came out, followed by the askari. The

179

Arab shouted to his zombis, and they went out with him.

The enslaved people of the place back from the farms and the river finished cooking their food on huge iron pots placed on open fires to the left of us, some ten steps to the left wall. Two of them, young women, brought us food. Then all of them came and sat near us with their food and began to eat.

"My brother," Abena said. Her head was turned toward the enslaved people of the place. She spoke loud enough for all of them to hear her, though she did not shout. Still no one answered her. "My brother," she tried again, "you the one closest to us, you staring at your food, not eating." The man did not answer. He did not show any sign of having heard any of Abena's sounds. Neither did he have the look of a person deliberately ignoring anyone.

"My sister," Abena said, addressing the closest woman, one of the two who had brought us food.

"My sister," the woman answered.

"Have his eardrums failed him?" Abena asked.

"He can hear."

"Why does he not answer?"

"He has no desire to."

"Is he always this way?"

"Since he was brought back."

"Brought back?"

"He escaped."

"He was beaten? Damaged?"

"Not that. He says he has no desire to talk of things he cannot do."

180

As for the man he ignored the two completely. They could have been speaking of the moon. He began to eat his food.

"What is his name?" Abena asked again.

"Call him the silent one," the woman laughed.

"Where did he go?"

"Home. Where else? He thought his first selling had been an accident."

"Who sold him?"

"Does it matter?"

"To me, yes," Abena answered.

But the other ignored her words. "It was no accident. He was sold again. This time they almost killed him outright. He talked a little when he was brought back, the first night. He said it was no use going back home. There was no home, just disaster waiting. He wanted something, not home, not this place either."

"He knew of such a place?"

"No, he was only thinking, telling us his thoughts."

"What made him stop?"

"Thinking? I don't think he stopped."

"Telling his thoughts."

"Ah, he said the thoughts he had alone were wishes only, a waste of time. A group thinking together could act, but a single person thinking would spread mere dreams—a childish occupation."

"Haven't others here tried to escape?"

"Most of us. Almost all. Yes, all."

"All?" Abena's voice carried surprise.

"All. The askaris say the whites prefer people like us for this kind of work. We have tried escape, we have gone home and been sold again. They say we know there's no life elsewhere for us to go back to. So we stay."

"Is it the truth?" Abena asked the woman.

"Is what the truth?"

"You stay. You don't want to escape anymore?"

"To what?"

Abena's question had been quiet, not hostile. Its answering question had been soft, just as quiet. Abena said nothing. She sat staring at the silent one. The woman rose. Three others followed her. They went to the cooking area and came back with water in large gourds and poured each of us a drink.

An askari shouted to us to get up on our feet. It was time to go. The woman Abena had spoken to came to the gate as we were leaving.

"I want to wish you safety," she said, "but how can I say that to you?"

"What is your name?" Abena asked her.

"Call me your sister," she said.

We travelled fast, urged by the relentless askaris. They seemed impatient to leave the forest behind, but even when we came to the more open land near the sea they did not allow us a more restful pace. On the outskirts of Poano they stopped us in the little forest to the rising till a man came running with some message, then they hurried us forward and would not stop till we reached the largest stone place. The guide spoke to the guards at the gate and they called to

182

someone within who brought a plank for us to walk on over the ditch on the side of the stone place. Inside, we were taken across a wide courtyard and pushed down stone steps into a huge cavern under the courtyard floor. It was there we spent what was left of that night. The air was bad in there and the soil beneath our bodies was moist. A smell of fungus hung heavy in the place, but exhaustion was stronger than our discomfort and we slept.

In the morning we were awakened long after sunrise. An askari led us up to the courtyard we had crossed in the night. It was immense, much wider than we had imagined when we came. Across from the opening leading downward to the cavern, near the wall to the rising, there were fires burning with a fierceness too intense for food fires. The guards directed us to turn left as we came out of the cavern and lined us up standing against the wall. A woman came with a large calabash. It was full of palm oil. Walking along the line we made she dipped a piece of cloth into the oil and smeared the left side of each person's chest with it. All this she did without raising her head to look into any of our faces. Abena spoke to her, calling her: "My sister, my sister." But this woman was another who did not seem to hear a word. The askaris marched us, directly forward this time, till we stood facing the fires.

That was when the tall slavedriver, he who was not a black man and not a white man, came through the gate and walked swiftly till he stood between us and the fires. He looked at us. In his hands he carried four long metal rods and a piece of coarse cloth. This new man who was neither black nor white looked slowly from one to another of us, then with an air of infinite satisfaction he examined the ends of the rods in his hands and placed them carefully in the hottest parts of the fires, one rod in each fire. He beckoned to the askari. The askari pushed two people forward from the end of the line. The man waited till the rods began to glow at their ends. Then, picking one up carefully with the cloth covering his palms, he turned to the captive closest to himself. The two other askaris held the captive by his shoulders, so firmly he could not move. The tall slavedriver pushed the burning iron against the captive's chest where the oil had been smeared and held it there a full moment. The tortured man yelled with pain, once. Smoke rose sharply from the oily flesh, then the iron rod was snatched back. Where its end had touched the captive's skin there was now raw, exposed flesh. The skin had come off in two pieces each as long as a middle finger and half as broad. One was in the shape of a bow not yet drawn, its string running alongside the central line of the captive's chest. The other was shaped like the top of an upright building pole cut off a short length beneath its forking.

The woman who had smeared our chests with oil returned, carrying on her head a calabash larger than the one before and in her left hand a horn. The slavedriver put the first rod back in its fire and took a second. The askaris brought another captive forward and burned the mark into her flesh. When we had all been burnt the slavedriver took the calabash and the horn from the woman, poured the

184

horn's contents, a grey powder, into the liquid in the calabash and shook the mixture. Then walking up to each of us he dipped a piece of cloth in it and rubbed our raw wounds with the mixture.

Even now Abena spoke to the woman who had brought the calabash: "What do you do here, my sister?"

The woman answered at last: "We farm, most of the time. There's a large farm up above Poano. Fruits, corn, white people's food. Other times we just work here, do anything they tell us to do. Feed the people they bring here."

Abena asked her: "They bring many?"

"Many," she said.

"My sister, what's his name?"

The woman, startled by the question's suddenness, answered with another: "Who?"

"The tall one."

"John."

"What is he?"

"A servant to the white men. But he thinks he is one of them."

"Did they bring him?"

"He was born here. Some passing white man. His mother is one of us."

"Where is she?"

"She died, not so long ago. Why do you ask?"

"Why is he so cruel?"

"With them he is gentle. With all things white he is gentle."

"Only with us, then?"

"Only with us. We say he wishes he had nothing of us in him."

"You say truth."

The third morning, after we had been made to run around the courtyard and then been fed, we were sitting chained, waiting. The slavedriver John had disappeared with no indication of when he would reappear to continue our torture. We were sitting, looking out across the stone courtyard from the side we had been brought to to the side with the highest houses, the side closest to the sea. We heard a noise as of many children, a loud, uncontrolled shrieking that should have been a song. Now from the gate to the falling came first an apparition exactly like a ghost: a pale white woman in white clothes moving with a disjointed, severe, jerky walk, like a profoundly discontented walker. Her walk was like that of a beginning stiltwalker, but an angry beginner. Her face was squeezed in a severe frown that had formed three permanent vertical creases on her lower forehead in the space between her eyes. She had no eyebrows. Eyelashes she had, but they were hard to discern, being white and therefore merging into the pallor of her face. On her head she wore a white hat. As she came in there was space before her, space to her left and right, space behind her: her figure seemed the shape itself of loneliness. It seemed impossible that she could ever be together with any other being.

The sun was high. The silence in between the children's noises, the particularly clear silence of bright daylight, together with her clothes and the way the white creature

186

moved, everything aggravated the sense of aloneness, created a desolation so thorough that it would have been easy to imagine the presence of this singular apparition had blighted all surrounding life into rigidity; that the white creature in fact existed only to perfect this general petrifaction before regaining some previous stony existence more proper to herself. Two things only worked against the strength of this impression: the noise of the shrieking children who were not yet visible to us, that and the flitting, nervous looks the creature cast behind her at irregular intervals as she walked her disjointed way across the courtyard. She looked like one trapped in a perpetual nightmare in which malevolent spirits had not caught her yet but were always on the very point of doing so. Each flitting, backward look was a desperate attempt to keep the object of her fear behind her. Yet for a time nothing was seen to follow. Then at last appeared the object of the white phantom's fear.

The entry of the prince Bentum, renamed Bradford George, was in total contrast with that of the white ghost preceeding him. Bentum came in with an exuberant walk. He seemed visibly to have to restrain his step in order not to leave the children too far behind—they seemed to have been placed directly under his charge, while the white apparition played some supervisory role above them all, Bentum and the children, from her distance. An enthusiastic, a positively energy-devouring smile, so exaggerated, so intense it made the beholder think the smiler could not last too long under such labour, enlivened the prince's face. Something in the rhythm of his walk, beside its sheer exhilaration, was also queer. Bentum was conducting the children's song, and therefore marched before them not straight forward but half turned to his destination, half to the children—a sideways walk. His dress was an arresting blue cloak surmounted by a wig of long, yellow destroyers' hair.

We stared long at the prince, the white creature and the children from around the stone place put under their charge, children neither black nor white. When they had disappeared into one of the rooms on the side closest to the sea Abena began chuckling—a soft, unrestrained chuckle so relaxed it startled us in this place. The rest of us feared to ask her the meaning of her amusement but after a while she herself broke our uneasiness.

"So this white ghost was to have been my rival wife." She laughed.

Ankoanda joined her: "It is funny if you can look at it like that."

"But such laughter hurts," Dovi said. He had been silent all morning, staring soft-eyed at Tawia. This was the first time he was opening his mouth. It seemed as if his statement was a challenge meant for Abena, for it was edged with a slight resentment. Abena did not answer. She and Pili, Kamara and Lini seemed now to have become possessed with a consuming curiosity. They looked attentively at everything around, like people determined to commit the details of the place to memory. They even rose to walk around the courtyard, stopping at each gap, each door, each grating in the floor, to see what was beyond it if that was possible. That was what they were doing when the slavedriver John returned. He turned his whip first against Abena, Pili, Lini and Kamara. Then as his fury fed on their pain it increased and the slavedriver hurled himself against the rest of us. At first we saw no particular reason for his rage against us: John did not seem to have noticed Abena, Pili, Lini and Kamara as doing anything unusual. We thought he was furious from something that had happened to him outside, some insult from his owners the white destroyers, perhaps. But before we took shelter in the cavern below we saw the cause: through the gate a line of brightly coloured persons was making its way into the courtyard where we had been. We saw them only briefly: Atobra, king of Poano, led the way; behind him the chiefs and big men, the parasites of the coast. We were not let out again till the morning of our departure.

We made a circle no more. They had arranged us in two lines.

"Going like this, we look like things," Ndlela said.

His words were true. We were being turned into things to be moved for use elsewhere, things bound for destruction, taken from our land to be broken up in strange places, and none of us knew of ways to halt this fatal progress.

Where land became sand we came upon the rock shaped roughly, accidentally, like a bird in flight, a thing unfinished by the carver. This would be the last thing we could recognise before the water, the last sign from days when we had a home and still looked forward to living for ourselves. Kwesi passed by the rock and cast a long look back at it. Before us the shore, and then the sea. Suma passed by the rock and turned to cast a look back at it. Before us a wave longer than any preceeding it broke on the distant sand then came racing beyond the wettest part of the beach before returning. Ude passed by the rock. He did not turn to look. On another journey he had spent endless moments near the rock playing, laughing with Manda. Pili passed by the rock. She cast a swift glance at it and moved on. The slavedriver John came hurrying down to the sealine, looking for his masters. Tawia came to the rock. She looked directly at it and stopped. Behind her came the others with her in the line: Ankoanda, Liamba, Makaa, Naita, Ona, Abena. Because Tawia had stopped they too stopped. Tawia looked again at the rock, then turned her back to the sea. A wail rose from her throat like a song of the dead: "I will not leave this land. Out there we shall only be destroyed!" Tawia reached the end of the rock farthest from the sea, around the neck of the bird where the rock made a kind of handle, and held it.

The slavedriver John, arriving angry at the rock, his face red with the fatigue of excessive zeal in his masters' service, seeing the cause of the line's immobility struck Tawia separately with his whip. Tawia did not move. John leaped up on the rock and stepped with his shoes on Tawia's fingers, crushing them against the hardness of the rock. But Tawia's hands, her arms, remained wrapped around the rock. Now the growing gap between that line and other advancing captives brought a white destroyer

190

hurrying to find out the cause. He too was angry on arrival. He grew angrier still on seeing Tawia's hands and finding them turned to bleeding pulp. The destroyer, redder in his anger than his slavedriver, screamed incomprehensible sounds at John, and at the height of his anger drew a small gun. Wonderful event if he had shot his own askari, but he did not. It was Tawia, her hands now useless, that the destroyer murdered in his thwarted greed.

The line of men had stopped alongside the line of women. In this line Dovi was the fourth. An immobility like the death of every living spirit within him had turned him stonelike at the beginning of Tawia's suffering. Among us all there was strong affection, but between the two of them the general love took on a great intensity. The sound of the destroyer's shot woke Dovi. Oblivious of the weight of others tied to him in the line of men he leaped forward, aiming for the destroyer. The others with him did not fight his motion but moved forward with him. Dovi reached the destroyer in one bound and brought him down. But that was all he could do. The slavedriver John, reversing his whip in his hand, smashed the massive metal handle against Dovi's unprotected nape and cut his breath. Other askaris came running up, their guns turned ready against us all, men and women in our lines, we who, stunned, had not found the speed of action to do anything to help the murdered Tawia and the unconscious Dovi, to do anything to help ourselves.

Tawia's body was cut from the line—so great was the destroyers' hurry. The ends of rope that had held her were brought together to join Manda and Ankoanda.

The white destroyers' hurry had been caused by their anxiety to take advantage of a rising wind. On the ship we were left tied together in the open space the first day and the next. The destroyers and their askaris ran like maniacs changing sails, all angry that the ship was not going forward faster. The third day they brought the ship to a halt. We could see nothing of the shore—one part of the ship the way it stood blocked our view—but before the sun began its falling we saw more captives brought to join us. The men came naked. The women each wore a skirt not much different from those our women wear. The slavedriver John looked at the new captives and shook his head. He went over to the hind part of the ship. Returning with a knife, he went up to the new women and began to cut the skirtstrings from their waists. Among the new men one just arrived, not yet bound again, with only the chains on his feet, watched the slavedriver keenly, a vein in his temple swollen with his concentration. John came to a young woman and stopped. She was barely a woman, small, slender, her graceful body not completely grown. The slavedriver cut off her skirt but after that he could not move his eyes, his hands away from her. John held her by the shoulder, touched her neck, her breasts, her belly, touched her in between her thighs. Without any warning sound the watcher leapt at John, so fiercely and with such force he knocked the slavedriver completely over the railing behind him and almost went down into the sea himself. There was something unusual in that man's face:

192

his eyeballs had a fevered yellowness in them. In his anger they were flecked with blood.

John did not drown. A rope was lowered for him and he was hauled up shaking from the water, his teeth chattering like an infant's though the day was warm. He had lost his knife in the water but when he reached the ship again he rushed at the watcher who had hurled him down as if he still had a knife to kill him with. The watcher was of slight build. Yet in that body he had strength enough to amaze us all, and skill for the using of that strength. Twisting himself to one side, he in the same movement took John by one flying knee and forced him crashing head foremost against the wood. Three askaris who had been watching like charmed snakes now forced the watcher down, while another took John below. When the watcher was completely subdued the askaris brought two knives and themselves completed the removal of the new captives' clothing. Mokili, best among us in the art of healing, looked at the watcher and shook his head: "That man is already destroyed," he said.

All the new ones were led into the belly of the ship. In the ship's immobility and ours on it the sun burned us with a hostile intensity that made some ask again why we were kept up here away from the shade below. Ah, ignorant imagination.

In the evening the ship moved again, a slow movement, but it raised a breeze to fight the sun's persisting fierceness, so that for the day's remainder our bodies knew the comfort between heat and cold. From where we sat the land became

193

visible, land with no forests, no trees to be seen on it, nothing except immense expanses of sand and water. In places the water seemed to have broken through the sand but the water gaps were small and the water coming into the sea came with little force, hardly ever colouring the sea the way the Su Tsen does.

Night came. Our bodies had lain unsheltered in the heat of day. Now they grew rigid with the night's cold and its wind. Another morning made us grateful for the coming heat.

At strange intervals we were given food and drink: corn cooked in salt, water as if we had entered the seventh season of some malevolent drought. The sand near the horizon gave way to something green, but this was bizarre vegetation: a thousand thousand dry-looking stalks pushing out of the water; coming closer we saw space between the stalks, but enough only for such as snakes and lizards. The ship came to a rivermouth, entered, then turned right into a long lagoon. There was wind here, wind surprising in its strength, blowing as if it had been forced from large open expanses into too small a space. Yet this wind was also fetid; it carried the smell of unnameable diseases.

Once from the land lining the lagoon small arrows fell in profusion against the front part of the ship. The white destroyers and their askaris seem to have expected this. Most took shelter below, while those remaining sought covered positions from where they shot bullets into the surrounding vegetation. But we saw no one emerge or fall.

A day's journey up the lagoon the ship reached a huge

194

place cut raw into the forest land. This was no stone place; it was built of wood and mud, but its shape was close to that of the stone place at Poano, and along its walls walked askaris always carrying arms. The greatest number of captives was added here. After this loading the ship went—slowly—out again onto the open sea. We too were driven down below. The ropes binding us were removed, but immediately we were each locked lying down into some sort of trap.

We sank into a leaden silence and lived in it for days we had not learned to count, our spirits numbed with the immensity of separation from each other, separation from our land, separation from our people and our way.

Among the men Lini emerged earliest. Talking gently, alone at first and unheeded, he asked if there were among us any who understood more than their own particular language. That question brought the first sound of laughter on the ship, for one of the others who knew our language asked Lini what kind of fool could be found alive who spoke only one language. Other mouths unsealed themselves. Seven languages, we found, were sufficient to reach every spirit there with us, and for these seven languages we had over thirty who could turn one into the other, experts in the arts of speech. So in that endless time below each group told the others of itself through its chosen spokesmen. Each group heard and understood every other's remembrance through its own interpreters, and separation lost a slight measure of its disastrous hold. Listening minds began to grow connections. The remembrances were

195

separate, but underneath them all ran connected meaning: our common captivity now, our broken connectedness before the onslaught of predators and destroyers, and for the times to come, our common destiny.

Heavy lay the sense of separation upon our mind. Children came down at night and told us we were still within sight of land, but every passing day the thought ran impotently through our mind: sailing into unknown seas, captives of destroyers, it would have been better if we had died. Some talking as if in sleep resolved to kill themselves if they found a way. Most were silent. A man with a soft voice, he the watcher who had almost killed the slavedriver John, said once it would be foolish for anyone to kill himself just like that. If we were truly resolved to die, he said, we should find ways to use our death to help those left behind. That would be the only intelligent dying. All who spoke after that agreed, but then one said it was difficult to know how to accomplish such things. The soft-voiced one said—without contempt—we could not complain now we did not have enough time for thinking of ways.

A child came with heavy news for us: we had passed a rivermouth turbulent with brown water, then towns, which he described, and that same day the hulk of a huge white ship had been left behind on our right. We thanked the child and fell silent.

"Why so quiet?" the soft-voiced one asked.

"That is our home we have left behind," Kamara answered him.

But soon the ship stopped again. We could see nothing,

196

except that new captives were brought in. Where we had thought there was no more space—a fantastic force is the greed of whites—the destroyers found room for thirty more. This loading took more time than any other. We asked the newcomers their news. They said they had tried escape right there on the ship. Ten of them had died at the destroyers' hands; three had leaped afterwards into the sea and held themselves under till they died. Now they had been defeated and the white destroyers were waiting for a wind.

It came fitfully when it came at all, the wind. Where we were trapped the strongest wind could only reach us as the languid motion of our own used air, but even that was a merciful thing compared to the total stillness of these days. The children coming down at night said the ship made only brief, spastic motions forward every day, then stopped. The air was heavy with its motionless humidity. Among us the sound of coughing, at first staggered and subdued, grew to be a strong, constant noise. Even the white destroyers in their greed grew alarmed for our health. They changed the method of our feeding. Now, except for the irons on our legs, we were freed in little groups, seven, ten at a time, and driven upward by an armed askari to take our corn. Water also we drank up there, after being made to jump and run for air and for the loosening of stiffened bodies.

Ask the destroyed. They alone can tell you, they who have been taken into whiteness, if they still have voices to tell you what they have seen they will let you know of time

197

ignorant of dusks, of time without dawns, time with no connecting motion from midday to dusk to night and dawn again. Ask the destroyed. Ask us, we who woke after sleep never knowing if nights had passed, or days; we who woke suspended on immobile water, breathing motionless air, we who woke immersed in the dirt of successive days and nights. Cleanness became a mere remembrance visiting our minds: the vision of an open courtyard swept in the early morning, the broom's passage traced out in transient repeated beauty on fresh sand, the easy feel of morning earth under rested feet—every remembrance of goodness brought frustration to the mind bound for slavery. Which remembrance of that dead time shall we pick for your hearing? Dirt then was our entire surrounding. The air itself had turned to liquid filth. Each body lay immobile in its own refuse. There were zombis sent down to clean our place, but they came not for work; they came to find entertainment whipping tied-down men. One of the zombis struck the soft-voiced one. He cursed them all, softly, but it was a bitter curse and the zombi understood its sting. The whip danced wildly in the centre of our space. Other voices cried pain but the zombi found the soft-voiced one again and this time did not lose him. By the time the zombi sought the air above us the soft voice had grown silent.

It spoke again, much later, and in a scream hoarse with ultimate fear. What had frightened the courageous soft-voiced one himself? He had felt his right side thinking to find blood from the wound left there. It was not blood he found but a thing that felt like a soft worm. After the first

198

scream he understood it was not alone. How had he lived with worms eating him so near the surface of his skin? What new disease had added itself to his pains and ours?

Now the soft-voiced one chuckled: "I will not reach their destination. I am destroyed already."

Lini answered him: "Tawia was right. Better to have died on our own land."

A voice unrecognized: "What will they do to us if we die so?"

Another: "They will throw us into the sea."

Again the first voice: "Ancestors, this death is so new. We cannot join you. We cannot even be wandering ghosts."

The answering voice: "No. This is a complete destruction, death with no returning."

Lini again: "Tawia was right."

Then Kwesi: "Tawia was right."

They threw one man out next morning. He died in the night. All that night terrifying screams broke from his throat. In his fear he begged the ancestors not to forsake his soul, but his prayers brought him no solace. In the morning they came to take him to throw him in the sea. One askari held a torch; two took the corpse. Behind them walked two white destroyers, their faces covered in fear against the diseases we lived in. On their way out they heard the soft-voiced one cough—an unnerving cough. The smaller of the white destroyers, he who must have been a sort of healer among them, asked for the torch and in its light examined the soft-voiced one as if he were some sick dog. Then the healer nodded to the taller destroyer. The taller destroyer nodded to an askari and shouted an order through the covering on his face. One of us near the entrance heard the order and understood it.

"They mean to cast you into the sea," he shouted to the soft-voiced one, "even before you die. Oh, ancestors!"

The soft-voiced one said: "They shall not."

There was fear among us, an uncertain fear unfixed in its cause. Now the discovery of the killing disease sharpened this fear, gave it intensity, gave it shape in our minds. The removal of lifeless bodies grew so frequent it tired the zombis working for the white destroyers and moved them to futile cursing. There was no telling which body would go next, for the disease could come sudden as a lightning stroke. Distance from those already dead gave no assurance of safety. The still air we all breathed was itself connection deadly enough between every still living person and those already wrecked by death.

The time has come for us to pause for breath. It is not that our remembrance fatigues us, no. This is no halt brought on by the tiredness of flesh or any weakening of our mind. In our remembrance this is no stagnant stop but a necessary part of our memory's flow in the telling of the way. For this time that has come, it is a time to be filled not with hollow sounds loud with emptiness. We have reached the time when we must speak of consciousness.

Of unconnected consciousness is there more to say beyond the clear recognition this is destruction's keenest tool against the soul? That the left hand should be kept ignorant of what its right twin is made to do—who does not see in that cleavage the prime success of the white destroyers' road of death? That the heart detached should beat no faster even when limbs familiar to it are moved to heinous acts— is that not already the severed atrophy of connected faculties, the white method of destruction? That our left eye should be set to see against its twin, not with it—surely that is part of the white destroyers' two thousand seasons of triumph against us? That the sight of the eye should be unconnected, cut off from the mind's embracing consciousness; that the ears' hearing should be blocked off from the larger knowledge of the mind, that the nose's smelling and the tongue's tasting should be pushed apart from the mind's whole consciousness—what is that but death's whiteness in delirious triumph? That the hand should touch and the knowledge of the substance touched should stay trapped in the touching hand alone; that feeling fingertips should each in itself alone contain the shut-off knowledge of members estranged from each other—could that be different from the blighting success of the white destroyers' road? That the passion and the thinking and the action of any one of us should be cut off from our connected consciousness by mere physical things, walls of wood or walls of stone—that would indeed be the manic celebration of death's white empire. For then in these surroundings dominated by the walls of whiteness built to separate sense from sense, to cut faculty from faculty, pull member from member and drive person against person, the passion and the thinking and the action of any one of us would stay impotently trapped in that particular consciousness alone, doomed to perish, a stream of useless visions, useless sounds, useless thoughts whose passage brings us no closer to our way, the way. In these surroundings built to separate each of us from the other, to turn each discrete one selfish from the whole, the seeing and the hearing and the thinking of each of us would find no understanding with any other, not even access to the general consciousness, and all our uttering would be like the wild, senseless cacophony of the market places brought against us by the white destroyers.

And then in that thorough death the single freedom of Sobo to roam the ship imprisoning us nighttime and daytime would have been nothing but the useless, fortuitous licence of the individual lopped off from our common destiny. Then in that saturating destruction Sobo's individual motion would have been cut off, unconnected with the larger purpose of the whole immobilized. His mind would have been nothing but the shrunken individual mind, with only enough capacity to think of the hustling salvation of the single zombi body, ignorant and caring nothing of the only worthwhile liberation, the rediscovery of our way.

And we the chained ones, our bodies and our minds held down under the white destroyers' walls of wood and iron, we would have had no knowledge of the silent, patient liberating plan, of the reasons why the proud Sobo himself bent in a wisdom dictated by connectedness, bent his pride to show the staring white destroyers that constant reassuring smile of humility, bent to follow death's white messengers like an overfaithful dog, till in overflowing confidence the white destroyers left him free to roam where he pleased on this ship imprisoning us, left him free to do what he might please because it was obvious to them his pleasure could never go against their destructive intent.

How, in the absence of connectedness, would any knowledge have reached us of Sobo's final wanderings that night on the ship imprisoning us, of his flattering the mirthful white watchers till a happy oblivion made both of them watchers no longer so that, still smiling, Sobo received from their very hands the wildly burning torches for his descent to the root of our liberation. How, in the absence of connectedness, would our consciousness have come by any vision of his quiet dance into the darkness where he connected barrel to barrel, connected barrels to the outer wall of our floating prison, connected fire to dormant power and danced silently back past the happy watchers still dreaming reassuring dreams, left them their used torches, and came silently back among us where no fragmented, unconnected self would have known to come?

That night Sobo came silently. But among us those still awake in our restlessness heard his breathing, heavy in spite of his silence. And then we heard the thunder he had prepared for the night.

In the absence of connectedness our minds too would have found no meaning in that liberating thunder, and like the white destroyers we would have heard in its fantastic loudness only an empty disturbance dependent on senseless chance. But connected ears heard that thunder, and our mind understood it. Ah, happy misfortune, fortunate disaster.

To return. The stillness around us in that ship took on the heaviness of doom. There had been some hopes this turgid airlessness would not last, but whole days passing with not the softest sound of any breeze erased that hope and left the white destroyers' ship stunned out there on the open sea, the destroyers themselves walking dazed with us their stolen victims below them. Now among us the fearful killing disease, the unmentionable itself, ran freely. It drove the destroyers past madness, for each passing day brought a multiplicity of deaths: human loss to us, loss of gain to the white destroyers.

The one by the entrance had been right. The time came when the soft-voiced one was to be taken out for throwing into the sea, and he was not yet dead. It was the slavedriver John himself who came, his face covered against our diseases like a white destroyer's, to carry the light body. The slavedriver carried the soft-voiced one like a beast hunted down and killed. The legs of the soft-voiced one, lit by an askari's torch, hung behind the slavedriver; his head drooped over the slavedriver's chest, to all appearances dead weight, nothing more. But half way to the open entrance all things changed. The soft-voiced one, he who had looked so like a lifeless corpse, became in a moment a determined, furious being, potent as some irresistible natural force. In a movement too swift for the following eye he braced his legs around the slavedriver's trunk. The slavedriver, surprised, tried to pry loose the legs. The soft-voiced one's wasted body, however, had acquired an extraordinary strength. It was flesh no longer but something immeasurably hard,

204

say rock, say iron, obedient only to the soft-voiced one's will. The slavedriver brought down his hands in a second attempt to shake the entwining legs from their constricting grip upon his body. That same moment the soft-voiced one raised his hands. His left hand, no longer flopping like a dead thing, took the back of the slavedriver's head while the free right hand groped for and soon found his chin. Holding the slavedriver's head in this way, the soft-voiced one ripped off the cloth covering the face with his teeth. Then, simultaneously, he pressed in the sides of the slavedriver's mouth, a thumb sunk into the right cheek, fingers digging into the left, so that the slavedriver's mouth fell open against his will, as if he were a child surprised. Now the soft-voiced one held open the slavedriver's mouth and in one movement of amazing speed swung his own exhausted, emaciated, tortured body upward so that the two heads were on a level, his mouth next to the slavedriver's. The slavedriver gave a shuddering jerk, but the grip of the soft-voiced one was strong. The soft-voiced one brought his mouth exactly together with the slavedriver's and then—incredible obedience to will—we saw him with our own eyes bring up all the bile and dead blood from within his body into his mouth, and this mixture he vomited forcefully into the slavedriver's now captive mouth. The slavedriver grew mad with a desperate rage. He tried to tear the sick man's head away from his. In vain. His chest heaved, refusing at first to swallow the deadly vomit from the sick man's mouth. In vain: the sick man's mouth was stuck to the slavedriver's like a nostril to its twin. It was not

205

to be separated by any force outside the sick man himself. The deadly vomit was twice rejected by the struggling slavedriver. Three times the dying man refused to let it escape harmless on to the ship's wood below. Three times the dying man held the virulent juices, rejected, in his own mouth and throat. Three times with increasing force he pushed them down the slavedriver's reluctant throat. The third time the slavedriver's resistance was broken and the sick man shared death with him, allowing not one drop to escape. Choking, the slavedriver swallowed death with the breath of remaining life. Then he fell to the floor with the soft-voiced one still inseparable from him.

It was now that two destroyers, the healer and the tall one, wondering no doubt at the meaning of the long silence, and impatient because the slavedriver had not returned above to throw their victim the soft-voiced one into the sea, came down to see what was going on. They stumbled into the two on the floor. It took time for their eyes to see all that was to be seen, longer for their minds to comprehend what they had seen. Then it was fear we saw in their movements.

The tall one shot the soft-voiced one dead. Then the destroyers summoned another of their own kind, a huge one, from above to carry out the corpse. That one came clad in white from head to foot, as if he had come to carry not a particular dead man but death itself. And he left with the body faster than he had come in. The other two, they stood just a little longer staring at the slavedriver John's fallen body. They did not help him. They left him

206

there, and after they had gone up the huge destroyer returned with another almost as large, and taller. Together they took the slavedriver and pushed him into the space the soft-voiced one had left, and shackled his body and his neck into traps like the rest of us.

The slavedriver John, he died that night. Not from disease, though the soft-voiced one had given death to him as surely as a white man lives to destroy. It was this that killed him: the shock of waking to find himself finally trapped with us his condemned half-brothers, not among his friends the whites. That night he called out to them thirty times like a frightened boy calling to his mother. We heard him in a violent struggle against himself, ending in an uncontrolled shaking that snapped his neck under its trap. In the morning the destroyers came again, briefly, and looked at him. In the light of their torches we saw him too. His body was already covered with huge red welts as if in some sudden bubbling out of yaws. The two huge destroyers took the body out and came back.

A sharp dispute now broke out among the whites. Those who had taken out the body refused to continue doing the slavedriver's other work. The dispute remained unresolved. The destroyers hurried out.

"They will be wanting one of us to take over the slavedriver's work," one of us said.

There was an answer: "Not me. I will not be the destroyers' tool."

Another: "Not me." Another, another.

"I will do it," said a voice, Sobo's voice. "It has to be

207

done, unless we all wish to die here like this."

"It is death any way," said a voice. But a different one asked Sobo a direct question.

"How will they agree to choose you?"

"Make a noise." The answer sounded ridiculous.

"What kind of noise?"

"Any kind. As loud and as long as you can make it. Stop only when I say so."

So when the destroyers came again and walked uncomprehending into a wall of noise they answered with anger but even whips were futile against determined, connected will knowing its purpose, and it was Sobo's voice alone that had the power to stop the noise. The destroyers left, but the counsel they went up to take was nothing drawn-out.

Such was the root of Sobo's freedom in our imprisonment, the small root that grew with purposeful care into a larger root.

How inadequate the seeing that remains broken off, unconnected to any larger perception.

How lacking in sufficiency the hearing unconnected to a greater knowledge.

How stupid the utterance cut off from the higher understanding of the connected whole.

Monstrous the barrenness of people when outside the lonely cut-off self there is no connection with the whole. Blood itself is impotent before the white perdition brought against us by the destroyers from the sea: the severing of each mind, the cutting of each soul off from the whole being of our people, the removal of each single present away from knowledge of our common past, our common destiny: against all this blood itself is impotent if it flows away from connectedness, away from our single way, the way. Ludicrous is the freedom of the slave unchained in his single body if his mind remains a cut-off individual mind, not a living piece of our common mind, our common soul.

For in the absence of that necessary connectedness of the soul that will live, what is any slave body's freedom but the destroyers' license contemptuously given to the slave to dance the jiving dance of his own death agony? Against the death brought by whiteness only the greatest connecting force will prevail: the working together of minds connected, souls connected, travelling along that one way, our way, the way. Connected thought, connected action: that is the beginning of our journey back to our self, to living again the connected life, travelling again along our way, the way.

Sobo was free of the chains holding us, of the traps we were still in. What meaning could his single freedom have had had it been the individual freedom of the unconnected soul? What could we, trapped below, have known of his thoughts, of his intentions and of his actions had he been merely an individual captive singy freed? How then could we have escaped the stupidity of the unconnected viewpoint, each forever petrified in his separate situation, each hardened in her cut-off condition?

Sobo worked with the energy possible only to those possessed by some transcending love of their work itself.

Working for the destroyers he returned fatigued deep into every night. Yet even in his exhaustion there was the feeling about him of a being eagerly searching, searching after some profound secret. His speech had become reluctant. Thrice only, in great excitement on his return at night, he muttered in answer to a question from someone—was it Mokili?—"Only yesterday the land was still in sight. There has been little motion. I saw the land."

How infinitely stupefying the prison of the single, unconnected viewpoint, station of the cut-off vision. How deathly the separation of faculties, the separation of people. The single agent's action is waste motion; the single agent's freedom useless liberty. Such individual action can find no sense until there is again that higher connectedness that links each agent to the group. Then the single person is no cut-off thing but an extension of the living group, the single will but a piece of the group's active will, each mind a part of a larger common mind. Then each eye inspires itself with visions springing from group need, the ear is open to sounds beneficial to the listening group, the limbs move and the hands act in unbroken connection with the group.

That is how in the end we came to know what Sobo saw, where he went and what he did there even before his single freedom burst into the fruit of greater liberation. For nights an unwonted pensiveness had held Sobo in its grip. Every morning he went up above us ready to show obedience to the destroyers. What they commanded him to do he did, taking perfect pains to leave no cause for the

210

destroyers' dissatisfaction with him. But his nights were sleepless. Once one of us asked him if he needed any help. The offer broke spontaneously into a chuckle of impotence, a chuckle unshared by Sobo. He simply thanked the offerer and fell back into his silence. That last night he lay in this restless quiet of his a long time, then he rose again. He was gone a pregnant time, and when he returned he lay down with no sound at all, as if he were a soul only, with no heavier substance left. All we could hear, those of us still awake that night, was his heavy breathing.

Then we heard the heavy sound of happy disaster. Our bodies underneath their traps in a pathetic sympathy of impotence shook to the rhythms of the ship's jarring vibration, and none of us dared ask aloud the questions on our mind, for still our liberation was not yet.

After the first thunderous sound itself, so unexpected, there came the longer, softer sound of water—water swirling, water sucked into airspace before closed against it. More of the eerie thunder followed; as for the ship it shook like an angered cripple. There was not just one sound then, not two, not even seven separate sounds but a long, multiple thunder like an unending tear in the sky's own fabric, broken at short intervals with the welcome unbearable loudness of whole new barrels exploding, caught in the advancing, consuming fire. The rest we heard—connected—later.

One askari, faithful to the destroyers beyond wisdom, had rushed with a night light to the thunder's source. The white destroyers had been sleeping in their high security

211

above. Now they too rushed in panic, ignorant as to what the cause of the heavy noise could be. The chief destroyer reached the powder store first among the whites. He arrived in time to see the faithful askari there with his burning torch, his consternation causing the whole of his face to shake convulsively. The chief destroyer was looking for the cause of this calamity. He saw the black body there with a burning torch among the powder kegs. He acted first and left confusing thought to tomorrow: with his small gun he blasted the slave spirit free of its body. There was nothing much else the chief destroyer or any other destroyer could do. Before him the kegs of potent powder blew up one after the other, those closest to the wood of the ship's outer wall exploding first, leaving open holes through which the seawater rushed and began to wet all the burning powder.

The destroyers made desperate attempts to save their powder. Their chief pressed them all into that urgent service. But against the rising water their numbers were far from enough. It was not only powder the white destroyers stood to lose: it was soon clear everything was threatened by the water, inexorably rising.

The chief destroyer decided to take a fatal step, a happy step. He would have us freed from our traps, first to help in the work of salvage, and secondly—keen is the greed of whites—to ensure that we ourselves, his goods, would not be lost to the raging waters. Freed, we were led up into the air above, then into the blasted powder store. Weak from confinement, our bodies grown alien, we struggled to haul kegs of powder, already wet, higher than the invading

212

seawater could reach as yet. Among us as we worked the experts in the arts of speech kept each warning from Sobo close to our mind, chanting it like a worksong to the rhythm of our labour. "Nothing yet, my sisters, nothing yet, my brothers. The time is not yet ripe; the time will soon be ripe."

Before dawn an undecided breeze started. As it gathered strength it brought a welcome coolness, for this was hot work. The breeze blew stronger as the sun began to rise. The ship began moving forward slowly, away from the rising and a little to the left. But returning from another of his anxious visits down below the chief destroyer in great agitation of body and spirit both shouted to the large destroyers and sent them hurrying at great speed up the tall poles holding up the sails. The ship slowed, turned reluctantly, then picked up speed on a crazy, jagged course backward into the rising sun, and quite sharply to the left. The chief destroyer strode from one end to the other of the labouring ship, furious with anxiety, shouting ceaseless exhortations to the other white destroyers and to their askaris.

What was the meaning of his shouts? Hau! Greater than any quality they have is the white destroyers' greed. The chief destroyer, his fear was about the sinking of his ship, the loss of what he chose to call his goods—our captive selves—and so of his sole worship: profit. This was the meaning those who understood him chanted for our understanding. The chief destroyer had decided to seek shallow water for his ship—a harsh avoidance of sure

213

sinking. The chief destroyer's plan? To load his goods—ourselves—into the boats his ship carried and to bring us shoreward where he hoped help from some other destroyer's ship would soon cross his path.

The sea lay open, a revelation of beauty that morning. To the rising, morning's first lights touched it, glancing off its thirty thousand calm hollows before reaching the hastening eye. The ship, dragging water, moved slowly like an ancient, bulky beast, and the chief destroyer wore despair on his angry face. We could not stop to look, but labouring under barrels of dripping powder we saw from above the shape of land over water, blue at that distance. The ship moved on. The blue land turned green, the green grew flecks of brown in places, till the ship at length shuddered to a stop on underlying sand. Distance still there was from the ship to land, but this was no distance to frighten any used to the sea.

The destroyers, aided by their askaris, made the large boats ready, sent them hurriedly dropping down upon the water. Among us the experts in the arts of speech moved with their unending chant: "Ready, my sisters, ready, my brothers. The time is not ripe; the time will soon be here."

Monstrous is the greed of the white destroyers, infinite their avarice. The chief destroyer, it was his intention to do all in his power to save us from death in the water—to save us for use as animals, to save us for his destroying people's future profit. The boats were lowered. The askaris, standing firm against our eagerness to reach the boats, counted thirty to go down into each, with two destroyers

214

holding guns watching in each boat. The future the destroyers planned for us was plainly visible: into the bottom of each boat the destroyers had ordered us first to throw the heavy traps and chains that had held us down all these many days.

"Let us," rose the chant, "let the experts in the arts of speech spread ourselves among the people. That way we shall have better understanding in each boat. We shall need to work close together." The chant was repeated, a happy worksong helping to lighten the destroyers' anxious suspicion, helping to prepare the way.

The boats were not enough for all of us at once. How many? Five is the number of our remembrance. Five boats on the sea. Thirty human beings unarmed, going in each boat, a white destroyer armed at each end. There was a third destroyer in the boat that took the lead. He also had a gun, a little one. In addition he carried in his left a ring loaded with keys to the traps and chains waiting beneath our feet in the bottoms of the boats. In the iron sound of these keys we heard all there was need to hear of the white destroyers' future intentions against us. Of their number and that of their askaris half, a little more, were left behind on the ship to keep watch against the rest of us, the larger part.

Standing straight at the forward end of the leading boat, Sobo broke into song. He sang a song whose light sound was a perfect wrapping for the heavy meaning of the words. He sang with an expression of utter happiness, so that the white destroyer sitting beneath him fondling his gun and looking up from time to time to see his face saw only the face of one so well enslaved he was happy to help his master salvage his wealth even from the teeth of such opportune disaster. Happy was the white destroyer, secure his trust in the faithful slave behind him singing in the wind.

Sobo's words counted the six nearest that happy destroyer and asked if they could summon all their strength. A hum answered him yes. Sobo's words told the six it was important to do one thing before any other: to seize the keys from the destroyer who had them, or, failing that, to send them to the bottom of the sea.

The boats moved heavily—they could not have been meant ordinarily to take so many people at a time—and the askaris rowing did not have the air of fundis at this work. Half the distance between the grounded ship and land the ripples on the sea began to rise and take the form of real waves. Ashale, who loved the sea and knew it with a lover's intimacy, was among those in the leading boat. He looked intently at the water and said with no betraying hint of excitement in his voice: "From just over there the sea's depth is not dangerous." Okai told those close to him in his language, and Kisa in her language also repeated the message. None raised their voices. They might as well have been muttering foolish, inconsequential words to themselves, for all any hostile listener could understand.

Sobo waited till the words had travelled round and been understood. Then he asked finally: "Who among us cannot swim to save himself?" There was only one, a boy, who answered. Where he came from water was not a thing to

216

play with, and not many ever learned to swim.

"Who is strong enough to stay with him and lend him strength?" Sobo sang the question. A woman and a man offered their strength.

So softly, like a man entranced into some private world, not concerned to touch any other being with his words, Sobo called out to his companions in the boat and asked each one if they felt they had strength enough for a struggle in which defeat would be death. All said they were ready. Sobo in his song called the six nearest the white destroyer carrying the keys, called them again by their names and reminded them they should think of nothing save the capture of the keys from that destroyer. Sobo called three more. Their aim should be the destruction of the second white destroyer with his gun. Another three were to take the third destroyer. The rest, according to their nearness, took it upon themselves to incapacitate the askaris rowing.

But now the white destroyer with the keys shifted uneasily and looked hard at his soft-spoken victims. He nudged his gun with his elbow in the manner of one wanting to assure himself it was securely placed, and then he looked out anxiously at the slow shoreline.

"Now!" Sobo sang, in the same gentle tone he had used from the beginning. Simultaneously he jumped up and twisted his body in the backward leap, aiming to reach the white destroyer with the keys behind him. But one foot caught a woman's shoulder and Sobo's impetus was lost a hand's frustrated reach from the destroyer with the keys. A look, not just of terror, but also of the sudden, belated

217

comprehension of those betrayed by the ones closest to them, came upon the white destroyer's face. The destroyer fired at Sobo's fallen body. He could not miss. Flesh was blasted off Sobo's right thigh and the skin on his back was scorched in a jagged line along half its length on the right.

But Sobo, he seemed to have no feeling left in his body, no fear of pain holding back his mind. He hurled his body forward with even greater force than he had used in his interrupted leap and this time hit the white destroyer with all that unbroken force and drove his head crashing against the raised edge of the boat. The six others reached the white destroyer with the keys that same instant. One tried to wrench the gun first from his fallen body, but the destroyer had a dying maniac's grip on his weapon and the first one pulled at it in vain. As for Sobo, he did not even seem to see the weapon. He did not seem to see anything, to tell the truth, save the keys now between his body and the white destroyer's. Grasping all the keys firmly with both hands, he forced them together with their leather rope off the destroyer's struggling form and wound the leather securely round his own bleeding body. The six others battered the white body under them. One more turned to help the first one trying to take possession of the gun. Together they pried the weapon out of the destroyer's reluctant hands before the broken body was hurled head first into the water.

The second white destroyer on that boat, he had no time to take accurate aim with his weapon. He shot his gun, but not before three of us, closer to him than Sobo had been to the first white destroyer, smashed bodily into him and fouled his aim, so that his shot flew past all the heads within the boat and wasted itself in the air. That white body was sent to join its companion in the water. There the three followed it and held it down till it had taken in its last lungful of salt water.

In the next boat the white destroyers, their apprehension risen to panic at sight of the confusion in the leading boat, fired their guns forward into that boat. Ignorant destroyers, they thought to help the other destroyers, and were amazed when their own victims flew at them. They fought, using their guns, now impotent, as clubs, and their fighting was desperate, but it was also brief. They too found in the seawater beneath us a final resting place for their murderous spirits.

The three boats following the first two, they were overturned, those of us in them rushing at once to one side, uniting all their weight and thus sending the askaris and the white destroyers and their guns, everything together into the water. What could wet guns do for the white destroyers now? They too joined their companion destroyers.

Up on the ship itself the fighting took longer, and it was far more bloody than on the boats. The white destroyers left behind, as they saw and understood what was happening in the boats, drew together with their askaris and put a deadly distance between themselves and their intended victims. As a warning first they shot two of us, a man and a girl just reaching womanhood. Then they stood watching to see which of us would try to move against them. One man among us, tall, possessor of a powerful body, shouted

219

to us to rush forward with him, but he himself was brought down before he had taken three steps.

"He was right," said a voice hidden among us, "but we must go against them all together. We shall need one to give the sound."

"You give it." This was not a lone voice.

The man waited the space of three breaths and gave the sound. At that sound it seemed as if all the white destroyers and all their askaris shot every gun they had into us. We halted and shrank back. Eight of us lay in the space still between us and the white destroyers and their askaris. Among us the fear of death rose and shook the courage of our recent preparation out of most. While we hesitated ten more bodies fell and those farthest forward hurled their weight backward against the rest of us. Then the voice that had given the first sound gave another.

It was a voice filled with courage, a voice to exorcise all ordinary fear, but the fear among us on that ship was no ordinary fear. For in the face of armed enmity is unarmed courage not merely another hazy name for suicide? That voice called; more strongly, the circumstances countered its call.

But then in the moment itself when deadly circumstance and the living urge of that lone voice held each other in such lame struggle a change came which none of us had allowed ourselves to look forward to.

There were eight white destroyers left on the ship. The askaris left behind were six. All, the six together with the eight, stood apart from us their victims near one pointed end of the ship. The space from the middle to the end opposite the white destroyers and their askaris was our space. The distance between the two groups was death to any trying to cross it.

We had thought that all the guns, the white destroyers' as well as their askaris', had now been fired against us. The voice urging us forward a second time shouted the whites and their askaris would need time to fill their guns with death again, and in that time we could be upon them. Before the full revival of our shattered courage two guns blasted the shaky calm. Those in the lead turned to each other wondering who had this time been hit, and they were amazed to see no new casualties among ourselves. We had seen nothing yet. Before us the vision was incredible. Two of the white destroyers lay unmoving on the ship's wood, destroyed by fire from their own askaris' guns.

It was impossible immediately to tell how many of the zombis had revolted, turned miraculously human and thrown death rebounding against the destroyers they were bound to protect from their victims. What we saw clearly now was the division of the camp of death. A gun whirled like a monstrous long club in the air descended faster than it had gone up. A third destroyer lay bleeding on the wood under stampeding feet. But the striker of that last good blow had struck his last. Three separate guns crashed into him, two colliding with his head between them, one sweeping his legs from under him, so that his body was hurled violently forward to meet us in our second rush. The twin blows had pushed that askari's eyeballs out from within his head. His body lay prone under us, the tongue hanging out a hand's length from its mouth, the eyeballs fallen so far they almost touched the hanging tongue; blood from the nose fell in a slow trickle down between the eyes on to the tongue.

All we had were our hands, but now they were sufficient. We caught one white destroyer almost ready with his gun filled with new death. He was not aiming it at us. His intended victim was a second askari. A crowd of us reached that white destroyer an instant before he could fire. Even in the agony of death that destroyer seemed concerned only to claw his way to the remaining askari whose happy infidelity had brought us life in the surroundings of death itself. That destroyer fought against thirty as if we the thirty were nonexistent in ourselves, as if the thirty were a mere obstacle in his path to the one askari.

As for the other askaris, like the zombis they still were they fought us, corpses possessed by the white urge to kill humans who had never harmed them. Before they died they destroyed one more among us, maimed two and wounded another five, but these last wounds were slight. Of the askaris' deaths nothing is left that needs saying here. They died foolishly, like zombis, defending evil against our own people.

But now there were five white destroyers left. There was not one of us, victims on that ship, who with our own hands did not strain to reach those five to take our vengeance for so much suffering in their greed. There was no need for weapons. Thirty victim eyes searched for each destroyer

222

and found him. Seven hands caught each ashen limb. One white destroyer was thrown into the water with not one of his limbs: these followed after. Another had his left thigh stretched away from the right till the bones between them cracked. He was hurled off the ship in the wake of the first. The third was strangled by so many pulling hands his neck turned longer than a chicken's, ungraceful in its slender death. The fourth and the last white destroyers, they went down together, bound tight with rope from the flapping sailcloth overhead.

Women leapt headlong from the ship, men leapt into the seawater from the side away from the destroyers' corpses in the joy of liberation and swam till they reached the others around the overturned boats. We pushed the boats till we came to the shore. There we righted them and rested to gather strength. Then those who knew about rowing went back to bring more survivors. Three times the boats went and came with people. The fourth time they brought food taken from the belly of the ship. The fifth trip was for barrels of wet powder and guns, thirty of them that had remained unsunk and undestroyed in the fighting. It was also now that children climbed up the ship's posts and cut down the heavy cloth.

This was wise. That first night on the shore it rained. There was no first gentle drizzle to warn us. The rain came sudden and abundant, did not last long, and stopped with just as little preparation as it had begun. We had had no time to build sufficient shelter. Had it not been for the heavy cloth brought from the ship we would have suffered greatly that first night. We were weak from the spending of our strength this past day, as also from the sheer unexpectedness itself of all these fortunate events.

Following the rain the night was a cold, silent night. The sea itself lost the heavy sound of its daylight surf and lay like a huge creature struck dumb by sudden misfortune. We lay under canopies of cloth stretched over high poles, on dry, sloping earth with ditches cut across the sides and top of our space to lead all that water off. The rushing water woke the first to sleep, but all again slept calmly once the rain was gone, all save those who had elected to be guards.

The morning was filled with beauty. The day before itself had been unbelievable, and the business choking it had left its truth unsavored. This morning we woke and were able to stretch limbs too long accustomed only to the miser motions imposed on us within slave traps. We were able to take in air that brought a welcome, unused fragrance into nostrils, mouths and throats too long abused with filth. We were able to raise our own eyes and see around us the world entire: earth, sea and sky broad, limitless before us. Some simply lay there on the grass and wept with thinking of the days and nights, the weeks that had gone before.

The first fire there we made with one of the white destroyers' guns. The askari Juma—that was his name, he who had turned against the destroyers his masters, destroyed them and survived them—he chose the driest powder from one barrel's centre, prepared the gun and fired it close against

224

dried leaves and faggots. This day also we rowed to the ship again, to bring all things we could use for cooking, all knives and implements we might find further uses for.

Thirty cut wood and softened earth for building resting places. Ten brought grass for thatching. Thirty took grain brought from the ship, sharpened fifteen stakes and planted corn from the day's middle to the falling of the welcome sun. Seven, the seven whose knowledge of the art of carving was surest, searched the surrounding forest for good wood. At the falling they returned with happy news: the trees growing in this unknown place, most were known already to some among us. Further, the carving experts said there was every tree here, every plant to serve the needs of work, of shelter, of food and of healing too. Seven more searched the forests for familiar food and brought back the yellow yam, together with great bundles of good leaves and edible mushrooms. The best water was not far. We built our shelters on high ground, a little away from the obvious path of the sweet water we had found.

Language was sometimes difficult between us, but the experts began to teach us all the language of common choice, and before the next new moon we were not strangers to each other's tongues, though the way to perfect understanding was still long.

"Askari," Abena said one day, "you should teach us all the use of guns."

"If you want to learn," the taciturn one replied, "but this name askari I do not like. It brings pain to my mind."

"We shall call you what?"

225

"Juma is my name."

"Juma." Abena called the name lazily. She seemed to be weighing the sound, to see if she could like it. "Juma, why is it so painful to your mind? Did you then not choose yourself to be an askari?"

."Let me forget now. Another time, when we have done things. Other things, so there will be no need to forget. Ask me then. Not now."

"I hear you, Juma," Abena said. "We can wait. But we can't wait to learn about the guns."

This was the time for the slow recovery of bodies maimed in captivity. As for the mind's healing that would take much longer, but for that too this was a definite beginning. At first the hunters, too depleted for the normal exertions of their art, learned from Juma how to use the guns and in this way they brought us all the meat we needed in that first season of our weakness.

It was the sound of the hunters' guns that brought us together with people who had come before us to this place. There were only five of them, four men and a girl, sister to one of the men. They had set a baitless panther trap for us along one of the new hunting paths, and though we saw the trap and waited for the setters they did not come out of their secrecy till each hunter had called out in every language known to him, assuring any listener we came in peace. Suspiciously, the one before the other, the oldest coming first, the young girl last, they came at last to a conversation with us.

Their news was this: sold into slavery, they had broken

away on the journey to the sea. They knew there was no way for them back home. For seasons they had lived their hard, suspicious life here, keeping far from the coastward roads to the rising, the roads used by slavers, predators and by chiefs. Their names? Kisa was the girl. The men were Tete, Mpenzi, Kesho and Irele.

They came with us. We had not known them before, but their mind's occupation was the same as ours. Their talk, like ours, was always of the terrible treachery of chiefs and leaders, of the greed of parasites that had pushed us so far into the whiteness of death. Their hope was ours: how to find paths to the uprooting of our betrayers, how to find paths to the destruction of our destroyers: not our specific destroyers, not our individual betrayers alone, but all their kind among our people, all the white destroyers.

This was the continuing work of our survival in that place: with knives and other iron taken from the ship skilled hands cut supple twigs for shaping into fishing baskets. We found the oduma growing in its wide spreading sufficiency. In the beginning, in the season of our weakness we did not need its shade. It was its bark we took. We ground it, threw it in the river far below our bathing water. The fish found their food, we found the fish our food.

Ehuka too we found, from its seed coaxing soap for bodies too long sickened with dirt. Not far from our new shelters three seekers found a stand of honton trees almost ready, they said in their joy, to roll into the river of their own accord. In another day half the new cloth was dry. The

227

other half we took out after the river had cleaned it more and turned it brown.

For canoes we hunted wide for the vuti, giant of all the forests, but here we found none. Still, there was enough of the smooth, black-skinned emeri. The experts in the carving art went up the river with helpers to live near the trees that would give them work till another new moon had shone and gone. They bit into the yellow lightness of emeri wood to bring out canoes hidden from the inexperienced hand.

For the further healing of our bodies too long immersed in the white destroyers' staleness and disease we found the slender, upright eyamdua, finished our asking and gathered its healing strength. The kahana also we found, taking its healing fruit together with its leaves, so that it was easy to drive out from our midst what still remained of the shaking, vomiting disease. Teeth that would have decayed in the white destroyers' filth found welcome twapea again. Of food there was enough from hunting even from the first. Grain brought from the ship sufficed till with the going and the return of seasons seed we had planted sprouted and reached a long-awaited maturity.

For the rest: women had found ehuka seeds for soap, the healers had drained the bitter water from kahana seed and leaf for protection from the needling sicknesses of cold nights and hot days. From the slender fale, clean, louse-hating tree, we received dark bark to give strength to weakened lungs.

Time there also was for women and men who had lived

together through destruction to utter to each other the things still hidden in our soul. Abena, for example, asked Juma to keep his promise and this time Juma did not plead pain.

"Ah, the white destroyers' kindness," he laughed a laugh of pain, "that kindness is always fruit inseparable from the tree of the destroyers' cruelties.

"Without a surrounding of utter cruelty what the whites call their kindness would be laughable indeed. But it is the time of their success: they have planted their cruelty all around us, so that in the hard strength of their cruelty the laughter of those able to remain undeceived by their murderous kindness is still laughter of weakness, the sheer bitter laughter of victims already trapped.

"Forgive me. I will say nothing of my own particular capture. Besides, you have all lived that as deeply as I or any of the people who were together with me on those journeys. So you know the truth.

"Our chiefs, our leaders, they have bellies and they have tongues. Minds they do not have. That is the white destroyers' happiness; that is why the white destroyers will exhaust their long knowledge of murder to keep our rotten chiefs, our bloated leaders on top of us. No one sold us but our chiefs and their hangers-on.

"The sea is strange to my people. We live far, very far from it. It would take a strong man many days, walking with the energy of his own determination, to reach the sea. But what would such strong men come down so far to seek? We were caught and sold. Our buyers, whites who came from the desert above us, forced us along unknown paths and strange rivers till we reached the sea. There we were sold to other whites.

"These white destroyers, they searched among us with shrewd eyes, took whom they needed and offered us a choice not open to the rest: 'You can escape the worst sufferings of slavery if you will become askaris for us.'

"Do you now see the white destroyers' kindness? 'Help us in the destruction of your people. That will be your individual salvation from destruction.' Ah, the life of the askari that I lived. That life."

The need for forgetfulness was still strong in him. No one pressed him any more. Of his own will he chose action as his best conversation with us.

These things Juma taught us: to take the gun and pour the potent powder down its neck, to push the wadding after the powder to hold it in its place, and after the wadding, to put the metal balls of death down the weapon's mouth. After, he taught us to hold the gun and keep the body not stiff with unfamiliarity but relaxed and steady; to look unblinking at whatever we would shoot; to put the strength of our legs and thighs and shoulders against the gun recoiling after firing. Then he taught us how to break each gun for cleaning and warned us against laying our weapons in wet places or near fires. He taught us all this and also the use of guns in the hunting of the slyest beasts. Beyond that he taught us not to fear the power of the destroyers' weapons but to learn quickly the use of that power against the destroyers themselves.

230

# 6

# the return

The pressing needs of the time after our first escape from the destroyers' proffered destiny left little time for rest, little time for conversation. That little time was consumed in the search of kindred spirits reaching for each other.

Of ultimate directions, along which paths we would turn the remainder of our lives, to the realization of what long vision we would bend our energies, of that we had had no time to talk. But a time of good harvests followed seasons of good work, and in grateful relaxation our minds at length reached matter central to our lives.

It was no hurried passage, this conversation of discovery. It took careful time, and at the end of this sufficient time we heard among us three kinds of voices uttering three separate visions.

First spoke the voices of tired bodies, voices seeing happiness in the present situation, unwilling to risk a return to the dangers of known pasts, afraid to follow any future vision. Those whose spirits found their utterance in the message of these voices chose to stay and continue in this new home. They were a third of us.

The second range of voices drew the most spirits, far more than a third of the whole. What dream did these voices utter? Returning was their dream. Strongest for these spirits was the call to return, the unequivocal call simply to go back to the places where mothers had borne them, places where fathers' brothers had dug holes to hold their navels. The call they heard strongest was a call from these places, from these homes, and it mattered little, the thought that destruction had reached into these very homes to blight them. To the listening ears of these nostalgic souls it did not matter, could not matter that it was at home they had first been betrayed into destruction's whiteness. Perhaps it was also their hope that their specific betrayals, their single sales were mere unhappy accidents, forgettable, easy to forget once the return home had been accomplished, once beloved eyes could see again the eyes of loving ones so recently betrayed, now miraculously returning, not wiped out, only grazed by death?

Ah, blind illusion of nostalgic spirits. Ah, self-murdering deafness of ears forever cut off from the quiet, reasonable call of our way. Most, far more than a third of the whole, chose to listen to the voices calling betrayed spirits back to betraying homes.

Far less than a third of us were left to drink in the meaning of the third voice. What was the meaning of this voice that called us?

Its farthest meaning, that meaning large enough to hold

all other meanings, was the meaning of the way itself: the call to reciprocity in a world wiped clean of destroyers, innocent again of predators. What was the meaning of the call to the way? Its closer meaning was destruction's destruction. Its closest meaning: the search for paths to that necessary beginning.

When the group that heard the voice of our way had taken long thought, from our conversation the decision rose that our path should lead us toward Anoa. Not back to Anoa, not back to any illusory home, but to the fifth grove, the secrecy of seers, refuge of hearers, keeper of the utterers. From there we would make a beginning to destruction's destruction.

This was to be no blind groping backward along any nostalgic road. This was to be nothing stupid, nothing futile. This was not to be a static holding on to that security— ultimately directionless—we had found in the present. The present station had been kind, more than kind: perfect for ourselves when rest was what we needed, when we were not yet recovered from the sicknesses leading into the whiteness of death. Remaining would be a choice of the permanent life of invalids. Better to leave the nostalgic along their backward road. Better to leave those frightened of vision in the static comfort they had found. Better to work out better directions, to follow better visions in our salvaged lives.

Now those of us who knew him remembered Isanusi again, remembered the words he had spoken of the need to keep the present world's available arrangements at a distance even if we found ourselves for a moment too weak to fight against these murderous arrangements. We had not understood him then. Now experience had lent us clarity and his words came back an echo to what we had lived to know. No, we would not return to homes blasted with triumphant whiteness. We would not remain here in invalid security. We would seek the fifth grove, seek Isanusi. We would seek the necessary beginning to destruction's destruction.

The askari Juma had a will to listen to the voice we heard also, but all this time he was prey to the sickly anxiety that rises against the will when it is harried between contradictory voices. A part of his will desired to take the journey back with us into the attempt at a new life close to our way. The other part was weary of all attempts. The sense of being a person already destroyed was so strong in him. True, in the killing of the white destroyers he must have expended prodigious energies. But that could be no explanation for the continuing exhaustion of his spirit. This was a tiredness with little of the physical in it.

Many days Juma seemed unable to will himself into the slightest motion, yet there was nothing diseased in his body. His spirit, so clearly falling deathward, drew ours too after itself and brought a sadness into each act of preparation for the long journey to the fifth grove.

Ankoanda, she who had come to feel for Juma something higher than mere gratitude, spoke to him: "You never worked for the white destroyers out of the freedom of your own desire, Juma."

234

"I worked for them."

"That is not all. You destroyed those you could reach when you could."

"Yes. I have done one good thing. But one good thing, what is the worth of that? You should leave me here in peace."

"Other good acts have followed that one. Others will follow."

"Where?"

Abena, listening, heard that question and breathed again, knowing the urge to life had not died in Juma. Abena added her voice to Ankoanda's gentle persuasion, and it no longer seemed so difficult to Juma to make up his mind. He would come with us.

The experts in the art of carving made fourteen new canoes. Five were ordinary fishing canoes; they would belong to those who had chosen to remain, to be used by the fishers among them. The remainder, nine long, deep canoes each with thirty strong oars, twenty for first use and ten for replacements, we divided between the people who had found no resting place here for our spirits. Most of those whose will it was to go back to families and homes would have a longer voyage before them. Some of their homes were far to the rising, in the last places we had been taken to before the destroyers finally turned their ship around. Five canoes would have been enough for them, but we found it wise to add a sixth, filling it with extra food and water vessels for the long voyage.

In the three remaining long canoes we loaded food and

everything necessary to its cooking, water to last us till we should reach fresh streams to break our voyage, our share of the weapons, the guns and the powder we had taken from the ship, together with bullets and wadding. We took in addition lengths of the heavy cloth from the ship, strong cover against rain. That was the beginning we made.

Who would call us to burden patient ears with long remembrances of our voyage back? The shapes of the shoreline running beside us took on an increasing aspect of familiarity. The lines of mangrove, our companions since the third day of rowing, first thinned out, then disappeared entirely. We had still to come to the long beaches of fine sand to the falling from Poano.

For two days we saw nothing but a rough coastline where rocks came all the way to the sea to end in broken heaps of smooth, dark stone. Behind the rocks the vegetation did not stand out distinctly. Bushes, a few, very few, tall trees. The rest was unclear to our sight and there was no time to row closer to the shore just to see what we could not see. When we stopped, it was only for long enough to take in fresh water and new food.

The twenty-seventh morning one of those who had chosen to come with us, Ulimboka, he whose home was days and days to the falling from Anoa, recognized an island. It was a small island not far from the land, standing high in the sea. We passed close enough to it, but on no side could we see any place where a person might climb up its rocky slopes without fantastic difficulty. On the island's summit stood a tree, tall, branchless till its very top, yet not

236

a palm; a tree for which none among us knew of any name. Even Ulimboka called it in his language simply the strange tree.

A day and a night from this island we reached the roughest shore. Here there were no beaches at all as far as anyone could see. The sea met land in hostile confrontation, along an abrupt, forbidding line of rock. In places the meeting was more than usually turbulent, from underlying rock making the seabed shallow and turning the water's flow into a sudden, massive, forward rush. But after these places we began to see stretches of immense, menacing calm where the sea took on the aspect of an ancient lake, a stillness far more fearful than the noisy turbulence.

"I know a place here," Ulimboka said. "I could show it to you."

"What is there?" Kwesi asked him.

"Emptiness. Just emptiness," he answered "Vast emptinesses in the rock, above the sea."

He was looking at the sea where it met the rocky land in this calm place, looking with a longing he could not have hidden from us even if it had been his intention to try to.

"What use are they, these spaces?" The question was Abena's.

"No use," Ulimboka said. "No one goes there. We found it by accident. It was our secret all the time of our growth. But the companions with me then are dead."

It was Abena's opinion we should go with Ulimboka to see his secret place. We agreed. We too had been thinking of future uses.

"We stop here," Ulimboka said.

It was an unlikely place. In the middle of a long stretch of calm sea and rock there was this whirling turbulence, pushing itself forward down a tiny opening in the rock face, its movement giving off a low sound like a moan. The space through which the water rushed in its disappearance was large enough to take the width of one canoe, no more. As, for its height it was so low that those in any passing canoe would have to lie flat to get past the opening.

Ulimboka looked at us and saw our anxiety.

"You don't know the place," he said uneasily. "Let two come with me. Let them be good swimmers, though I tell you there is no danger. Give the two rope, and give them a knife. If they find danger let them cut the rope. That will be a warning to the rest. If all is well the canoes can follow us. We shall pull seven times at the rope."

We agreed, asking Ulimboka to forgive the sourness of our necessary suspicion. Ndlela and Ona chose to go down first, and Ulimboka led them while in our canoes we waited a distance from the whirlpool's beginning. We did not wait long. Seven pulls on the rope told us we could follow—seven pulls so strong, so enthusiastic Kenia laughed and said the three had surely gone lunatic with joy in there. Three more went in. They too pulled seven times, harder even than the first three.

In threes we all went in, saving fifteen to come in last with the canoes, five in each. The fifteen lay flat in the canoes, the first person standing upright long enough to bring each canoe's point to the exact middle of the opening, then lying back as the water's movement itself drew the canoe forward, down the hole and into the beauty of the calm space within the cave.

We were amazed. Here was beauty to madden the soul with happiness. Here was space for wandering, here was cool darkness to soothe each spirit seeking quiet. Here also was light reaching rock and water from hidden, subtle openings above. Leaving was torture, but stronger than our pleasure here was the call of the future, and the future called us to leave now, saving these spaces for impending use, not for the instant's enjoyment.

Thirty days and thirty nights we spent on the way, cutting a huge half circle on land, avoiding the coastland. Always three walked ahead looking for paths away from travelled roads. They left a good route for us by leaving dead leaves against wrong turnings; where there was a confusing abundance of leaves they cut a single four-sided figure into tree trunks near the paths we should avoid. At each day's end the two slept and left a third to watch and to call to us on our approach, using the ancient call of the vulture. We reached them in their safe, hidden resting places every dawn. One among us joined the sleepers and set off with them on their next day's journey while the last watcher slept with us. Days we rested, prepared food for ourselves and for the travellers in the lead.

From the twentieth day recognition had grown to be a more frequent companion; by the thirty-first day everything around us was familiar, known to the nineteen who had grown up in Anoa.

We had been away merely a few seasons but changes enough for many lifetimes had flowed over us. And the fifth grove itself, about that also something had changed. We did not find Isanusi where we thought we would, where we had left him in his old shelter.

It was the morning after our arrival we found him. We had gone in search of water from the pond below the waterfall. There at the exit, before we emerged from covering vegetation, we saw Isanusi bathing at the lower end of the stream. Isanusi was not alone. With him in the water was Idawa, she whose beauty had maddened a greedy king, she whose intelligence had spurned the stupid circumstance of royalty. We saw Idawa and Isanusi in the water, and there was no longer any mystery remaining in any of our minds, no wondering to find the secret of Isanusi's survival in the face of banishment, of his endurance above exile's sour despair.

Lying on the bank where it was sandiest Idawa and Isanusi rested after the sweet exertion of swimming. Sunlight danced on their bodies' blackness, was caught by the gathered water there, lost and caught again. Idawa and Isanusi swam again, then they came out of the water, turned left at the waterfall and disappeared from us.

We went to the water now and drank. Sunlight had sucked up all real dew. Following the water of their still wet bodies we found Idawa and Isanusi in their new shelter. We did not startle them in their relaxation but from close to the entrance to the shelter we left a trail of signs known to Isanusi from the days when he tried to teach us truth and we heard only the beautiful outer sound of his words, knowing nothing of their meaning. We laid the trail to bring the knowing discoverer to our secrecy: the small, simple sign of the vulture in flight, and the circle of regeneration now burst with the invading line of destruction. Following these signs Isanusi came.

A restlessness had possessed Abena for days before we first saw Isanusi again. She was waiting on the path for him when he came. He saw her alone and seeing her like that made him unhappy.

"Abena."

"Isanusi."

Isanusi halted completely and stared again at the figure before him. His look was a question, but Abena gave no answer. She looked directly at him, her gaze promising nothing.

"You have come." Isanusi said. Despair broke his calm surface, and in that moment the body that had in its recent abandon been so oblivious of itself, absorbing warmth from the sun and comfort from the water, Isanusi's body shook like an infant body caught on windy mountains in the night, and Isanusi bent double with the pain he held.

"But you have come alone."

"Not alone," Abena answered Isanusi.

Mokili walked from the shadow of the trees. Ankoanda followed him. Suma came next, then Dovi, Ndlela, Pili, Kenia, Kwesi, Liamba, Ude, Makaa, Ashale, Ona, Kamara, Lini, Naita and Sobo. With Manda came Ulimboka.

"This one I do not know," said Isanusi.

241

"He is one of us," Manda said. "Ulimboka is his name. He comes from far to the falling. He is a finder of hidden paths, a truthful man." Isanusi studied Ulimboka and gave him the greeting of welcome. There was doubt in his eyes, but it was not suspicion.

"One I knew is not here," he said at length.

"Tawia," Kamara said. Sorrow made his voice uncertain, weak. Isanusi looked but did not continue asking. There would be time for all this heavy remembrance, time for recalling disasters not yet escaped. Isanusi came to know Juma, came to know Kimathi, Soyinka, Dedan, Umeme, Chi, Mpenzi, Inse, Nandi, Kibaden, Kima, Mensa, Ngazi, Kisa, Tete, Kesho, Irele, Okai, Ankonam, Akole, Kakra, Nsa, everyone of us in turn.

"Come with me where I live," Isanusi said. "It is small, my shelter, but it is near the sweetest water. I have a visitor, a companion."

"We know," Abena said quickly.

"Hei!" Isanusi uttered his surprise. But understanding came swiftly to him and he laughed. "Hau! There are spies even in the fifth grove, hau!"

We walked with Isanusi back to his shelter. Idawa came to us out there in front of the door. When she too had heard all the new names she remembered herself and said: "Ah, but we even forgot to give you the water of welcome. Wait, I shall fetch it."

"Do not go," Mokili told her. "We have drunk it already."

Our conversation that first day was long. Always, Isanusi's questioning turned around one thing: what was it we desired to do, and why we desired to do it now—whether it was mere rage of vengeance animating us, or a clearer vision beyond that.

When we had told him it was our desire to work, to live entirely against destruction, he was again anxious to know if we knew it clearly in our minds that we ourselves would not outlive the white blight; if we knew no one now working, living against destruction could be sure of any sweet decline into a natural end to life; if we knew clearly that in the glare of the white destroyers' power it was parasites, not creators, who found long lives to live?

When Isanusi knew we understood ours would be merely the necessary work of preparation against destruction, that for us there would never be any triumphs in the public place, even then he asked again and again how we had come to decide that the work of creation, the work of finding paths again to our way, the way, that work had enough attraction to bind our spirits together for the rest of our lives. Heavy on our minds was the weight of Isanusi's doubt. But we knew—how well we knew, how enormously well—he had reasons enough for the deepest doubt.

There were days of rest, days of quiet, patient building, days of planting, days of conversation, days also heavy with remembrance.

"When shall we talk of work?" Abena asked.

"When all are ready," Isanusi answered her.

"We have all been ready," Ankoanda said.

"There will be much for us to learn first," Isanusi said. "About our enemies, the white destroyers; about the

243

things that make them strong, their weapons; about those of our people who help the destroyers through their willingness to be used against us: the rulers and the parasites."

Juma had been silent since our arrival. He would sit or stand with us, but his attention seemed absorbed in matters distantly removed from the present. Today he spoke.

"What I know," he said, "is about the white destroyers' ways of terror. I know their weapons. I have lived with them. I have served the destroyers." His unhappiness sounded almost as deep as in our first days on the shore far to the falling. "I can continue to teach the handling of the destroyers' weapons, of the ways to use them."

"We shall need to learn all you can teach us," said Isanusi.

"When shall we begin again?" Juma asked.

We chose the day. With the powder, the bullets and the guns we had brought Juma continued the teaching he had begun. With great care he taught us each the best way to hold our weapons standing, lying, running. In forest clearings to the falling, where no man would ever hear our noise he taught us how to conserve bullets while fighting, firing straight at chosen objects smaller than half a human body, starting close and moving steadily back till we learned to hit still objects farther distant than the breath of the river Su Tsen a morning's walk from the waterfall below our spring.

Then it was time for Juma to teach us to hit objects in motion. We cut tree trunks into pieces half the size of a human figure. Juma set each piece rolling gently downward on sloping paths, and facing it we shot at the advancing wood till we grew skilled at hitting it with every shot. We prepared longer, steeper slopes, rolled more of the pieces downwards and fired faster as they came hurtling toward us.

After that we learned to shoot from beside the slope, arranging ourselves on either side in such a way it would be impossible if we missed the rolling wood to hit each other through any mischance; we found it took far greater skill and infinitely more patience to hit the wood running across our line of vision than when it had been coming straight at us. That skill and that patience we also mastered.

Then Juma taught us the use of trees and rocks, of everything in our surroundings, as cover for our bodies. We learned noiseless motion, and from the hides of animals we shot for food we made sandals for our feet, tougher than aheri bark, flat so they left no mark on hard ground, and even on soggy earth they left only a slight impression that disappeared moments after we had passed.

All our conversation with Isanusi turned about a central understanding: remembering the thousands upon thousands of seasons of our people's existence, remembering the thousands upon thousands of days spent journeying to find new resting places, remembering ancient and present assaults against the soul of our people, and remembering the harsh division—division yet to find resolution—between suicidal contention and desperate flight, we saw this vision plainly, heard this sound clearly: we have been a people fleeing our true destiny.

Peering into our mind, into our people's soul, what was this destiny we saw after so long spurning? This. It is our destiny not to flee before destruction, not to wander impotent, our soul turned coward, our bodies mere vessels for the demonstration of a massive impotence. This is our destiny: however far in our blind anxiety we may think to fly, however distant the places we reach seeking an unconscionable quiet, there the predators, there the harbingers of destruction will find us.

It is our destiny not to flee the predators' thrust, not to seek hiding places from destroyers left triumphant; but to turn against the predators advancing, turn against the destroyers, and bending all our soul against their thrust, turning every stratagem of the destroyers against themselves, destroy them. That is our destiny: to end destruction—utterly; to begin the highest, the profoundest work of creation, the work that is inseparable from our way, inseparable from the way.

This has been no useless explosion of rage animating us, hurling us singly into the brief, senseless acts of momentary, particular revenge. In us has been the need to spend life against the present killing arrangements, destruction's established system; to spend life cutting through deceiving superficies to reach again the essential truths the destroyers must hide from spirits if their white road is to prevail; to spend life acting on the truth against destruction's whiteness; to spend life working with our people, searching for paths to our way.

This should be the lifework of spirits still open to the

remembrance of the way, capable already of visions of its rediscovery, willing, determined to make it a living way again.

Vision is the aim of this vocation: the clearing of destruction's pale, thick-lying pus from eyes too long blinded to every possibility of the way. This lifework, its fruit should be the birth of new seers, other hearers, more numerous utterers. And the fruit of all our lifework together: that should be destruction's destruction.

And the passage of seasons? What of that? This is no hurried hustle hot with the sweaty anticipation of impatient profit but a lifetime's vocation. This is work of undying worth, the only work of worth in these surroundings blighted with death's tinsel, in all truth. It is not the passage of seasons that concerns this vocation then. It is the thoroughness of work, the trueness of the search for our way, the way.

Isanusi spoke to us of another fear, the fear of the urge to hurry forward blindly once our real work had begun. As if he knew already, he spoke more than once of the danger of too rapid growth, of the acceptance of mere pretenders to our vocation. But it was not his habit ever to push his own doubts against important work. The time came at last when the only reasonable speech left was action.

Ulimboka, chosen keeper of the stores, said: "We have used up half the powder we brought with us. Of the bullets we have only a third."

Juma thought again: "We should get more. We will need more, all we can get."

247

Kisa asked: "How shall we find it? From the cave? From the hiding places in the forest? Shall we not deplete our stores that way?"

Isanusi said: "Nowhere could we find as much as in the big stone place at Poano." A silence followed.

"He is right," Ashale said. "It should be the stone place first."

"That will be difficult, impossible, I should think." It was Dovi.

Ashale continued: "We could go a long time on what we take from there, if we take care to keep it well. Our own stores in the forest would be easy, but is that not mere waste? We could take a smaller place first, like the place where we were taken first. But what we could get there would not last long, and after that first attack the destroyers would be warned. Whatever we do after that will be more difficult. They will be far more careful."

"He is right," Juma said. "The best time to attack the stone place is in the beginning."

When the conversation turned to possible helpers, possible friends in our work, a heavy silence descended upon us. It was Isanusi who decided to break it.

"I know a man", Isanusi said. His voice was filled with doubt, but he went on. "He is not one of us, though if he had a mind to be he could find reason enough. He is not one of them, the princes and the parasites, though many times it has seemed to me that in his heart he yearns to be among them. That is the source of my deepest doubt about doing any of this work with him. For I have known him a sufficient time, during my stay in Poano. In everything he did and said I saw a divided soul. It is some time now since I knew him, but I will always have my doubts whether in this world there can be found any clay, any metal that will make that soul one, abolish the cleavage within it. He helped me more than a few times, for his gravest fault is not a lack of hospitality, and I also had occasion to help him in full measure. Whether it would be wise to bring him into any of our work, that is a decision we shall have to take together. But I shall tell you about him. Perhaps some here among us have already heard of him.

"Kamuzu is his name. The bitterest enmity runs in his blood against the princes of Poano and their parasites. There is some talk of their having cheated him in some immense, unforgettable way. I tried, but never was I able to get direct truth from his tongue as far as that heavy matter was concerned. I asked others, but few knew anything, and of the few that knew only one, reluctantly, told me this: Kamuzu once helped Atobra, king of Poano, his three princes and his parasites at court to deceive, capture and then sell a large number of slaves to the white destroyers, only to have the king, the princes and the other parasites hold back from him his agreed share of the prince paid for women and men. Kamuzu's anger against the king, the princes and the parasites is that kind of anger, anger with nothing pure, nothing good in it. Kamuzu does not hate the enslavement of our people. What he hates is his own exclusion from the profits of the trade."

"You are certain, though, of the sharpness of his anger

against the king, the princes and the parasites?" Abena asked Isanusi.

"More than certain. It burns his blood."

"There is nothing quicker than anger for giving energy," Abena said.

"True."

"We should try him," said Suma.

"We should," said Abena.

"Yes," Isanusi agreed. "But the ancestors help us if we become dependent on him for our success."

This was our first preparation: fourteen went to the nearest of our hiding places and from there brought dry powder and bullets enough for twenty. Guns they also brought, though we had enough already with us.

Three went secretly to Poano bearing a message from Isanusi to the man Kamuzu. Kamuzu welcomed them, gave them the fullest hospitality and most useful help in their search for knowledge there at Poano. After fifteen days the three came back to us knowing how, when and where entry into the huge stone place was to be sought, where the slaves of the place were kept, where arms were stored, and where the destroyers themselves lived. The three told us what they knew. For three more days we considered what could best be done now that we had all this necessary knowledge.

The white destroyers from the sea, these are a people of dead stone. What they have in place of a soul, that thing finds its solidest expression in the places of heavy stone they have built here, outposts for the destruction of our people, centres to continue the destruction of our way.

Our decision was to take the stone place at Poano, but the method could not be a sudden, brutal assault from without. For two more weeks seven chosen from among us lived near the stone place, came and went within it. Three watched and took minutest note of every little detail we would still need to know. Three went in as guests of Kamuzu, men who had come a long journey to see him and to live with him for a time. They lived with Kamuzu in his house, an imitation of a white destroyer's shelter not far from the walls of the stone place. Four went in unknown to Kamuzu. They were craftsmen skilled in the working of all kinds of wood, and it was their skill that gained them entry.

For the thirty who chose to go into the stone place with Isanusi and Kamuzu on the final day there was difficult work, sweet work of preparation. Juma found and taught a new way to push bullets down each gun's neck: a quicker way than we had ever used, for in the enterprise ahead quickness would be life; any clumsiness, any slowness would give the white destroyers a terrible victory.

The week before we moved Kamuzu did not betray Isanusi's hesitant trust and ours. He went to the white destroyers in the stone place—for he knew them well, and they liked him—went to them and smiled good news to them. Kamuzu told the white destroyers he had an old friend, a chieftain living far off, but not too far off to reach the coast with as great a retinue as it would be worth a great man's while to bring. This chieftain, a neighbouring

251

people had angered him, insulting him beyond the endurance of his proud spirit and even going so far as to rob him of a portion of his immense wealth. Whence his decision—fastened to imminent action by irrevocable oaths—to destroy the angering people completely.

The three among us who had been with Kamuzu in the stone place came back full of praise for his dissimulating art, and we all rejoiced in the success of its use against the white destroyers. Kamuzu himself, they said, breathed the full fury of his imagined chieftain friend, cursed the offending people and with overwhelming eloquence pronounced his friend justified in his determination to exterminate every single one of the unrepentant people. Kamuzu rose to the high message of his speech. His friend the chieftain needed arms to give solid force to his determination. This chieftain friend, he was a direct man, with a sense of honour any trader would find assurance in. He would come to Poano himself with a number of his trusted nobles, warriors all. Gold they would bring, enough to pay for half the bullets, the guns and the powder of their need. The other half of their trade debt they would pay promptly on the effective use of the new guns in the extermination of their enemy.

The destroyers listening to Kamuzu, they laughed till blood reddened their skins, then they grew serious. They asked if the offending people themselves were known to have guns also. Kamuzu with the greatest show of contempt told them those people did not even know the proper management of spears. The destroyers grew dead still on

252

hearing the extermination of the unfortunate people would be a certain thing if they gave Kamuzu's unseen chieftain friend the guns he wanted. They asked to see this friend. Kamuzu said his friend was a severe man, not one to waste a journey. He would come only if he knew for certain there were guns awaiting him. He would not come merely to talk. If there was any further assurance the destroyers wanted, Kamuzu pronounced himself fully empowered to give it them.

The destroyers told Kamuzu the cause of their hesitation: guns they could give, but gold they did not want so hotly at the present time. If Kamuzu could dissuade his raging friend, prevail upon him to use the guns he wanted not to kill all his enemy but to defeat them and bring them to Poano, there to sell them as slaves, if Kamuzu could persuade his friend of the wisdom of such a change, the white destroyers would give him all the guns he needed and not demand even one ackie as his pledge of honesty.

Kamuzu pretended chagrin, asked the destroyers three times to reconsider. The destroyers were firm: guns for slaves, not gold. Kamuzu gave in at last. He would vouch for his irate chieftain friend, and in a matter of sufficient days he would bring him down to the stone place, together with his trusted nobles, warriors all.

The day came. We were ready. So well, so thoroughly had Juma prepared us for the coming work we had a full day to rest in quiet secrecy after we all reached Poano.

Thirty of us went with Isanusi: for Kamuzu's angry chieftain friend, the fabled one thirsty for hot blood, he was to be Isanusi himself. Fantastic we looked in our special robes—robes capacious, robes so ample a sufficiency of bullets hidden in the folds of each made no sound at all. Incredible we all looked, but none more amazing to sight than Isanusi himself. Hau! What an imbecility always is the high ceremony of state and royalty.

Shall we risk laughter again at such a time in our remembrance? Is it not enough just to say Isanusi was dressed with all the foolish magnificence of royalty? On his head he wore a high, gilded hat, woven in imitation of a crown. A rainbow would have turned white with envy to behold his long robe. Red of fresh murder was the most abundant colour, but not the wildest. Fool's gold glittered hoarser than the red; a deep, false blue struggled to push the brighter colours into obscurity. White strips crossed the cloth ostentatiously every breath of a hand. But the most unashamedly royal adornment was this: pieces of broken metal, even bits from some white destroyer's shattered mirror, all were sewn in patches into the screaming pattern of the gown proclaiming brilliant royalty. That was hardly all. On the wearer's ankles small, high-pitched bells tinkled with every step he took. Nor did Isanusi forget to add to his accoutrement a long fly-whisk, indispensable tool of all flyblown leadership.

What need is there to spoil time with further laughter in the description of the noblemen's clothes we wore that day? Long did we laugh when our dressing was complete, laugh to behold each other so stupidly attired, till Isanusi, hearing Kamuzu's step, reminded us with exceeding seriousness we were aristocrats today, and therefore should not have brains capable of seeing through the folly of our state.

Kamuzu, on his own grim initiative dressed in robes he had kept safe for some special occasion, looked a fitting friend indeed for the brilliant-hued Isanusi. We curbed our laughter and followed him. Kamuzu led us into the stone place through the same gate we had seen the prince Bentum, renamed Bradford George, enter on a different day. But this time we did not stop in the courtyard; we crossed it and were taken directly into a room raised above it, but lower than the level of surrounding walls.

There were in that room five white destroyers come to bargain with Kamuzu and his wild, brilliantly coloured chieftain friend. Kamuzu told us why there was such an air of furtiveness about the things the white destroyers did and said that morning: the whites were servants of other white destroyers, their own princes and parasites, and it was for them they traded here with our princes and parasites. But from time to time these white destroyers here in the stone place, they too sought means to enrich themselves directly by turning the trade of their princes and parasites to their own account. Whenever they did this they had to take immense care not to arouse the suspicion—or if that was already awake, the envy—of the lesser white destroyers in the place. Hence the need for secrecy.

Kamuzu had already made it clear he would be coming with his irate friend for guns alone. Yet even on this day itself the white destroyers—a tremendous monstrosity is the

255

greed of whites—tried to make him change his mind. They brought out large quantities of useless, shiny things and urged their usefulness on Kamuzu and Isanusi both. But Kamuzu did not betray us then. He resisted his own impulses and refused to consider anything but guns.

At length the white destroyers had the guns brought out, one for each of us. Isanusi looked with profound skepticism at the guns. Then with great emphasis and for a long time he shook his head.

There was puzzlement on all the white destroyers' faces. They looked to Kamuzu for an explanation of his angry friend's strange behaviour. Kamuzu told them his friend the chieftain was a severe man, and a man grown cynical from long experience of treachery: he doubted the guns would work, and he wanted concrete proof.

The white destroyers pointed eagerly to the guns, pointed to their new wood and their shiny metal parts. Still Isanusi shook his head and the white destroyers, anxious, turned again to Kamuzu. Kamuzu explained. He told the white destroyers there was not one breath of trust in his friend's breast for anybody in the universe, absolutely none; that the angry chieftain suspected the guns could be old and useless things merely polished to deceive the unwary eye.

Kamuzu himself turned angrier as he talked, and in the end he made a loud, fiery declaration of his intention to take his angry friend immediately out of the stone place again unless the white destroyers gave him incontrovertible proof the guns were new and good. On seeing him so incensed the white destroyers had begun murmuring uneasy words to each other, but when near the end Kamuzu said again his chieftain friend intended the capture of thousands of slaves and he could not begin such serious business with defective weapons, the white destroyers looked significantly at each other. Their faces relaxed again and they even smiled.

On the white destroyers' orders powder was brought in a barrel from a room immediately to their left. One of the destroyers, he who had one good leg and wood in place of the other, took back the ring of keys from the askari who had been ordered to bring the powder, and dropped it heavy into a large pocket on his right. Carefully, obeying instructions from the one-legged white destroyer the askari loaded each gun with powder but added no bullets.

"Test them, friend," the one-legged white destroyer said.

Still Isanusi shook his head. Kamuzu explained: "My friend the chieftain has heard of guns that make a noise loud enough to frighten fools. Noises do not interest him. He wants to see how well your guns can kill."

Without leaving the destroyers too much time for thinking Kamuzu took a bullet of his own from the magazine hanging openly from his waist and pushed it into the gun nearest him. Isanusi had been pacing in front of us as he talked in his high simulated anger to the white destroyers through Kamuzu. Kamuzu now gave Isanusi the loaded gun.

Isanusi held the gun just as if he were looking for one among us to test the killing power of the weapon on. He pointed the loaded gun at Oko, then at Tomfo, then at

257

Soyinka. The gun moved down the line of us, the rhythm of Isanusi's walk growing more rapid, more impatient. Once, one of the white destroyers made an irritated sound, but immediately after that all of them laughed, waiting for Isanusi to shoot one of us dead.

Isanusi passed the middle of our line. When he reached Okai he brought the gun closer to his body, ready. A sigh, audible with long relief, escaped the white destroyers. Great then was their chagrin when instead of shooting at Okai, Isanusi turned the gun and aimed it for one steady moment only at the lone askari, and from just three men's length fired at him.

The askari, surprised, dropped his gun before he fell. That same moment each of us raised our guns and drew a first bullet from beneath our ludicrous, magnificent robes. The second of the white destroyers had rushed forward to the askari as he fell, not to succour the dying zombi but to retrieve his gun. Soyinka sent a hard bullet straight into that destroyer's body just as he touched the fallen gun. The third destroyer rushed upon Badu, but Ankonam fed another bullet into him before he could reach his murderous aim. Before us lay two white destroyers. Blood from their wounds came in thin lines on the uneven floor and filled the small cracks in between blocks of hewn stone. The askari's body lay a little distance apart from theirs. The other two destroyers and the one with one leg ran in a panic making for the door closest to them. Umeme and Mpenzi moved faster and blocked their path.

Now that the fighting had become an open thing we took

258

the best covered positions we could find. Whoever came through any of the doors would have to walk through bullets.

Umeme, Chi and Juma put their own guns down to turn themselves into loaders for the rest. Mokili, Lini, Kgosana and Ndlela became passers.

What followed was most surprising in its ease. We had expected the destroyers and their askaris, defenders of the stone place, to make immensely difficult the capture of the place. Three more of the whites came rushing into the room at the sound of shots. They came running as if the very possibility of danger in this place was a stranger to their minds. We sent them hurrying to their soulless ancestors, sent them with their own instruments of death. Seven askaris came next, running even faster. We waited till they saw us, for it was our intention to find out what they would do. They gave us no cause for further hesitation. The sight of their masters lifeless on the stone at our feet filled the askaris' eyes with blood. They hurled themselves against us. Our weapons found their entrails first, all of them.

No one else came in after that. Carefully we went out ourselves, moving in protected sevens to search the entire place. We found many, but among them few had the urge or the fighting strength to resist our taking of the place.

We found the highest of the destroyers in his room on the side directly above the sea. He did not seem entirely un- aware of the fighting that had been going on outside the safety of his room. Whether it was for courage or as a continuation of some long entertainment, he was drinking

259

rum, taking it in huge draughts from a spacious chalice when the first of us burst in upon him in that room. He wore one thing: a kind of tunic reaching down a little below his waist. He was not alone. A woman who in every way visible was in a state of passage between blackness and whiteness was there in the room with him. She was altogether naked, and it was plain she stood in need of no more rum. This chief destroyer, he was not truly surprised at our arrival. He even smiled a kind of smile before reaching languidly, like one interrupted in the middle of better things, underneath a pillow. He had no time to bring out the little weapon hidden there. Okai shot him in his chest, and a bullet from Kibaden, almost simultaneous with Okai's, sank into his brain and stopped his breath completely. His woman stared wide-eyed at everyone and everything, took a last draught from the chalice left beside the bed, and sank chuckling back in repose as if she had just seen some novel entertainment. Only Kamuzu stayed behind to gape at her. We moved on.

Others we found, destroyers and askaris both. Not one escaped execution at our hands. The prince Bentum also we found. His room was between the destroyers' and the askaris'. Something had happened to his white ghost of a wife just before our entry. What exactly there was no telling, but her body showed sufficient signs of some fantastic spasmic struggle, something that seemed to have frightened Bentum, renamed Bradford George, into total forgetfulness of everything around him till the moment he saw us enter. Fear, not courage, urged Bentum's unthinking leap against

Oko. A most unfortunate leap it was. Oko, disdainful of his own gun, stepped back slightly, measured the body suspended in the air and struck with his hardened left hand against the open throat. His right, similarly hardened, came down upon the neck and broke it. Bentum reached the stone floor head first.

The prince Bentum, renamed Bradford George, did not die. We took care to send him, a permanent invalid, dressed in the most ridiculous finery, back to his father Koranche in Anoa. With him we sent a message by the messengers who carried him, a message to his father the king: Remember those you have destroyed. They remember you.

We opened the locks holding slaves in the caverns below. Some captives we found already unchained, mainly those kept to work there at the stone place. One, a woman, came afterwards to Abena, looked at her long, shook her head and would only say: "Ei, my sister!" Many were for returning to their remembered homes. We told them our doubts but held no one back. Ten in the end remained who understood our purpose and had in themselves the urge to work with us. When in the fullness of time we left Kamuzu raving in the blazing stone place these ten also came with us.

In the weeks we had to work in before our departure from the stone place we were fortunate in the fulfilment of our aim. Each night five canoes slid along the far lagoons to the falling from Anoa, sought unused entry to the sea taking guns and powder, bullets and wadding to increase the stores we had hidden along the safe half-circle from the cave to the fifth grove.

We kept the white destroyers' flags flying above the stone place before Kamuzu in his swollen pride of self had them brought down, kept the usual number of guards—four in the morning, eight at night—pacing the walls, our own people dressed in the clothes of dead askaris to lure destroyers' ships still ignorant of the capture of their strong stone place.

Ships came from the rising loaded with slaves, from the falling with the white destroyers' weapons and their goods. We let them come under the walls of the stone place before they understood there had been a change, for in the weeks of preparation we had spent careful time learning about the firing of the big guns, and at first we used them well. Seven ships came, three back from the rising, four from the falling, the destroyers' own direction. The four ships from the falling brought enormous quantities of rum, but also guns and powder, then smaller amounts of the white people's goods for trading. With the motions we had taken care to learn we welcomed them. The first was a small ship, one back with captives from the rising. The destroyers came down from their ship and made their way to the main gate, but before they reached it they must have seen something, for suspicion seized them and they tried retreat. Too late. We destroyed the destroyers there before the gate. When afterwards we went to their ship we found the captives on it near death, most of them. The ship was small; where we found the captives there was no breathing space.

After healing all the survivors wanted to return back

home. We warned them, gently, they would find themselves betrayed again, but the homeward pull was strong among these also, and our counsel was mere words, mere wind. We bade them farewell when they started out together, aiming for the rising.

The taking of the second and the third ships, both also from the rising, was similar to the capture of the first, except that the destroyers now came within the stone place before understanding hit their killer brains. The fourth ship and the fifth we destroyed on the water with fire after taking all the weapons and the powder kept on them. The sixth carried little else beside rum. We sank it. The seventh ship anchored in peace outside the stone walls. The destroyers from it came confidently up into the stone place. We let them in, and after that we drew the bridge. Arrived in the courtyard, they finally looked round with open eyes and saw in the whole place not one face they could recognise as a destroyer's. They too tried to fight. We executed them all. Their ship contained a strange mixture: captives and all sorts of goods. We freed the captives, kept what could be of future use among the goods, and sank that ship also there beneath the stone walls, a thing that was to add to Kamuzu's rising anger against us.

Prophetic indeed had been Isanusi's doubts. In the beginning, before the actual fighting for the stone place, Kamuzu had thought it would be prudent if he took no active part. It was not personal courage he lacked, for he was in that way as brave as he was generous in his hospitality. His disease came from a poverty of vision: he truly feared

263

we would never succeed against the white destroyers there in their own stone place. The greatest good Kamuzu did was this: he suppressed his doubts long enough to help us, and his help was most significant.

Where he had thought we would fail we succeeded. Kamuzu survived his astonishment well, so well it became his high pleasure to strut about the stone place day and night as if he had always himself owned the place. In truth it was his belief he had come to achieve ownership at last, for in the end what could we be in the eyes of one such as he was except tools to power, to be discarded after the achievement? To him we could never have appeared possible sharers in the use of power; the uses we saw were so strange to his mind.

Terrifying is the still clear soul's disgust at sight of the once destroyed aspiring not to abolish destruction but in their individual selves to become destroyers. Horrible is the sight of slaves hustling to place themselves on their master's stool.

Kamuzu had suffered long under the keen burden of ambitions suppressed in impotence. Now that the stone place was in our hands the highest of his ambitions surfaced abruptly in all its grotesque mediocrity: Kamuzu wanted to live forever in this hard stone place; more, he wanted to become a copy of the chief of the white destroyers we had found in this place, the one they had called the governor.

This is what Kamuzu did in his hot pursuit of this infant dream: the governor had a concubine who survived him, that same woman who was neither of us nor of the destroyers but a mixture with a body part black, part white, inhabited by a soul frantic in its denial of the portion that was of us. He had had a wife from his own people, the governor, but this had been a woman remembered by those who had the frightening misfortune of seeing her as something white like leprosy triumphant, her body bloated in a watery way, much as if she had been made out of a single giant yaw, and given to frequent confinement with some ill-defined shaking disease, severest, so it was said, whenever she chanced to catch the governor tasting darker flesh able, as hers was unable, to satisfy his lust. The sickly female destroyer had died in a cataclysm of anger one riotous night at the stone place. The half-black, half-white woman who had helped her hurry to her ancestors from then on resided permanently at the stone place, to be the governor's chief diversion.

Now we had sent the governor to join his bloated spouse, leaving the concubine behind. Kamuzu felt the call deep in his spirit to help himself to the departed destroyer's leftovers, and he did. Not only did he take the used woman for his own; he also coveted the dead white destroyer's servants, his clothes, everything he thought could make him more like a destroyer.

Kamuzu raged at us, at our decision to keep the white destroyers' flags flying above the stone place. We told him our reason: we hoped to lure more of the destroyers' ships. Kamuzu's rage grew hotter. It died only when in the end we agreed to have him put up flags of his own design. Ah, pity the soul destroyed. Kamuzu had a fantastic flag made:

a likeness, supposed to be of himself, standing huge in an attitude of triumph above adoring heads below. Above the heads another figure, equal to Kamuzu's, a white destroyer's. Pity the spirit hollowed by destruction.

Kamuzu's most disastrous habit was his affection for the sound of cannon. We stood against this craving of his, but when in the end he won his way he shot cannonballs into the air on the most ridiculous of pretexts. He fired cannon for ships seen far on the horizon, for ships seen coming near, for ships at anchor far off, for ships refusing to stop. Often Kamuzu shot cannonballs to express his anger against the king, the princes and the parasites of Poano for old wrongs they had done him. Sometimes he fired cannon for no other reason than to indicate to the world and to the sky above that Kamuzu was pleased with himself that moment. We watched this tremendous squandering of gunpowder and grew anxious. We knew no one who could teach us how to make it. Our best hopes lay in keeping large quantities of the potent powder stored.

From the first day we had made plans to remove powder, guns and bullets from the storerooms of the stone place to our own half circle of hidden places. It was now necessary to accelerate these plans, to remove in days only quantities of arms and powder we had hoped to move in the passage of whole moons. Secretly, yet at great speed, we did the moving. A few only among us were needed to keep Kamuzu's small mind asleep. For in the passage of these days all he required for his happiness was that his person be subjected to endless praise.

266

We took turns composing, took turns singing the most extravagant praise songs to Kamuzu's vanity while every night secret lines of our women and men carried what we needed out through the smallest of the gates in the back wall of the stone place, across shadowy open spaces, across the groves around Poano and to canoes waiting on the neglected arm of the long lagoon Essei. What spurious praise names did we not invent to lull Kamuzu's buffoon spirit?

Osagyefo!

Kantamanto!

Kabiyesi!

Sese!

Mwenyenguvu!

Otumfuo!

Dishonest words are the food of rotten spirits. We filled Kamuzu to bursting with his beloved nourishment.

What we removed from the stone place we hid not in any single discoverable place but divided among the seven secret places we had prepared, going from Ulimboka's cave in an arcing journey ending in the fifth grove outside Anoa.

Thirty days we had in the stone place before Kamuzu's greed and his vanity turned to treachery and we planned our withdrawal. In that time we took powder in a hundred and seventy kegs, fifty small, the rest each of sufficient weight to give carrying work to two adults. Three hundred guns we found in unopened boxes. We took them all. Bullets and their containers we counted in the thousands and hundreds. Those we also took. Hiding everything in the nearest secret place, we found time later to divide guns, powder, wadding, knives and firestones among all seven separate hiding places.

But what winds of breath we wasted reasoning with Kamuzu in the days before we had made a firm decision to abandon him to his headlong doom! Kamuzu thought we should aim to keep the stone place permanently. He even called it, after the manner of the white destroyers, his castle. In his opinion, the stone place was the new seat of power over our people in the new arrangements brought by the whites, and whoever held it would be the person in ultimate control. We tried to reason with Kamuzu. We explained it was not power over our people we wanted, but the liberation of all of us from alien power; that if we were content, eager, in fact, to move into the seats of alien control ourselves, then we could not be liberators but traitors, another set of rotten chiefs taking advantage of our own people's immobilization to impose ourselves on them; that it might be easy enough to grasp such power at the moment, but once we succumbed to that traitorous temptation we would quickly find ourselves forced to keep faith not with our people—always the victims of this power—but with the white destroyers from the sea—the real establishers of this power.

Kamuzu's argument was unchanging. Power, he informed us, was a thing always to be taken as it was found, just whichever way it was found, not as the taker would wish it to be. We now had power in our grasp. If we were

268

interested in finally moving away forever from victim situations, we should not be hesitant to step into the white people's shoes.

Exasperated with his blindness, we decided to humour him, not to awaken his suspicion. We chanted his praise songs for him and watched his spirit bloat itself in the most remarkable ways. Kamuzu ordered the lighting of thirty special torches at his table—for like a destroyer he had taken to eating at their table—every night, torches not placed against the walls but held by those slaves of the stone place who, trusting us in the first days, had not left for their homes with the others but had stayed in the hope a new day was coming.

To soothe him while our work continued we chanted more elaborate praises, but his vain appetite only increased with satisfaction:

Osagyefo, courageous, skilled one who arrives to pulverize the enemy just when the enemy is exulting in imminent victory;

Mzee, wisdom's own keeper;

Kabiyesi, leader of men;

Kantamanto, faithful one who never broke an oath;

Mtengenezaji, what a multitude of things would remain unrepaired, forever broken were it not for you!

Katachie, commander supreme!

Thirty such resounding appellations Kamuzu accepted for himself with overflowing joy. Nor was he satisfied merely with our proffered services as praise singers: the buffoon must have suspected some humor in our chanting. He found

269

an old singer with a high, racing voice to sing for him, and a hireling drummer brought from Poano beat out the words on mercenary skin for his flattery.

When he was not steeped in self-flattery Kamuzu raged against us for our continued hostility to the white destroyers. In his new day of power he said he had discovered something we could not know about in our deep ignorance, something he called diplomacy. Kamuzu began to send out invitations to the parasites of Poano and others from nearby to share his meals with him. It was these feasts he used to begin secret contacts with the whites, with the king Atobra and his courtiers. To him these were beginnings of alliances between one great man of power and other men of power, secret pacts designed in the end to drive us out of the stone place and to keep Kamuzu supreme there, a black copy of the head white destroyer. Kamuzu pacted with the parasites he ate with to contact the white destroyers and indicate his willingness to enter a partnership in trade with them. The white destroyers proved most agreeable, provided only Kamuzu would promise to find ways to get rid of those the destroyers called troublemakers: us. Kamuzu indicated he would like to, but could not. The white destroyers and the princes and the parasites sent Kamuzu a message: they would be willing to help him if he would be willing to help them. Kamuzu asked them how? Now the white destroyers and the princes and the parasites sent messages to Kamuzu informing him of a plan, and Kamuzu liked the plan. Now Kamuzu took on for our benefit the air of a man deep in statecraft. There was nothing we said to him that was not naive, even the little we did choose to say.

The night of betrayal came and found us ready. Kamuzu had given a key to a small, unused side gate on the town side to his friends without, for their invasion. Kamuzu's secrets were our secrets too; our secrets were inaccessible to him. Using the side entrance opposite the main gate we left the stone place in that same safety of the dark night Kamuzu had planned to use against us. Before we left we set advancing fires to the remainder of the powder in the cavernous places below.

We were out on the sea already, far beyond the Essei's opening, when the first brilliance of that night's explosions began to light the skies behind us. On the highest wall we clearly saw a frantic figure, Kamuzu's, waving its arms in the lurid air. He must have been shouting heavy words to someone, but between himself and us the distance was so far.

In the aftermath of the stone place's destruction that night it was the king of Poano, Atobra, and other kings from around, together with their parasites, who pacted with the white destroyers to force our people to labour rebuilding the place. As for Kamuzu the demonstration of the destroyers' and the princes' and the parasites' gratitude to him was swift: they hanged him in the huge public place to the falling from the stone place. His crime, the new interpreter the destroyers had found was told to say, was something called presumption.

More of the work of preparation awaited us, work for minds, work also for bodies. Juma taught us silent motion,

271

flat movement along the earth, making impossible the upright killer's aim. He taught us the arts of hiding, and the art of choosing places best for the trapping of unsuspecting pursuers. He taught us to fight impatience, not to shoot until we were absolutely certain of our aim. More than all this he taught us. He taught us how to keep sudden sorrow at the death of a companion checked till each battle was over and fallen friends could be buried, those merely wounded given to the healers' care. He taught us to kill in ourselves the spurious, impetuous courage that urges the fighter to spectacular personal deeds carrying more risk than usefulness. He taught us the frailty of small groups, taught us to move always in overwhelming numbers against small groups of our attackers, then to disappear, to seek another insufficient group and wipe it out.

Isanusi also taught us. His teaching tended to matters of the soul. Isanusi spoke to us of the need to persevere even in the present triumph of the white destroyers' road. He spoke to us of the possibility, terrifying in the absence of deep thought, that the white destroyers' domination would grow even heavier, lasting beyond our individual lives, swallowing up whole generations before at last their glaring day was ended. He spoke to us of the constant need for thorough preparation before each new piece of work: the gathering of truthful news concerning the destroyers, the support they enjoyed from the princes and the parasites, the numbers of their askaris, the quality of their weapons, and the nature of their intentions. Above all Isanusi reminded us that all we did would be nothing, less than nothing, if we forgot the way away from which all action is waste motion, if we forgot to seek the people's understanding first.

After preparation of the body, after the mind's preparation we were again ready for the continuation of our work, ready for motion tending toward the way.

Purpose lends wings to the traveler. To them that know their destination fatigue is a brief stranger merely passing in the glare of day. We have ranged far. Farther than the cave to the falling, farther in that direction even than all the lands of Ulimboka's knowledge before he came with us, we have travelled in the work of our one purpose. Farther to the rising than the last station of the white destroyers' ship of death we have gone seeking paths to the living way. But of the thousand days of work behind us which shall we call back for remembrance now? Shall we remember the days of waiting, days that in our eagerness began to seem unending, the days of waiting for the predators' long boats on the brown river Osu, far to the falling from the first home of our survival, Ulimboka's cave? Or shall we recall the single day of the liberating ambush that followed another patient wait? Or the day another predator, closer here, driving humans to slaughter, counting already in his head the things he stood to gain, found himself staring straight into the unblinking eyes of our avenging justice? Shall we remember the white destroyers' surprise when askaris they thought they had newly found brought against them the living force of a violated people's anger?

Those first days of the long wait Abena's patience was

endless. Weariness made the greater part of us prone to impatience, but Abena went about the work of preparation, completed, repeated, perfected each necessary detail. And always, even after the seventh day of unrewarded waiting, her voice carried the same message: "They will be coming this way. They have no other route." That we knew well enough, but what was it held the predators back so long?

Our connected eyes had brought us news of their passage down the river to its mouth, toward the sea and the markets brought there by the white destroyers, rowing their monstrous boats, at that time slow and hollow of human captives. Connected ears heard and brought us news of the predators' well-tried plan: to go with gold and elephant tusks stolen in sudden raids from our forest people down to the coast, where predators meeting with destroyers would trade their stolen property for rum and shiny tinsel from the destroyers' lands. Whence, rowing their ungainly boats like some sort of immense, bloated serpents along the towns of the spreading delta, it was the predators' intention, made firm through successful habit, to seek the several kings and chiefs and princes and leaders and assorted parasites there thirsting for the white destroyers' drink in their unthinking bellies and for the white destroyers' trinkets to lend their mediocrity substance. These leaders, these chiefs and kings, their kingship, their chieftaincy, their leadership knew only two methods: the waste of their people in foolish internecine wars seeking humans to give predators and destroyers; and, failing success in these wars,

274

the treacherous sale of their own people to waiting predators, waiting destroyers.

When, after the long wait beside the river Osu where it bends narrowest before reaching the easy coastlands, when the predators came at last, their captives forced to row upwards against the river, the sails on their long boats now unuseable, the reason of their slowness finally lay plain: their boats were near to sinking with their human booty. Such loads of crime must have taken long days to collect, long days spent threading the delta's waterways.

There were five boats taking humans to the predators' land, land near the desert but not yet turned completely desert itself. The predators, such was the news, needed work done on their stolen land, extensive work, consuming work. The predators, we have always known, hate all work, hate all reciprocity. Not for them the giving of care to the land so the land may give in patient return. Their women first, then any strangers they encounter on the road, they turn into slaves to do their work: for that stupid injustice is also a sacred part of the predators' religion, that religion that is the cult of slavery.

There were five boats coming up the river. They came close together, abreast almost. Each long boat carried a hundred men—more, maybe thirty more. The captives sat below their captors, their bodies immobilized from the thighs down by rigid planks of young bamboo tied in measured bundles across the width of each boat. Only the captives worked at the oars. The predators stood over them and swung their whips at them as the spirit moved them,

275

whips made of iron chain, not leather; or they simply rested in the shade of shelters on the boats. Each boat carried ten predators. Only ten.

We waited till they reached the river Osu's narrowest part, where only one of their boats could pass easily at a time. There they broke apart and formed a line. Seven shots cracked the afternoon silence. Beautiful shots, they brought down five of the predators in that first boat alone. In that moment the predators had yet to see us. The five who remained standing in the first boat seized their guns, but instead of shooting in our direction they commenced a massacre of their captives. Abena and Ona reached a decision simultaneously. Moving from their safety they showed themselves plainly to the predators in the boats. For Ona the decision was close to fatal. The first predator to see her took swift aim and shot at her. It was an expert's kind of shot. Ona fell toward Abena. Abena went down beside her and held her flat against the earth till Sobo and Nsa reached them with help, crawling on their bellies to keep under the predators' deadly fire.

Now that the predators could see us they turned from their captives and aimed all their guns at us. Surprisingly good the predators were at marksmanship, but they were on water, caught between the river's pinching banks; we were on firm land.

The first boat reached the left bank first. Only two of the predators were left alive on it, and already they were bleeding so profusely it was clear they would not see another of their Allah's days.

276

It was work of extreme difficulty reaching the first boat. On the others the surviving predators—three were left on the second, six on the third, two on the fourth, four on the fifth—placed themselves next to the rowing captives, using them as shields. We could not continue shooting; any attempt we made to reach the stranded first boat would expose us to the fire from the surviving predators.

It was the captives themselves who ended their captors' hope. In the second boat and the fourth we saw the captives, as if they had breathed together in the planning of the move, stop rowing to seize the predators now cowering so close to them, then attempt to strangle them. The struggle was most unequal. The captives were fixed to the boat from their waists down, and only two could join strength against their fully mobile captors at a time. Still, determination gave the captives strength, and the six in the second boat holding the three predators would have finished strangling them had not the other remaining predators returned to their abandoned plans for massacre. Still using the captives as shields, but taking care to stay safe from their reach, the predators now turned their guns solely against the captives.

"Shoot, then!" Juma told us. Our aim was good, but still the massacre of captives was terrible before we had wiped out the last predator. Of captives there had been six hundred and more. Those left were five hundred only; death had eaten too well.

Of the five hundred thirty after hearing our news chose to come with us: twenty-four women, the remainder men.

All the rest, memories of home called them also back to the shattered life. They returned. We returned. There was more work, unending work against destruction.

And the first ambush: here the predators had ravaged seven peaceful towns, towns still ignorant of guns, and they had taken fifty humans, marching them toward another bargain with the white destroyers on the coast. Four long limbs we turned ourselves into that day for fighting, and we stretched them, two on either side of the predators' road. Juma led the first arm, Abena took the second. Across the road from Juma Kakra led the third arm. This was the first test of her readiness: a happy test. Down the road from Kakra the people in the fourth limb listened to Ulimboka.

We had all learned and come to like this dance taught us by Juma, and we danced it well. Juma and Kakra waited till the line of fifty captives bound to wood had passed them completely. Five predators, together with eight askaris, drove the slaves. Doubtless they hoped to find more victims before they reached the coast.

When their line was exactly midway between Juma and Abena, between Kakra and Ulimboka, Mokili listening to Abena fired the first shot. A silence followed that. Alarmed, but unable to judge the magnitude of danger to themselves, the predators called their line to a halt by the left side of the road. They pushed the captives down in the tall grass away from sight, then stood ready to fight the invisible source of danger. Two askaris were left standing over the captives, watching. The rest, six askaris, five predators, began to move circumspectly forward along the left side of the road.

278

Another shot. This time it was Ude, listening to Kakra, who fired. It was a distant shot, but Ude has a wizard's eye. One predator fell. Like a beast in panic the predators together turned in the direction of that second shot, forgetting the first. They began running in that direction. They did not run far. Naita, listening to Ulimboka, fired now. Immediately, Kenia and Kwesi from the same direction fired too. From up the road Juma waited till the predators and their askaris were moving toward Ulimboka's limb. Then all his group fired and two more, a predator and an askari, stumbled to the ground. Now the predators and their askaris had become a gathering without centre. Wheeling and turning to face each new shot, they exhausted their remaining strength in futile motion. Before we descended on them to finish their execution they had used all their bullets hunting phantoms.

Three of the captives we freed—two women, one man—joined us. The others heard calls from home. They went.

But we should not stop the onward flow of work with overlong remembrance of single battles won, of new people welcomed, of the increase of courage for the journeys of the way. For this is mere beginning, not a time for the satisfaction of sweet remembrances.

# 7

# the voice

The time also came when the sickness of nostalgia descended tearing at our group, caught one of us and turned him backward and made him a child again hankering after situations forever lost, craving the love of blood relatives better in his remembering mind than they could ever have been in their own flesh. It is possible to bring the adult spirit out of unreasoned nostalgia, but what energy of mind can move the contrary spirit so strongly drawn into infancy that the call he hears becomes inseparable from that of filial duty?

Dovi was the one who went from us; went blindly, in hope, back to Anoa and all the arrangements there, oblivious of our safety, past caring about the unprotected beginnings of the paths to the way. Dovi went, and by his going raised the suspicion of parasites against us and brought our future rushing headlong into a present not yet completely ready to receive it.

It is true Dovi had suffered—but if the pain of one single

person preoccupies our mind and obliterates our judgement, what shall we bring to the understanding of a people entire turned prey to white destruction? Dovi had suffered, but who is it saying any of us have been alone in our suffering?

Among the twenty of us who in that last season of initiations went beyond the last of the open initiations still unsatisfied with what we knew and found the cause of our continuing mindhunger in the fifth grove, among the twenty there was the closeness of separate bodies breathing from a single soul. Within that oneness of the best of friendships there were minds and emotions drawn to each other with a strength intenser than the general love. Between Dovi and Tawia there had been just such a power of affection.

Dovi's spirit was always one to find its most frequent centre outside of himself. In life Tawia was that most frequent centre. But that day when we were forced onto destruction's ship Tawia's spirit refused the threat of exile. John, the zombi eager to do the destroyers' slavedriving work, together with his master the destroyer killed Tawia at the rock that searing day and Dovi himself, his head was cracked with a whip's heavy butt. Dovi's body recovered, but his spirit never came out of the despair of the bereaved, for the balance of his spirit was gone with Tawia. Without her his will became a mere wavering thing between the things the growing adult knew he should do and the enchanting comfort of infancy remembered blindly as a time of love unmixed.

In Dovi's wavering he was often overwhelmed with a

massive feeling of his own ingratitude, a sense of having abandoned the providers who had sweetened his infancy. Reasoning words of persuasion were mere impotent air before the strength of his feeling. The safety of other seers, other hearers, the longer keeping of the utterers' secrecy, so necessary in the time of our preparation, none of this had any force against the push of Dovi's deep nostalgia wearing duty's face.

The day came when Dovi broke his usual silence and told us again he had made up his mind to go. No one tried any more to turn the spirit whose urge was now so clearly, so strongly away from us. No one tried any more to remind Dovi of our continuing need of the protection of secrecy until full preparation should give us necessary strength to move harder against destruction.

One of us only, in momentary anger, said it was our duty to our own survival to force Dovi to remain. Abena talked long against this anger, and Isanusi gave her words support. Better, they said, better to lose the whole advantage of our secrecy, better to forego the hope of completely surprising the destroyers again together with their zombi allies among our people, than to keep an unwilling soul with us in our work, blasting our necessary unity, negating our strength. The spirit straining to go from us, we should let it go.

We left Dovi with the knowledge of our acquiescence, left him to himself. In three nights he was gone.

Fragile indeed the strength, small the quantity, low the intensity of energy springing in the mind alone. Against it how potent, how huge, how crudely powerful the energies surging from the body's blindest needs. How should we rail against Dovi's dangerous weakness as if it were some peculiar crime of his lonely self? Many still within their minds recognise what is good, what they would want to do if . . . If their bodies' demands, if the needs of the stomach and the more constant needs of the heart, if these heavier needs were not of a kind always to overwhelm the mind's most beautiful recognition. If . . .

Dovi was not ignorant. His mind knew the possibility of the way, saw the inherent beauty of a new life lived together with other minds dedicated to finding paths against the white destroyers' road, against the white promise of our perdition. But joined to a creator's mind Dovi had a consumer's feelings: dense, heavy, crass, even their energy a lumpen force, their inertia dragging his uncertain mind from the immediate difficulty of the tasks of creation, enticing him to let his soul sink sweetly into the solidity of the present, potent ugliness of the destroyers' white road. He saw the choice before him. We held out to him a companionship whose root was not in the potency of perishable things but simply in the mind's recognition of our own good even in this present time of our continuing destruction. This is no companionship with matter for attracting heavy bodies in their downward motion to their graves. This is no dance for zombis. Ours is a companionship of the mind willing to find our way again against the luring softness of immediate situations made garish by the white destroyers, the better to blind unwary lookers; ours is a companionship of the spirit willing to use its energy to

283

survive the immediate harshness of efforts to find liberating paths to our way, the way.

So our appeal was to Dovi's mind. Being such, it depended —so pathetic, yes, is the first dependence, that necessary dependence of all creation's beginnings—on the strength of his mind, on how clearly, how constantly that mind itself felt called to a vocation along our way, the way.

But the call of death, the white destroyers' overwhelming noise, is powerful beyond the resistance even of the creator's mind in this present situation if the creator be trapped alone in spirit. The call of death is a multiple call, a noise of triumphant loudness potent because it does not need dependence on any delicate beauty of the mind's recognition; the white road is triumphant now because it is not attached to the long, difficult striving of the soul against the simple mortality of the flesh it inhabits. The white destroyers' noise is a heavy appeal, the call of stone, a leaden beckoning to flesh already inclined to death. Locked to the heavy body's every craving, the white road rejoices in the use of all the abundant energies servant to such craving: that is one root of death's potency.

Our call to Dovi was a welcome to mere truth needing no decoration, truth taking all its sweetness from necessary action against falsehood. Against our call the noise of the white road had skill to merge itself into the sweetness of infant dreams, the illusion of remembered love even where there had been nothing but a fearful possessiveness, the hallucination of love in a universe of cut-off people, the magic dream of beauty when all real beauty—the working

284

together of our whole people along our way—had long been murdered under the heavy stones brought against us by the white destroyers stalking this land.

Ah, the perception of beauty is so dependent on the soul's seeing, on the soul's hearing. A shrunken soul, shrunken from the way, may see the disaster of families cut off from other families around and still think their fearful huddling together against others is some kind of love, not hate made visible. Shrunken souls, turned from our way, may see the frightened efforts of lone men, lone women, lone little blood groups, to survive in surroundings turned dangerous by the white destroyers' instruments of triumphant hate, and in their shrunkenness such souls can call the disaster beauty, call it love. For souls reduced near death can see beauty even in the triumph of ugliness itself, can see love in all-pervading hate: so far is their vision cut off from any truth, so far are they from the way.

We depend on no such potency. No illusions brought us here, none support our work. We offer none of the comfort destroyed minds find in lies. We could not hold Dovi back, for his soul was open only to the loud shout of tired blood.

"My mother . . ." as if in this whole universe there were no mother but his particular mother.

"My father . . ." as if he were the only son, his father the only father in the world.

"My family . . ." the selfish desire of the cut-off spirit was so strong in him.

So in the end we did not try to keep him away from his desire, not even in consideration for the safety of our work, after we were certain of his soul's direction. Our way is not a road for unwilling souls. The way is not the road of coercion.

What we could do in the knowledge of Dovi's going we did. The places we had shared with him we took care to make safe against surprise. Where defense was uncertain in case of attack we abandoned the place completely. A guard stood awake along each possible path to our secrecy, while we continued, hastened the work of preparation.

Of Dovi himself what more is there to say? Idawa went to Anoa. On her return she brought us saddening news only days after Dovi had gone home thinking he could stay peacefully in that particular enclosure. He had expressed no desire to see anyone, anything beside the circle of his particular blood family. It was this blood family itself that worked his betrayal.

Hau! What a shrivelling there has been in the spirits of our people; what a destructive fragmentation of our soul! Hear this: Dovi's father and his mother too, it had been their long hope to see their son grow into something to ensure their survival in spite of everything, their private comfort—just so short, so mediocre, so normal their vision was. After the king Koranche had sold us to destruction Dovi's parents walked in the general ignorance of our real fate, and they felt keenly the sorrow of the bereaved. That sorrow, it grew gentler with the flow of succeeding days, but the fear of hunger, it grew greater, not less. The king, on the advise of the flatterer Otumfur, did a clever

286

thing. Pretending ignorance of our fate compounded with sorrow on our account, the king Koranche offered all our parents the option of his support and his protection. Most in taciturn suspicion preferred to keep their distance from the court, but some, Dovi's loved ones first among them, had accepted the lazy offer.

Surprised now at their mourned son's reappearance, a reappearance so menacing, and feeling completely disoriented by even the little he chose to tell them of the truth, they regarded him with the pity of the sane and felt it their duty to share the secrecy he so craved with their friend the king.

Koranche the king became afraid. Already wild dreams had punctured his rest too many moons going, too many coming. In these dreams a figure such as the mad Isanusi followed him inexorably and even without opening his grim mouth threatened the fleeing king with dissolution. Now such was the strength of Koranche's obsession with Isanusi his spirit prompted him to find out from the surprising Dovi only one thing: where was Isanusi?

To a casual question asked about the rest of us Dovi had told the king Koranche a storm had drowned us, he alone surviving, how, he could not say. The king had not been concerned about the truth or falsehood of that wonderful salvation, but to Dovi's initial denial of knowledge concerning Isanusi's secrecy the king opposed an unshakeable disbelief. In the end the king had Dovi given a whole calabash full of the water from boiled etsa bark.

"Drink," Dovi was told, "then tell the truth. The truth will free your entrails and you will know no harm."

287

Dovi did not drink the etsa water. He told the king Koranche where in the fifth grove Isanusi could be found, told and in the telling wept tears of childish rage. Now the king Koranche swore to find Isanusi, for, said the king, Isanusi had used the craft of sorcery to plague too many of his nights, and he was certain he the king was bound to die unless Isanusi could be found.

Seven successive nights the king Koranche woke screaming after dreaming a recurring dream. In form his nightmare changed; its essence was always the same. In it Isanusi sat implacable upon a mountain high above the palace staring downward at the king, and cold was Isanusi's anger. From his open eyes something dark flowed as Isanusi continued to stare. The dark substance reached the ground at the foot of the mountain, came down and flowed steadily, inexorably against the palace and against the king within it. When the dark thing reached the palace the king Koranche saw clearly what it was: a living stream of men without end. Each looked exactly like Isanusi. Each approached the king in his palace with the same steady, direct, disrespectful look Koranche had hated so in Isanusi. The king tried escape but his limbs refused him movement. He shouted for help. No one came but the impotent flatterer Otumfur. He shouted more loudly for help. From far beyond Poano a thousand thousand white men began their coming in a thousand ships with a thousand thousand arms to help the king. But the white ships must come over slow expanses of water, and the endless black flow of Isanusi's coming over land from the mountain down, the first among them

288

were already inside the palace. Fear made the dreaming king scream—a loud scream waking all in the palace, the sweating king himself last of all.

The king Koranche consulted every healer who did not arrange to disappear at news of his need. His nightmares continued. The king Koranche sought counsel and aid from his friends, the white destroyers. The white destroyers asked the king Koranche a simple, direct question, a question flying straight from their spirit's nature: why not make immediate plans to kill the man Isanusi? That answering question turned the king into a praise-singer singing the white destroyers' wisdom.

The great gong was beaten. Those who went to hear the king's message were told brave men were being sought to penetrate the groves, even into the fifth grove itself—a gasp—for the capture of the mad Isanusi. The people stayed silent till there were no more words to hear. Then they went home.

Koranche in his embarrassment turned as usual to his counsellors the white destroyers. What courage and a sense of duty had been powerless to do, said the white destroyers, greed could be counted on to do. The lesser gong was beaten. Children returned home to their parents with the king's message: whoever on his own sought and destroyed Isanusi and brought his head to the palace would for the balance of his life be given all the food, all the white men's drink he could ever crave for himself. Whoever chose to undertake Isanusi's killing was to go first to the palace. There he would be given a gun, powder and sufficient

289

bullets, for as for arrows and spears, the king had it reported they could do nothing against Isanusi's wizardry.

One happy fool, son of another flattering parasite, seeing for himself a future choked with food and drink, turned himself into a tool for cowardly royalty. This young man Bofo, two groups older than ourselves, undertook to be a killer—for things. He went to the palace for his promised gun, his powder and a belt of bullets. He also remembered to ask for a jar of the destroyers' drink, for Bofo was not fool enough to trust his own natural courage. Thus completely armed, the killer started out, seeking in the heat of his greed something he had never before thought to seek: the fifth grove. Idawa preceded the killer, told us of his coming, and helped us prepare for him.

The fifth grove is not a place of visible paths. Dwellers there have always been quiet movers, disturbing nothing they need not disturb. Yet even here the eye searching for easy access is drawn naturally to openings between plants, openings that would be the beginning of paths and obvious passages if others than seers, hearers and utterers had heard the voices of their soul calling them this way.

Of these openings we selected the easiest to the lazy eye, the one that gave most direct access from Anoa. In one afternoon we built a shelter of old, dry wood and grass, badly hidden among the trees at the grove's beginning. Under the tree closest to the shelter we cleared a space and cleaned it, a perfect place for a tired body's rest. There was work for carvers, brief work, for the likeness they made of Isanusi did not have to be exact. The mercenary killer would not seek closeness to his quarry; in his mind the image of Isanusi was already strong. It would not occur to him to doubt the sleeping form was his. There was work for everyone, heavy work, for the hole we dug before Isanusi's effigy had to be too deep for any man to climb out of unaided, and three grown men's length across its centre. All that earth we carried away from the hole. Above the hole we spread thin soil on chenchen cloth sewn together, and above the soil rough patches of fresh moss.

The killer Bofo had no eye for traps, for he was stalking an easy victim when he came. We watched him come from the second grove, in a hurry till he penetrated the fourth. At the margins of the fourth he grew more circumspect, though still reluctant to lose his headlong speed. Then he saw in the distance the lone form lying in repose underneath the tree in the prepared space. Like an ancient panther Bofo stalked nearer the lifeless form, careful of noises, trusting in the power of his gun. He drew closer than the length of twenty adults. He raised his gun, took eager aim and fired. Shaking with the beginning hunter's excitement he filled the gun again, aimed and fired, filled, aimed and fired a third time. Underneath the tree the form made no motion. Among the watchers none of us made the slightest noise. The whole grove belonged to the killer to triumph in. In his elation, his task to his mind already accomplished, he threw down the now useless gun. He did not go directly to gather up the victim he had shot. First he danced a happy little dance to gratulate himself. Music he did not have there, but his lone voice was sufficient to his purpose:

he gave himself resounding appellations of bravery, praise names borrowed from the remembrance of our greatest fighters gone—the killer Bofo took them all to boost his manic leaping. The dance over, the killer bounded toward his silent prey, bounded and fell headlong into the hole awaiting him.

Isanusi had asked one favour: we should let him fight his would-be killer to the death. We had counseled a direct execution, for Isanusi was a thinking man arrived at the necessity of fighting, not a natural fighter who had been forced by circumstance to learn to think. Oko begged Isanusi to let the work of fighting with the hands devolve upon himself—in vain. Isanusi found our fears for him insulting first to ourselves—that we could think we could not do without him, and to himself—that we assumed he was bound to lose against his younger enemy. Against the force of Isanusi's words we had no reasonable answer, only our mute affection.

Isanusi walked from his safety among the trees, walked till he reached the hole and jumped into it to face his would-be murderer. We ourselves, all save the watchers over the paths, we came out from the secrecy of the grove after Isanusi. When we came to the hole's lip we stood above the two within and watched the killer and his prey.

The fight itself was brief. Fear at first immobilized the killer when, after seeing the man he supposed he had killed descend into this hole after him, he raised his eyes and saw above him seventy steady, staring eyes where he had expected no humans at all. Yet despair did not sap the killer's strength; it increased it. His body, already much fuller if its growth than his mind, was gorged with the blood on anger and the fear of danger. A heavy body it was, far more massive than Isanusi's slender frame. In the fighting the killer's aim was plain: he would fling his weight relentlessly against his prey, force him down with the sheer weight of his mass, then choke him dead. The first time he leapt at Isanusi it was with a cry part way between fear and defiance. Isanusi, he fought like a dancer, calmly, always waiting till another moment's waiting would have been disastrous, then stepping aside and letting the killer's impetus take him past in frustrated violence. The killer turned, leaped, missed, turned again and leaped again. He missed a third, a fourth and a sixth time, but he did not change his aim. His hope in fact grew higher, for every successive miss brought his timing just a little closer to success. The seventh time he actually brought his body crashing into Isanusi's, and Isanusi had some difficulty twisting free. Isanusi stood waiting in the centre of the hole. The sweating killer had hurled himself with such force he had reached the side of the hole opposite from where he had sprung. Now, turning with no perceptible rest, he charged back with fantastic force, surprising us the watchers with his speed and strength, filling our minds with fear.

Isanusi did not move to escape the killer's thrust. It seemed to us he too had been surprised by the killer's suddenness. The killer's body drove itself with brute violence against Isanusi's. Isanusi fell backward in the hole, fell under the killer's massive force. This was no simple fall of the vanquished, however. In his falling Isanusi had taken care first to take firm hold of the shoulder straps on the hunter's uniform the killer Bofo wore. Falling, Isanusi also bent his left knee and placed the foot against the killer Bofo's groin. When Isanusi's back touched the ground he pulled hard, once only, on the killer's clothing. In that same motion he pulled his left leg straight and upright. The killer's body, sent hurtling with its own speed and that imparted to it by Isanusi, rammed like cannon shot into the hole's stone-studded side.

So much violence, so much force had gone into that single throw. The killer hit the wall first with the top of his head, just above the occiput. The impact went full against the line of his spine. Thick and heavy the killer Bofo's neck was, but not thick enough to save him. The string of his brain itself was snapped. A bone stuck displaced, peering through a hole in his neck, just above its junction with the head. Not much blood flowed from the broken killer's body, and even that little flowed from incomprehensible places: the eye, the ear, the anus, but not the killer's mouth, not his nose.

We took ropes and brought Isanusi out, and then the killer. Life still remained in that body, but it was life on its road to death. We built a carrier for him. Eight men taking turns carried him with quiet, careful speed into the most frequented part of the second grove. There the killer, without his gun, without his bullets, his life now completely gone, his eyes still surprised, his mouth gaping bloodless, was laid to rest, ready for quick discovery.

294

Abena shuddered with the day's remembrance long afterwards. Weeping she told Isanusi he had done a heady, foolish thing, and she did not rest till she had raised a conversation at the end of which we all agreed we should not make the destruction of destroyers and their tools a thing of chances, but should always find the quickest, surest way to wipe them out. Isanusi admitted he had been at fault, that it had been a risky thing to do. But he repeated there had been that in him which would have remained forever paralysed with doubt had he escaped that particular confrontation that day. Against such words no one brought more words.

Only one other imbecile came individually to hunt Isanusi in hopes to win himself a lazy life. This was a man unknown to any in Anoa, an adventurer from Poano, one of that breed of parasites with no purpose in life save the running after money and things. This man had heard there were prizes to be had for a killing, and he had come. He too was given a new gun, powder and a sufficiency of bullets. He did not reach the third grove even. From an alari branch Kenia placed just one bullet dead between the second would-be killer's eyes. We took the body and left it in the second grove, in exactly the same position as his predecessor Bofo.

The quick death of the king's hired murderers, together with the general lack of knowledge concerning the real circumstances of their end, turned the king into a full-blown, raving lunatic. Contradictory impulses invaded him close upon each other, often simultaneously, and pushed him into endless activity. He could not sleep, no matter what large quantities of the white destroyers' drink he imbibed to tranquilize his raging spirit. Voices urged him to the doing of wild things if he wished to escape instant death. One voice he heard ordered the confined Dovi freed. He had him freed. In another half day the same voice had turned against Dovi and Koranche was howling for his blood, but Dovi was not to be found in Anoa.

Dovi returned seeking us. Wandering lost near the shelters he had known, he was caught unresisting, brought blindfolded into a clearing he would have no way to recognise, a place between the fifth grove and the fourth, but out to the falling. There in the clearing we let Dovi see and hear again. What he saw was our indifference to his fate, answering his to ours. What we told him was this: in his going he had made it absolutely clear his personal happiness was greater in his mind than the group's continuation in our chosen work. As long as he had supposed there was something still left for him in the old life at Anoa, he knew no care for the group. For him then the group was merely a thing to be used in the pursuit of his individual happiness.

We asked Dovi no questions. We told him simply there could be no possibility of any new understanding between himself and us. We told him he could be of no help to us seeking us out in his confusion. We told him to the extent he forced us to defend ourselves against his selfish turmoil, we would not hesitate to do so. Ashale could not help advising Dovi to go join the white destroyers' and the

296

king's askaris or their traders; we were not dealers in articles of personal comfort. We sent Dovi on his way out of the grove again.

The third attempt against Isanusi was longer in its preparation. Two weeks passed after the execution of the lone adventurer from Poano before Isanusi's and our safety was threatened again. This time six men came on the hunt: five black men, three of them askaris, two of them young relatives of parasites, all five listening to a white destroyer, the hunter living by the river near the landing place. The six, they too had expected to find a lone quarry. Even so, the white hunter had taken care to place himself far behind his helpers—that was how he escaped. The battle with the five cost us two lives—Ngazi fell with Inse—and took time, for the five knew something of fighting and were skilled in the finding of expert cover. The white hunter fled back to his safety when it grew clear there was not only one man here waiting to be killed. We had grown beyond another piece of our secrecy.

That night, after the execution of the five askaris and the flight of the white hunter, in the best darkness of that night a voice crossed Anoa, a voice clear, unhurried yet secret still, and untrappable. It was a voice speaking to the people, calling memory to a remembrance of our way, calling vision to its lost clarity in each succeeding day. The voice spoke to the people of a people flowing into destruction. The voice urged a turn, a turning against destruction's whiteness and the accomplices of its success: bloated kings and parasites, bodies depleted of soul, minds

297

unconnected to the whole, unconnected to the way.

Other voices, secret voices, sought open ears every day among the people, sought them speaking in quiet whispers, requested secrecy and began with them the long, patient work: work of persuasion, work of remembrance, work preparing paths to the way again.

Soon it was not the smallness of our beginning we feared but the dangers of too rapid growth, for our work itself brought growth. True, even the slaves caught in their own homes and delivered into captivity, most, far the greater number always turned homeward on finding their unexpected liberation. Into whatever illusions they were fated to walk, we could only talk gently to them of what we knew, then bid them good journeys. But the strongest, the quickest in mind and body, they chose to stay. From the lands to the falling, far beyond even Ulimboka's knowledge, we came back first with thirty, ten another time, twos and threes later. Here in the fifth grove itself many have come who have helped us in secrecy at Anoa, and from Poano we have taken in small groups as accident or treachery threatened their useful secrecy.

Nor is that all. A happy discovery this: that even among zombis working for the white destroyers a body is found now and then inhabited by its own spirit living still though six-sevenths murdered, a spirit willing to move if it can find its destination, a spirit still able to move. Juma has not remained the only one. Two more askaris have come to us, and four more work still among other askaris, their secrecy not yet broken.

Anxiety there is: always there are those spirits forever hypnotized, eternally trapped to work for the white destroyers, their wills a plaything in alien hands. Always they will be thrown against us, ah! the heavy weight of remembrance. Isanusi is gone, his secrecy shattered by the false zealot Fosu. And yet our work is no vocation to suspicion against ourselves. We shall continue trusting those among us in whom the spirit has not entirely lost remembrance of the way. We shall call to them. Some we will find whose intimations of remembrance will turn intenser, turn into conscious thought, turn from thought to action. That is our vocation, not the crippling suspicion that brings the fear of motion. We are not a people of stagnant waters. We are of the moving stream, rememberers of the way.

To return. The king Koranche and his princes and his parasites, following counsel from their friends the white destroyers, began to swell the number of their askaris. A hundred and more new men they found, some bribed with promises of easy food and drink, some coerced by remissions of long, intractable debts. The older askaris taught the new the stiff walk of death and also the firing of guns. At night the askaris were set to guard the palace, the white destroyers' homes, the few places in the town where relatives of parasites fearful for their safety lived, and above all to comb the town searching to silence the voice telling truth in the darkness of nights.

It was at this time that Fosu came to join us—heavy time, heavy in the end this coming was, but how could we have known? It would have been unreasoning suspicion not to believe him those first days of his coming. It seemed so true then, what he had to say of his own family, the loss of loved ones. And the news he brought us of the king's preparations, of the numbers of white destroyers newly brought in to give counsel to the king and his princes and his parasites at Anoa of the forcing of strong men into an army to be sent against Isanusi, even of the bringing of slave askaris from the stone place at Poano, now rebuilt—all that was true. How could we in those days have known that Fosu's furious coming and his unctuous vows of undying fidelity, that they also were a part of the preparation for Isanusi's destruction?

It was the zealot Fosu, false traveller along the way, dog working for destroyers, who betrayed Isanusi, delivered him into the hands of death, and taught us the bitterness of deep suspicion. Fosu had come to us speaking words of fire. The king had shattered his family, he claimed, sold a generation not yet tested, and blighted all his future hope. One present hope only he still had left: vengeance against the king. He had heard the voice in the night, the untrapped voice calling together those determined to clear the land of destroyers and the parasites, helpers to destroyers. Other, secret voices he had sought out had given him nothing definite to follow, but their quiet news gave him sufficient indications to put him on his desired path.

Ankoanda had looked directly at Fosu's face that first day and declared: "Our trust should not be so quick." But then Idawa next time she returned brought news, and

300

the news supported the newcomer: his family had indeed lost numbers, though not a whole generation, and in all of Poano no one seemed to know where they had disappeared. It was hard, those days, deciding between a just suspicion and the unnecessary caution of those afraid of motion. In the end we decided for motion, for the acceptance of new members hearing the call of the way, provided they too were ready to move with us, ready to test themselves in necessary action.

Fosu brought us serious news: the destroyers, seeing a future imminent with trouble for themselves, had lately brought in a heavy load of arms in preparation for coming strife. These arms had not been brought into Anoa itself— there was great uncertainty about the palace as a place of safety—but had been hidden on a hill not too far from the river, on the side to the rising.

Three chose to go with Fosu as their guide to examine the place: Isanusi, Juma, and the girl whose precocious skill had begun to amaze us all, Kisa. They chose weapons and set out in the evening.

Fosu led them into a trap. The waiting destroyer and his askaris waiting on the river bank did not have patience enough to wait for all four to get down from the canoe. Fosu had gone down first. Isanusi was about to follow when three guns sounded at once from the trees above the canoe.

Isanusi's understanding was quick. He himself got down after Fosu to make sure the traitor could not escape to bring final misfortune against all our group. Isanusi in the instant of his landing turned his gun against Fosu and shot him dead. Then he pushed the canoe with all his strength back into the river's stream. A peremptory shout told Juma and Kisa to return at once with the heavy news of betrayal. The two rowed past the overhanging cliff beyond which no askari bullet could reach them. As for Isanusi himself, how he died we do not know exactly. But this we know: he held the askaris and their master the white hunter impotent to chase after Kisa and Juma after he had killed the traitor Fosu. Nor was Fosu the last zombi he killed. There was a funeral for two askaris the day following, and when finally we surprised the white hunter we saw he too had been wounded—there was no doubt on which day.

Juma and Kisa came back to us late, for they had had to go a circuitous journey to get back. We worked fast breaking shelter where Fosu had known us, while ten of us went circumspectly across the river at the first ford above Anoa and circled down to the place of betrayal. Signs of recent struggle were all that remained: blood on the soil, bruised saplings, the beaten undergrowth. There were no bodies, neither Isanusi's, nor the traitor Fosu's, nor any other.

Before anger at Fosu's treachery, before sorrow at Isanusi's death could turn into the ashen paralysis of will that makes all action impossible we moved against our sorrow's cause, against betrayal's instigator. In our motion we took the most dangerous first, descending from the hardest of our tasks into the easiest—our meeting with the king Koranche.

The white hunter, he lived on the river bank below the palace, not far from the landing place of the white destroyers' ship. We took him first. We found three askaris that night guarding the white hunter's yard. From our secrecy among the trees Oko took a huge stone and with all the power in his arms tossed it crashing against the back wall of the hunter's yard. Leaving the entrance, two of the askari guards went right, and right again, seeking the noise's cause. Oko waited till they had finished their inspection, found nothing and returned to the entrance. Then he tossed another, huger stone. The noise it made was louder. The night was dark. One askari went within the yard and came back with a flaming torch. Together with a companion he went again from the entrance seeking the noise's source.

"Shoot into the light," Juma said. Ashale fired, Abena fired, Kwesi fired, Kgosana fired, Sobo fired, Kamara fired, and Juma fired, so fast and so close together the sound was like one long rent in the night. The torch fell sputtering on the ground. In a moment it had died completely.

"Now, before they bring more of their lights," Juma said. We moved, quietly but swiftly, to the left of the entrance, away from the askaris' path. We waited by the side wall there till the commotion within the yard died down and men rushed out carrying torches. We heard their voices, but not the hunter's. We waited till the servants and askaris with their torches had run out in the direction of the fallen askaris, then we raced into the yard itself.

The hunter's room was not hard to find—there was only one complete house in the yard, the rest being only sheds and large storerooms. We did not enter the hunter's room. We stood outside the door, waiting. A short wait: the

303

hunter had merely been getting himself ready. He strode out through his doorway muttering destroyers' words to himself. Five bullets entered his huge body, and the askaris, confused by the swiftness of everything this night, could do nothing to delay our withdrawal.

We found the white trader's place closed—no great surprise—and only two askaris, one already sleep, remained at the gate. We left them alone. This feast night we would find their master at the palace.

At the palace it had not been our intention to start the fighting at the gate, but an askari chancing to see Kibaden and Okai climbing the back wall fired at them. Juma gave us the sign for a change of plans and we rushed through the gate—a dangerous action, but now unavoidable.

The king Koranche had been feasting with his friend the white trader. There was another destroyer with them, the priest of their childish religion. They had eaten long since, drunk their fill and now were merely playing with dregs, looking heavy-eyed at young dancers dancing the dance of virginity at this strange time. None of the revellers had felt disturbed at the sound of shooting outside, to judge from the mood we caught them in, though all must have heard everything clearly. Perhaps they imagined it was merely something unimportant to them, the askaris shooting people in their own excitement. Immense was their surprise in the light of all the torches at their feast to see thirty armed avengers burst in against their pleasure.

As for the king Koranche, we did not shoot him there and then. By the time we had finished destroying the destroyers his guests together with the askaris still intent on murder, it was nearing dawn. We brought the king Koranche, Otumfur his chief flatterer, together with Tumbolangu, Buanyi, Kuondo and other flatterer parasites from the court to the largest of the public places. We had found the great drums and brought them also. Unusual time this was, but we beat the drums and the people woke to find out what new message could have come with such unwonted urgency.

The first to speak to the people was Abena. To begin she asked forgiveness for the suddenness of their awakening this night. Of the events of this night themselves she spoke briefly only, then moved on to causes. She told the people the causes of these events and other recent events were distant, deep as our roots themselves. She called the people to remember the recent voices crossing the night, to remember the truth they carried. She spoke of the disease of parasites eating our people, inviting whites to bring destruction against our land. Then she asked who remember-ed the dance of love, the dance of our age's final initiation, asked who remembered its aftermath. But the people had no wish to utter their uncertain knowledge. In wonder they asked to hear the truth.

"Ask the king," Abena said. Calm her voice was, sure her step as she took Koranche's hand like a loving mother. "Here stands the king. Ask him."

He did talk, the king Koranche. Why, it was impossible to tell. Nor was it false, the confession he made, though he sought now to blame the drink he loved so well, now the greed of his courtiers. He told the assembled people of the feast he had arranged for us his children on his white friends' ship, of its aftermath, and even of the wealth it brought him and his courtiers. The king told of other disappearances among our people, other trials for uncommited crimes. All the while he stared at those of us he could see, at Abena most amazedly. It seemed from time to time as if he would interrupt his confession to ask Abena something, but always his question ended at its beginning: "But how . . . . how . . . . but . . . . how?"

Abena herself shot the king Koranche dead at the end of his tale. The parasites also we executed immediately after they had given witness of their service to destruction. Abena could speak no more, so heavy was the grief brought by remembrance, but Ndlela undertook to finish the explanation she had begun.

"We have been thrown into death," he told the people, "we have seen its whiteness and yet escaped it. The further meaning of our lives is the halting of this white destruction turned against us, the removal of parasites whose greed welcomes destruction's white empire. Endless our struggle must seem to those whose vision reaches only to the end of today. But those with ears connected to our soul will hear a message calling us to a better life, to a life closer to our ancient way, to a preparation for the best, the only living way. It is not vengeance for our own single selves we have been seeking in this work. Those who can see, those able to hear, let them hear this: we are preparers of paths to the way that was our way; it will be our way again."

Dawn had come. The night's work was done, and we would have our dead to attend to. Voices crossed the dawn together, protected voices prophesying against destruction sitting heavy on our land; voices awakening the still sleeping against caretakers now turned sucking parasites; voices calling the living to the work of preparation, work against the road of death.

So that was the way Koranche the king died, confessing crimes he had sought to hide from our people. Laughable is the courage of kings and parasites, ludicrous indeed their puny bravery beside their greed's immensity. Now among the surviving hangers-on at court a fiery rivalry raged over the inheritance of the corpse's wealth. For the body was not yet in its shame-filled grave when disputations started between the parasites, each claiming to remember of a sudden some long promise made to him by Koranche of cloth or trinket or of rum. In the end they simply leapt beyond quarreling and fought each other seizing whatever their greed could reach. But what an enormity of senseless goods Koranche had accumulated in his palace! Under his own room he had had a huge cavern made. A thousand casks and hundreds more came out of that cavern, casks not of powder but of Koranche's beloved drink, the destroyers' rum. Cloth of colours bright to fascinate children's eyes set in adult heads; a thousand strings of beads and a hundred chains of falsely glittering gold and silver; brass pots and pans: the parasites scooped frantic armfuls and ran in trembling haste to hide their stolen goods at home.

307

The prince Bentum, renamed Bradford George, a cripple since his foolish leap against the fighter Oko in the stone place, unable to rise, watched the flatterers who should have helped him raging to steal his inheritance. Outside the palace walls the people stood in a comprehending silence, watching their caretakers eaten with the greed for trash. Bentum, Bradford George, lay powerless all through that day and the night following. With the next dawn the heat of recent events cleared from the minds of two of the parasites. Their greed satisfied for the present, they thought of the future and thinking frightened them. In this fright they went, the two, to the crippled prince and asked what new service he wished them to perform for him. Even in his resentful impotence the prince was obliged to be grateful. His wish was simple: send to the stone place at Poano to the whites in their rebuilt safety, and ask for help.

In three weeks the help the prince Bentum sought arrived from his friends the white destroyers: five new destroyers, soldiers all, together with a hundred new askaris carrying guns. The people watching saw naked the root of the new cripple king's power, saw and remembered the meaning of the voices walking secret among them in clear nights and quiet, whispering days. A ship came up the river to the landing place. On arrival it vomited a stream of guns and powder barrels.

Now the great drums and the great gong, the lesser drums and the lesser gong were no longer beaten because the king wanted them beaten, but because white destroyers wished their commands known. Bentum was a limp thing lying helpless wherever he was put, unable even to tell the spokes-men what was to be said. The great drums were beaten. The people were told the king wished—not the destroyers wished but the king wished—every home to send two grown men, for the king wished to expand his army. Strange army, not an army of all the people armed, but an army for the palace alone, an army obedient to the purposes of white destroyers. The voices walking in the night had spoken of the coming of glaring days, of the imminence of a whiter destruction. The voices crossing Anoa in the night called to listeners and asked if there were any left uncertain of the need for fighting against the invading white road.

We too have not been immune to the calls of the flesh, calls to tired minds to give up thoughts of creation when all around has become a praise song to destruction. Against the testing hardness of life on paths to the way strong and sweet indeed to the blinded mind are the calls of despair, and often has our contemplation of this present world and its arrangements lent heavy weight to such despair. Always, the counter to that despair has been in deeper contemplation of the universe, in contemplation bearing action. Let despair run its course; there is no need to cut it short. The present chances that frighten, let contemplation of these same chances be definite, clear, sustained and deep. That is what removes the fear. For the knowledge of all the chances piled against us fighting against death is also sure knowledge that if fear turned us from fighting the chances would not decrease just for that. They would increase. That other call, the raw fear of death? That too is strong, overpowering almost, at times. Again the exit from fear is to let the mind enjoy its freedom to thrust deep, contemplating that most frightening eventuality known to the cut-off self: death. For the mind untrammeled reaches this knowledge: that in these surroundings usurped by destruction the distinction is not between those dying and those not dying in our physical selves, but in the quality of the deaths we choose. There are those whose physical death is at the same time the triumph of destruction's road. There are those whose physical death is a necessary preparation for a profounder life, life of our people, life of our way, the way. And the call of cut-off love: the soft, abandoned, peaceful closeness of the bodies of loved ones even when the destroyers' triumph already whitens all love with hate: strong call indeed as long as the vision is truncated, small, detached from our larger wholeness, that call only serves the surrounding, alien glare of death. The call to procreation, the urge to leave peaceful life behind, to go back physically among our captured people, take love within the limits permitted it by hate, to create new life physically in the pallid glare of hate: again let the mind go forward into deeper thought. Parents willing to be slaves should have children born to be slaves, for they have deserved them. We do not refuse the call of love, but let it be love growing along the way, and if the paths to the way are all now the hard paths of constant fighting against triumphant destruction, we crave no other procreation than that possible along these paths. The children we aspire to bring here, we should not be for them merely a horrid warning. How beautiful if, growing up, they saw us always fighting death, and by their natural learning grew also along our way, and saw the way as the natural aim of life! The call of love, the call to procreation, we do not reject. But away from our way all this stunted love is hate wearing disguises, and away from the way procreation is not creation any more. Away from our way, the way, it is but stupid dross, the trap of death made spuriously enticing with thefts from the way of life itself.

In Anoa also the white destroyers now had a stone place built by humans forced to work, and they filled the place with guns against the surrounding world. The destroyers' commander told the parasites and the askaris of a plan to make all our land safe for the destroyers' road.

"We shall throw a ring of fire round the danger of rebellion here in these your forests," the destroyers' commander said. "Daily we shall make the ring smaller, tighten it till the last rebellious soul within it is choked, and the alliance of whites and the kings, the princes and the leaders of this place can progress in safety."

"We shall throw a ring of fire round the rebels," echoed the cripple king Bentum, renamed Bradford George.

"We shall throw a ring of fire around the brigand rebels," echoed in their turn the parasites.

Another of the white destroyers intoned—for he was the priest: "Our coming here is a high favour unto you, o heathen people. We bring you whiteness, which is godliness itself. We bring you the miracle of belief to save you from the damnation that is doubt. How could you have known before our coming unto you that a god invisible, unheard, but still known to us the whites, created this universe? How could you have known before our coming unto you that this god sent his only offspring to be a teacher unto you, an expert in how to suffer without resistance against those who make you suffer, without bitterness even, a teacher to teach you to aim for excruciating deaths after lives of pain? How, abandoned to yourselves, could you have known? Come and be saved. Come to the church, come into whiteness, come into purity. Throw your names to oblivion. Take white names, and denounce those who would fight against the whiteness of our new road. Rebels against whiteness they are, rebels against god."

The parasites—ah, how perfect for their lousy spirits they found christianity, this other religion for slaves—echoed the white destroyer priest: "Yes, we too believe there was this virgin who yet bore a baby to teach us suffering. This we believe for have not the whites said so? Who refuses to believe this is a soulless one, a rebel. The whites will help us clean the earth of rebels."

The white soldiers trained mercenaries and forced slaves in the crafts of death. The white priest clawed the air four times and pronounced assembled hundreds blest for the work of destruction, and destruction's forces came thinking to throw their ring of fire around us. Did the destroyers think the utterers fighting along paths to our way would stay gathered, easy prey to death? We spread so wide over the land their ring of fire could only be a thin, broken line of

312

stragglers peering through dark, beautiful nights searching for avengers they could not see. They came against us dragging the slow heaviness of power. Against them we turned the potency of swift movement. They came to surround us; we surrounded them in our nights, disappeared in daytime's glare, surrounded them again at night. They came to attack; they retreated defenders. They sought penetration; we welcomed their penetration till extension strained the destroyers' penetrating member, then we cut the member from its source.

True it is, the destroyers' thrust has also left holes bitter to remembrance. Death took the fighter Oko, disdainful of weapons, trusting most his hands and his natural strength. A destroyer's bullet found his eye and closed it. Suma too, and Pili, they are gone. Naita calls to Makaa in the night—in vain; that long companionship is also broken. Ndlela too has fallen seeking paths to the way again. Where is Ashale, where Kamara now? Soyinka, Kisa, Kakra, Okai, Badu, Ankonam, Ata also; new women, new men now take your pace, but our remembrance will always be heavy with your absence, and the presence of the things you did.

Know this: we continue. Destroyers have sent their thousand zombis against us. A hundred have run back to safety leaving guns and bullets for our use. No white destroyer was wise enough to tell them they would find not cowards but men breathing purpose, pathfinders along our people's way. Know this also: discouraging is loss, discouraging even the mere contemplation of the destroyers' massive weapons of death. But we have seen

313

the destroyers' force hurled against us turn to strength against the hurlers, and we know our way lies beyond despair: far beyond despair our way, the way.

"See the disease, and understand it well. It is important," Isanusi had said before his death, he too wondering how in the face of the invading strangers' success a deeper commitment could bring larger numbers to the way again. He had talked of another potent tool of death, the people-killing fascination with things, the hypnotism of the white destroyers' shiny things. Things not to bring people together, things not to be shared, things not to be the joiner of people's spirits, but things to set people apart from people, because such is the destroyers' arrangement—these are things only a few can have, things the many have to be without, corrosive envy's source. Against the disease Isanusi saw the cure: the hope of the way, creation of what is necessary, creation sufficient for sharing, creation that makes sharing easy, natural, reasonable, not an unbearable sacrifice, creation for community. How far lies the present road from that healing creativity, how disastrously far this invasion of goods deliberately made scarce, so that their mere possession raises men of the lowest mind and rapes the eyes of multitudes to ignorant admiration.

Idawa had answered Isanusi, and her answer had been a start on hopeful journeys, an answer bringing greater understanding. She spoke of those needing the white destroyers' shiny things to bring a feeling of worth into their lives, uttered their deep-rooted inferiority of soul, and called them lacking in the essence of humanity: woman-

314

hood in women, manhood in men. For which deficiency they must crave things to eke out their beings, things to fill holes in their spirits.

But understanding is a bare beginning only. Around us everything shouts loudest for despair, and our spirits in their rising must push against the heavy solidity brought against us by the people of stone. It is a hard rising, but we should not lose this clarity and turn into stupefied haters of things and forms, leaving intact destruction's cause itself. A people are already trapped in spirit when they agree to the use of things to hurl themselves separately against each other. The root of the disease is not in things themselves but in the use of things; the disease is not in the abundance of things but in relationships growing between users. The people using all things to create participation, using things to create community, that people have no need of any healer's art, for that people is already whole.

Since how many seasons gone have we needed healers to reveal to us the secret of all healers' work? The body that is whole moves always together. No part of it goes against any other part. That has never been a mystery to us. If then the white destroyers thrive on our disintegration, what surprise? Yet there is no call to murder hope. Why should the informed hearing be so discouraged by destruction's loudness when already even the destroyed fragments begin to call out for healing, when aleady there is healers' work to do?

True it is, we have known other sources of despair: the knowledge that a people may flee predators only to find destroyers, escape whiteness coming from the desert only to collide with worse whiteness emergent from the sea. Yet here too understanding takes the mind beyond despair, takes it active into healing work. For did not Abena and Isanusi, did not Juma and Mokili spend revealing time making loud the thought that those gone before had also suffered from a blindness no less dangerous than the present atrophy of vision? What else could it have been but blindness, the inability to see that there is more than the choice between becoming predators and staying prey, more than the choice between hunters and the merely hunted, between destroyers and the destroyed? Why else did they not think to beat new paths to the old way? Why could they not see that those whose vocation it is to destroy destroyers do not through their work become destroyers but the necessary, indispensable finders of paths to the way again? Why were they so blind to this, that in the triumph of desruction's whiteness the destruction of destruction is the only vocation of the way?

Our people coming down found a kind of beauty in this place itself; we will find it again. But movement alone was no lasting answer. The way, the highest beauty, did not come again at the end of that long journey from the desert's edge. Instead, what a scene of carnage we have come to live here! Here we have had quarrels, bitterness, strife, so that the life of our people is become a tattered thing and we are everywhere in shreds. That long flight then has only varied, only prolonged our disintegration. That flight was also part, not a denial, of the two thousand seasons prophesied against us.

316

And yet it happens that the beginnings of creation are hard to tell apart from mere destruction. This too should not escape our remembrance: the way is not an old road ready for consumers to travel on; the way is a call to creation. Easy it is to fall into the trap of loneliness if we forget that our people are not just of the present, not just the walking multitudes of murdered souls and zombis now around us, but many, many more gone and many, many more to come. Because it is useless to locate hope in the already destroyed; it is the method of the lazy hypocritical soul, courting despair so as to spare itself the necessity of action. As reasonable it would be to visit cemeteries there to wait upon the dead to rise to our conversation. Yes, there are many whose semblance of life is all trapped within the present death. But what are we if their numbers alone should depress us into immobility? What are we if we see nothing beyond the present, hear nothing from the ages of our flowing, and in all our existence can utter no necessary preparation of the future way?

Certain it is decay runs exulting through our people, certain we have fallen into a grotesque dance of death, the dance of whites and kings and princes and other worms and parasities. But shall we call Idawa foolish urging us to remember even mortal bodies can destroy the lice infesting them? That our people will live, and will necessarily destroy the white destroyers infesting us together with their helpers the parasites? Shall we forget Isanusi's words: that left to ourselves our people would have the means and the will to destroy the parasites, but for thousands of seasons we have not been to ourselves, and if a path is to be found against the parasites that path must be laid deep enough to go against those bound to help the parasites against our living soul: the people of stone, the white destroyers?

Some despair, Isanusi said, has but spurious cause; beware the quick anger against a sleeping people for not breathing a quicker breath. In the beginning this can only be the anger of those already tired of the difficult, patient work of healing, work innocent of praise songs. This is the anger of those seeking receptacles for blame. For he is no liberator whose skill lies in calling loudly to the bound, the trapped, the impotent enslaved, to rise upon their destroyers. The liberator is he who from a necessary silence, from a necessary secrecy strikes the destroyer. That, not loudness, is the necessary beginning.

Soon we shall end this remembrance, the sound of it. Soon it will end. Its substance is what continues. The ending of our remembrance should give greater force to the continuation of the beginning flow in search of our way.

The white destroyers: what a scene of carnage, what utter desolation they have already left stretching over this land! What a destruction of bodies, what a death of spirits! But the reign of the destroyers cannot reach beyond these two thousand seasons. The predators from the desert, they who found so much to do among us turning living bodies to carrion, what are they now? A bizarre sort of egrets feast impudent on their very eyeballs in other deserts they once called their own. Thirty hundred seasons consumed in the lazy oppression of other peoples have killed their

318

minds. All they can be now is willing instruments of worse predators than themselves, of destroyers even greedier. And the white destroyers from the sea, the worst there are, what of them? Their reign is surely bound within the two thousand seasons of our oppression. For their greed is preparing deep graves for them; it will raise against them the torrential wrath of all things in the universe, all bodies, all souls still with the seed of life unkilled in them. Were they not on their way to spread death elsewhere when their gluttony brought them here? Their greed is far-flung, far beyond our land. Other lands have burned in their insatiate avarice, other peoples have died in the whiteness of their greed. In those other places surely other survivors have awakened from the whiteness of the trance of death. Others devoted to life will surely find that between the creation of life and the destruction of the destroyers there is no difference but a necessary, indispensable connection; that nothing good can be created that does not of its very nature push forward the destruction of the destroyers. And in that urge to life, in that fight against destruction's ashen blight each people of the way will find every other people of the way.

Dangers there will be in the newness of this discovery, dangers like the headiness of too quick, abundant faith from those too long sold to despair; the pull of old habits from destruction's empire; the sour possibility of people helping each other turning in times of difficulty into people using each other to create a selfish ease. Real dangers, but nothing beside the present danger of despair in the face of the illusion, massive, stone-like, of the permanence of this white destruction.

We do not utter praise of arms. The praise of arms is the praise of things, and what shall we call the soul crawling so low, soul so hollow it finds fulfilment in the praising of mere things? It is not things we praise in our utterance, not arms we praise but the living relationship itself of those united in the use of all things against the white sway of death, for creation's life. That is the beauty of the seers' vision, that alone is music to the hearers' ear. That is the sole utterance of utterers conscious of our way, the way. Whatever thing, whatever relationship, whatever consciousness takes us along paths closer to our way, whatever goes against the white destroyers' empire, that thing only is beautiful, that relationship only is truthful, that consciousness alone has satisfaction for the still living mind.

But still, in the present what a scene of disintegration, what a bloody desolation the whites have stretched over this land! What a killing of souls!

Whose will is it to make utterances of despair simply because our physical eyes have not lived at the very end of destruction's two thousand seasons? Who is the seer of such hazy vision he pines in regret that his ears of flesh will not be the very ears of flesh that hear the music of that definite creation? Where is the hearer so deaf he has not heard it does not matter which mouth of flesh and blood utters creation's onset as long as every seer treading paths to our living way, every hearer, every utterer of the way has even in the two thousand seasons turned all living energy against

320

the whiteness of destruction's sway?

There is no beauty but in relationships. Nothing cut off by itself is beautiful. Never can things in destructive relationships be beautiful. All beauty is in the creative purpose of our relationships; all ugliness is in the destructive aims of the destroyers' arrangements. The mind that knows this, the destroyers will set traps for it, but the destroyers' traps will never hold that mind. The group that knows this and works knowing this, that group itself is a work of beauty, creation's work. Against such a group the destroyers will set traps for the body, traps for the heart, traps to destroy the mind. Such a group none of the destroyers' traps can hold.

Soon we shall end this remembrance, the sound of it. It is the substance that continues. Soon it will end. Yet still, what a scene of carnage the white destroyers have brought here, what a destruction of bodies, what a death of souls!

Against this what a vision of creation yet unknown, higher, much more profound than all erstwhile creation! What a hearing of the confluence of all the waters of life flowing to overwhelm the ashen desert's blight! What an utterance of the coming together of all the people of our way, the coming together of all people of the way.

*Dar es Salaam*
October 1971–August 1972